India Studies in Business and Economics

The Indian economy is considered to be one of the fastest growing economies of the world with India being among the most important of the G-20 economies. Ever since the Indian economy made its presence felt on the global platform, the research community is even more interested in studying and analyzing what India has to offer. This series aims to bring forth the latest studies and research about India from the areas of economics, business, and management science. The titles featured in this series will present rigorous empirical research, often accompanied by policy recommendations, and evoke and evaluate various aspects of the economy and the business and management landscape in India, with a special focus on India's relationship with the world in terms of business and trade.

More information about this series at http://www.springer.com/series/11234

Gayithri Karnam
Editor

Public Budgeting in India

Principles and Practices

Springer

Editor
Gayithri Karnam
Centre for Economic Studies and Policy
Institute for Social and Economic Change
Bengaluru, Karnataka, India

ISSN 2198-0012 ISSN 2198-0020 (electronic)
India Studies in Business and Economics
ISBN 978-81-322-3915-4 ISBN 978-81-322-3917-8 (eBook)
https://doi.org/10.1007/978-81-322-3917-8

Library of Congress Control Number: 2018950940

This Springer imprint is published by the registered company Springer Nature India Private Limited
The registered company address is: 7th Floor, Vijaya Building, 17 Barakhamba Road, New Delhi 110 001, India

To (Late) B. S. Bhandary

The initiative to bring out a publication on public budgeting putting together the principles and practices was taken by Late Mr. B. S. Bhandary who happened to be an avid follower of budget discussions and writings. Mr. Bhandary was trained in Economics and held many positions in many organisations including Karnataka government, Vysya Bank, Vijaya Bank etc. He also had a training stint at Barclays Bank International Ltd. He edited the chapters of Mysore State Gazetteer (Raichur District) and also was a co-editor of a volume in honour of Prof. S. L. N. Simha. His untiring efforts in persuading senior civil servants and academicians to contribute to the present volume and a regular follow-up has culminated into this present publication. It is unfortunate that he is not amidst us today to see this volume being published. This book is in his honour and fondly dedicated to him.

Foreword

One of the earliest references to the basic principles of formulation of a Budget for the State may be found in Kautilya's *Arthashastra* written between 300 BC and 150 AD. In the chapter dealing with Budget, Audit and Accounts, it is laid down that "the Chancellor shall first estimate the revenue of the year by determining the likely revenue from each place and each sphere of activity under different Heads of Accounts, total them up by sphere of activity ...and then arrive at the grand total." (Rangarajan 1992, p. 275)[1] In this treatise, it is laid down that expenditure shall be shown under the headings (i) budgeted day to day expenditure, (ii) unbudgeted day to day expenditure, and (iii) foreseen periodic (fortnightly, monthly or actual) expenditure.

Altekar[2] states that Sukra, in *Sukraniti*, provides information not to be found in other works on polity in the post-Kautilya period. The portfolio of different Ministers under a King is given in this book for the first time. Sukra also gives details about the percentage of the State income to be spent on different items. Fighting forces claimed 50% of total income; Reserve Fund or Treasury claimed 16.6% of total revenues; public debt or State loan was unknown.

In English writing on parliamentary proceedings relating to taxation and finance, the word 'budget', said to be derived from the French word, 'bougette', meaning a small bag, was first used by a member of parliament in the year 1733, when then Prime Minister Robert Walpole placed before the Parliament a proposal to shift the burden of taxation "from landed wealth to consumption", which would have hurt the middle class and the poor. Incidentally, in England of those days, opening one's budget also meant something like 'bringing out a box of tricks'.

However, the word 'budget' in the sense of an estimate of revenue and expenditure of the national government did not come into regular use, until a few decades after Walpole's taxation proposals. Apparently, by 1764 the practice of

---

[1]Rangarajan, L. N., 1992, (ed) Kautilya_The Arthashastra, Penguin.

[2]Altekar, A. S., 2001 State and Government in Ancient India, Motilal Banarasidass publishers private limited, New Delhi.

presenting a budget as an annual event at which the Chancellor of exchequer gave an account of the State of National Finance came to be well established.[3]

In France, during the Napoleonic era, a strict budgetary control system was in operation for expenditure on the Army. Thereafter, a detailed system of estimating revenue, 'calculation of cost' of various items of government expenditure, Public Debt Management, procedure for preparing accounts and auditing the same was put in place by early nineteenth century.

In the USA, Alexander Hamilton (appointed first Secretary of the Treasury, in 1789 during President Washington's administration) set up the Department of Treasury developed the system of financial management including taxation, debt management, etc. He also presented the first US Federal Budget.

The US Constitution, which embodies the doctrine of Separation of Powers and the principle of checks and balances lays down the detailed procedure of preparation of budget, passing of the budget, the appropriation bills, the role of the President and the Congress in the budgetary process, etc. The President is assisted in the process of budget formulation by the Office of Budget and Management while the Congress is assisted in the scrutiny of the budget by the Congressional Budget Office, established in July 12, 1974.

In the British administered India, the first budget was presented by James Wilson, on Feb 18, 1869. Mr. Wilson was the Finance Member of the Viceroy's Executive Council. He was also the founder of the influential British Financial and Political Magazine, the Economist.

Independent India's first budget was presented by the then Finance Minister, R. K. Shanmukham Chetty. It is worth noting that when Shri. Shanmukham Chetty was engaged in preparing the first budget, the Budget Scandal of UK of 1947 had broken out, leading to the resignation of Hugh Dalton as the Chancellor of the Exchequer. Dalton was not only a Labour Party politician but also an economist of repute who had written a standard textbook on public finance. He had to resign from his post of Chancellor as he had inadvertently mentioned some details of his budget to a journalist while walking to the House of Commons before delivering his budget speech. This incident is said to be the cause of great secrecy maintained about budget formulation in the UK and probably more so in India.

The credit for presenting the maximum number of Union Budgets in India (10) goes to Shri. Morarji Desai. Some of the memorable budgets or budget related polices since 1947 include:

- The budget presented by F. M. John Mathai in 1949–50 which was accompanied by an announcement regarding formation of the Planning Commission. Thus began the era of Planning, dividing budgetary expenditure into 'Plan' and 'Non-plan', and debates regarding raising resources for the plan, fixing the size of the plan, determining central plan assistance to the States etc.

[3]Please see "the History of Parliament", posted on the Internet, March 7, 2012. https://historyofparliamentalogy.wordpress.co.

- The budget speech of C. D. Deshmukh for the year 1956–57, which talked of the need for raising investment: income ratios from 7 to 12%, a plan size of Rs. 4,800 crore, the need for raising resources for a plan of this magnitude.
- Introduction of expenditure tax on the recommendation of Nicholas Kaldor, a Cambridge Economist, in 1956 with a view to curb consumption and raise resources for the plan. The expenditure tax was first introduced by T. T. Krishnamachari (the then Finance Minister) in 1957. After being abolished in 1962 by Morarji Desai, it was brought back again in 1964. It was finally abolished in 1966 after which Chaudhary Charan Singh tried to bring it again in 1979 but failed.
- Introduction of compulsory deposit scheme in 1963, after Sino-India War 1962. The President promulgated the Compulsory Deposit Scheme (Income-tax Payers) Ordinance, 1974 on 17-7-1974 to provide for compulsory deposits by certain categories of income-tax payers in the higher income brackets. The Act came into force with effect from 17-7-1974 and the Scheme with effect from 15-11-1974.
- Indira Gandhi's 'Garibi Hatao' Budget of 1971 which is linked with the ideological division in Congress Party, split in the Party and deepening the socialistic orientation of the Congress Party. Fourth Five Year Plan emphasized the strategy of 'Removal of Poverty' and 'Garibi Hatao' was the slogan.
- Charan Singh, Deputy Prime Minister and Minister of Finance in his Budget of 1979–80 giving rural and agricultural focus to the budget. The budget highlighted the presence of great poverty and unemployment in the country, particularly in the rural areas, and agriculture sector's potential for generating employment, and the need to provide purchasing power to the large majority of the people. It focused on increasing the growth rates of agriculture and industrial sectors with enhanced investments. The budget also highlighted the relevance of efficiency in expenditure; hence it intended to appoint an expert committee "to examine the impact of public expenditure on the promotion of growth and reduction of poverty and recommend ways and means of making public expenditure more effective in solving the problem of poverty" (ibid. p. 11).
- Long Term Fiscal Policy (LTFP) statement was rolled out by V. P. Singh in 1985. Government's new approach of increasing tax collections was not by raising rates but by making the structure simpler, through better compliance and, above all, by levying tax at rates that are generally judged to be reasonable. It also included the policy measures like introduction of Modified Value Added Tax (MODVAT) after consultation with expert committee recommendation. "The LTFP, for the first time, gives the breakdown of broad aggregates like Centre's resources for the Plan and the head wise breakdown of sources of financing for each of the five years of the Seventh Five Year Plan. It also

contains a statement indicating the directions of reform in the area of the Central government's finances, especially taxation." (Bagchi 1986, p. 639)[4]

- Chidambaram's dream budget of 1997 aimed at enhancing the tax base with a recourse to moderate tax rates and voluntary disclosure of income (VDIS) Chidambaram states' "I believe that the time is opportune to introduce a Voluntary Disclosure Scheme. This would be a simple scheme where, irrespective of the year or the nature or the source of the funds, the amount disclosed, either as cash, securities or assets, whether held in India or abroad, would be charged at the revised highest rate of tax. Interest and penalty will be waived. Immunity will be granted from any action under the income-tax, Wealth tax and Foreign Exchange Regulation Acts. The date of commencement of the scheme will be notified separately, but the scheme will end on December 31, 1997.[5]"
- The most momentous budget of Manmohan Singh for the year 1991–92 involved dismantling industrial licensing policy, initiating economic reforms and liberalization of the economy. The then Finance Minister Manmohan Singh had stated, "There is no time to lose. Neither the Government nor the economy can live beyond its means year after year. The room for maneuver, to live on borrowed money or time, does not exist anymore. Any further postponement of macro-economic adjustment, long overdue, would mean that the balance of payments situation, now exceedingly difficult, would become unmanageable and inflation, already high, would exceed limits of tolerance. For improving the management of the economy, the starting point, and indeed the center-piece of our strategy, should be a credible fiscal adjustment and macro-economic stabilization during the current financial year, to be followed by continued fiscal consolidation thereafter. This process would, inevitably, need at least three years, if not longer, to complete. But there can be no adjustment without pain. The people must be prepared to make necessary sacrifices to preserve our economic independence and restore the health of our economy."
- Pranab Mukherjee's Budget of 2009–10 announcing the policies to to counter the negative fallout of the global slowdown, 2008 on the Indian economy. Pranab Mukherji stated "the Government responded by providing three focused fiscal stimulus packages in the form of tax relief to boost demand and increased expenditure on public projects to create employment and public assets. This fiscal accommodation led to an increase in fiscal deficit from 2.7% in 2007–08 to 6.2% of GDP in 2008–09. The difference between the actuals of 2007–08 and 2008–09 constituted the total fiscal stimulus. This fiscal stimulus at 3.5% of GDP at current market prices for 2008–09 amounts to Rs. 1,86,000 crore."[6]

[4]Bagchi, Amaresh, 1986, Budget and long-term fiscal policy, Economic and Political Weekly Vol XXL No 15. April 12, 1S85.

[5]Government of India, 1997. Union Budget Speech.

[6]Government of India, 2009–10, Union Budget Speech.

- Passing of Fiscal Responsibility and Budget Management Act in 2003 aimed at imbibing fiscal discipline by framing targets of zero revenue deficit and a 3% fiscal deficit. Government had very effectively implemented these rules till 2008, which resulted in rapid reduction of revenue and fiscal deficits. But 2008 global financial crisis resulted in announcement of massive fiscal stimulus measures, which made the government to miss the targets. With respect to States' fiscal responsibility, Karnataka was pioneer in passing the Fiscal Responsibility Act in 2002, which is one year prior to the Central government. The Act is effectively implemented by state government which has made the Revenue Deficit State into revenue surplus one and the fiscal deficit of the state is less than the target fixed in the Act. Further, Karnataka is very strictly following the its debt: GDP ratio too which is less than the target of 26 of its GDP since its inception.
- Arun Jaitley's Budget of 2017–18 announcing the dismantling of the Planning Commission, abolition of Plan and Non-plan schemes in the Union Budget contained some major structural reforms. It is stated, "the removal of the Plan and Non-plan distinction the focus of budgeting and expenditure classification will shift to revenue and capital expenditure, as has been envisaged in the Constitution of India. A clear distinction between capital and revenue expenditures is also essential for analytical purposes, transparency, and efficient policy decision-making. The distinction is fundamentally important for the assessment of the operating costs of government and the investments made by it along with measuring the efficiency of government activities. Moreover, developing a performance-oriented approach requires separation of running costs from capital expenditures. The emphasis on distinction between Revenue and Capital expenditures is therefore, not only a constitutional requirement but also an essential ingredient for policy formulation and efficient resource allocation."[7] (GoI 2017, p. 2)
- Introduction of Goods and Services Tax (GST) is a major indirect tax reform in the economic history of India's tax reforms ushered in July, 2017. GST is hoped to integrate the country into a common market and enable a smooth flow of goods from one state to the other by removing barriers across states. It has subsumed various indirect taxes levied by the centre and the states to bring in a pan-India uniform indirect taxation system. GST, a destination-based tax, helps eliminate cascading effect of taxes.

In the context of this global historical account of budget preparation and execution several following issues and concerns need to be addressed:

1. The need for a proper constitutional and legal framework for formulation of budget proposals, approval of the budget by the competent authority, method of budgetary control, etc. Many countries have passed what is known as organic Budget Law, but some countries, as in India, the foundational principles are laid down in the constitution, the details are provided by executive instructions

[7] Government of India, Union Budget Speech, 2017.

issued by the Union/State Governments. There is need for a public debate about the efficacy of organic Budget Law.

2. After abolition of Planning Commission of India and abolition of Plan and Non-plan schemes in Union Budget, what should be the consequential changes in the State Budget, how capital budgeting should be dealt with in Union and State Budgets, whether there is need for a separation of revenue and capital account in budget? How to ensure adequate funding for multi-year projects of assets creating nature.
3. Poor fiscal marksmanship. Very often revenue forecasting is done in a casual unscientific manner, resulting in over estimation of resources and over provisioning for expenditure. Similarly, while forecasting expenditure for a project/program all the components are not taken care of, unit costs are not calculated diligently and other lacunae are found in expenditure forecasting. The result of all these failures in proper forecasting of revenue and expenditure, is cost and time over run in implementing projects, projects languishing for years together for lack of funds and poor service delivery to the citizens either in providing social services, like health or education or in building infrastructure. The Finance Ministry, as well as the other Administrative Ministries and Field Departments have to develop capacity for scientific forecasting of revenue, formulate projects/programs delineating all components in detail, do appropriate costing of each item of expenditure, prepare a time bound program for implementation, and precisely calculate the resource requirements for each year of program implementations.
4. Institutional changes required to make the budget more realistic at the Union/State level. The need for something similar to the Congressional Budget office, staffed with competent persons, at both Central and State level. Similarly, there is need for making the subject committee/standing committee on finance (both in Parliament and State Legislatures) more active and empowered to scrutinize the budget proposals and suggest changes where felt necessary.
5. The need for independent Fiscal Authority (as in UK) to scrutinize budget forecasts regarding resources, and underlying assumptions regarding rate of growth of GDP, elasticity of taxes, etc.
6. Even though the Planning Commission at the Central Government level has been abolished, the State Governments have not abolished their planning machinery i.e., State Planning Departments, Planning Boards, etc. The Central Government has set up a NITI Aayog, but the role, if any, of NITI Aayog in maintaining links with State Planning Machinery is not very clear. Similarly, it is not known if the NITI Aayog is going to perform any role in project formulation, project appraisal, inter se prioritization among projects, giving guidelines to the State planning organizations in these areas, etc. In the situation of such a vacuum, how proper expenditure management can be achieved at the Central and State level needs to be analyzed. Without proper mechanism and scientific guidelines regarding project formulating project appraisal, project management undesirable projects are likely to be included in larger number in

future budgets, on political consideration or due to irrational exuberance of budget frames for fancy eye-catching projects.

7. Nitin Desai, a former Chief Economic Advisor to the Government of India, has in a recent article published in the Business Standard ("Restore the real purpose of the Budget", Business Standard, dated 22 February, 2018), has pointed out, "over the years government, is eager to use the wide media and public attention that the Budget presentation attracts, are making it a propaganda vehicle for sketchy sectoral initiatives that can capture media attention". After citing several such Budget announcements in the sectors like Health, Housing, Power, Skill Development, etc. he warns that "using a secrecy-surrounded Budget process for announcing sketchily planned sectoral targets and policies is dangerous." There is need for detailed case studies relating to such grand announcements of sketchily formulated unrealistic plans and programs and their final outcome, so that appropriate lessons can be drawn for the framers of the future budgets.
8. Over a period of time, several sectional/identity based/inter-sectoral components have been introduced in the Budget, both at the Central level and the State government level. Some were started at the initiative of the Central government and adopted by all State governments, some were introduced by the Centre and adopted by a few States, some were introduced at the initiative of one or two State governments and then probably discontinued. We are referring to Special Component Plan (for the welfare of the SC Population), Tribal Plan/sub-plan (for the welfare of ST population), "Gender Budget", "Agriculture Budget", etc., It is not known to the members of the public, what are the guidelines regarding preparation of such plans/sub-plans, whether care is taken to ensure that there is no duplication in schemes prepared under the special provisions and the regular Departmental Plans of the Departments of SC/ST Welfare, Women's Development, Agriculture and Horticulture etc. There is need for detailed study of such special plans/sub-plans and formulation of model guidelines for the benefit of Central Government Departments/State Government preparing and implementing such plans within plans or 'Budget within Budgets'.
9. From time to time several innovative ideas have been introduced, practiced for some years and then given up for something considered to be a better idea, in areas of preparation of Budget, and in evaluation of success in implementing Budget proposals, etc., reference many be made to the concepts of incremental budgeting, Zero Base Budgeting, Performance Budget, its modified/improved version of Program Performance Budget (PPB), Monthly Program Implementation Calendar (MPIC) in Karnataka, Result Framework Document (RFD), etc., It will be useful for the practitioners, academics and the general public to find a review of the working of these innovative practices across different countries and different States of India, over the last two/three decades. This will help in formulating realistic/purposeful Budgets and in ensuring that Budgets are result oriented and appraisals are outcome-focused.

10. Since all Budgets have to be based upon certain macro-economic assumptions regarding GDP growth rate, growth of consumption demand, investment rate, money supply, estimated Inflation rate, employment/unemployment rate, etc. there is need for strengthening the data collection and analysis system and in general the statistical system in the country. At present, there is a lot of confusion regarding the appropriate method for calculating GDP (whether in the agriculture manufacturing or service sector), how to compare GDP calculated in recent years with the GDP of earlier period, how to estimate employment/unemployment rate, job creation in formal/informal sectors, etc., All these issues are important because revenue forecast for the coming year will depend upon estimate of GDP growth, inflation rate, etc. Similarly, Government expenditure policy will depend upon its objectives and if job creation or unemployment reduction is an objective, government should have objective, reliable information regarding the employment situation the economy. While all these issues cannot be resolved immediately, there is need for open discussion and debate among the officials and the experts, with all available data having been brought in the public domain.
11. There are several other issues relating to preparation of the Budget documents, need for adequate discussion or debate in the Parliament/Assemblies on the Budget proposals, proper system of accounting to be adopted in Budgets (cash vs accrual), strengthening Budget preparation and scrutinizing capability at the sub-national (State, local bodies–urban and rural) level, appropriate steps to be taken to see that Fiscal Responsibility Acts have some more teeth, that fiscal deficit (appropriately defined to avoid various subterfuges in which Finance Ministries/State Finance Department and being adept over time) is kept under control, proper institutional arrangement for debt management, what should be the relative role of the Finance Ministry. The Reserve Bank of India in managing public debt issues of debt sustainability etc. which require in-depth analysis. It will be desirable if on several such issues white papers are prepared by the Central Government and the State Governments creating public awareness and generating more debate. Hopefully such discussions and public debate will help formulating better policies in these important areas.

The present volume discusses many of the issues raised above. The publication of this book owes its origin to the initiative of (the Late) Shri. B. S. Bhandary, formerly of the Vysya Bank and the Southern Economist and Dr. K. Gayithri, Professor of Economics, ISEC, Bangalore. They felt the need for a book, based on Indian experience at the national and sub-national level, which will deal with the important subject of 'Budget' which is at the core of the theory and practice of "Public Finance". Dr. Gayithri and Shri. Bhandary were instrumental in collecting these articles written by academics with background in law, economics, international expert in public finance, and civil servants with long expertise in fiscal management. Dr. Gayithri who has decades of experience in analysis of fiscal policy, public expenditure management and in specialized areas like performance or outcome budgeting, has herself written two articles and also the introduction, which follows this Foreword. (Late) Shri. Bhandari, has contributed one article on expenditure management. He was an unusual gentleman, who had carried within his heart, his lifelong passion for economic studies and had pursued the matter of collecting articles to be included in this volume very quietly and patiently over a period of about 2 years. It is indeed unfortunate that he could not see the publication of his volume, which was the dream of the last years of his life. The book is dedicated to his memory.

I am confident that both researchers and practitioners in the field of public finance, and the general public who are expected to be the ultimate beneficiary of a good Budget, well implemented, will find the book interesting and useful.

Bengaluru, India

B. K. Bhattacharya, IAS (Retd.)
Former Chief Secretary
Government of Karnataka

Contents

Editor and Contributors

About the Editor

Gayithri Karnam is a professor of economics at the Center for Economic Studies and Policy, Institute for Social and Economic Change, Bangalore, India. She is a specialist in the areas of public economics, industrial economics, and public policy studies. She has conducted extensive research in the areas of state fiscal studies, public expenditure planning and management, and budget reforms. She has served as an advisor on a number of state government committees and as a consultant to international donor agencies like USAID and DFID for state-level fiscal studies. She has been a recipient of the Shastri Indo-Canadian Faculty Research Fellowship twice for undertaking comparative fiscal studies at the Carleton University, Canada. She has undergone training in the Duke Center for International Development, Duke University, Durham, USA, on aspects relating to "public budgeting and financial management." She has also participated in the executive education program on "Public financial management in a changing world" in the John F. Kennedy School of Government at Harvard University, Boston.

Contributors

M. R. Anantha Ramu Fiscal Policy Institute, Bengaluru, India

B. S. Bhandary Vijaya Bank, Bangalore, India

S. K. Das Bengaluru, India

Gayithri Karnam Centre for Economic Studies and Policy, Institute for Social and Economic Change, Bengaluru, Karnataka, India

V. S. Mallar National Law School of India University, Bengaluru, India

Gopalkrishniah Nagesha Post Graduate Department of Economics, Government First Grade College, Yelahanka, Bengaluru, India

A. Premchand Hyderabad, India

N. Sreedevi Centre for Economic and Social Studies, Hyderabad, Telangana, India

M. R. Sreenivasa Murthy Bangalore, India

C. Vijaya Kumar Comptroller and Auditor General of India-Field Office, Bangalore, Bangalore, India

List of Figures

Chapter 4

Chapter 6

Chapter 7

Chapter 8

List of Tables

Chapter 4

Chapter 5

Chapter 6

Chapter 8

Chapter 11

Chapter 12

List of Charts

Chapter 12

List of Boxes

Chapter 12

Chapter 1
Introduction and Overview

Gayithri Karnam

1 Introduction

Government budget is a statement of resource and spending proposals for a specified period of time. As per the Indian Constitution, the Central government (Article 112) and state governments (Article 202) are mandated to present their Annual Financial Statement (AFS) before the Parliament and State Legislatures, respectively. Budgets are instrumental in translating the socio-economic development goals of the governments into reality by way of resource provisioning for the professed development. Translation of policy goals into reality is largely dependent on how well the planning process, resource allocations, and execution of schemes synchronise with one another. Public budgeting has undergone dramatic changes over the years with the diverse roles assumed by governments from time to time, as a fall out of which the scale and nature of public spending has been undergoing major changes. Fiscal operations of the governments tend to impact the economies in a significant manner depending on the nature and extent of intervention, be it raising of revenue or expending the resources. Budget preparation is a complex and challenging exercise given the multifaceted and at times conflicting goals, involving a number of demands on limited resources. Factors underlying such a major role for the governments in India are many. Rao (2015, 59) states "…. there are several reasons for the state to embrace a much larger than the minimalist role public choice proponents would recommend in a country like India. These include the need to overcome large social and physical infrastructure deficit, provide correctives to missing and imperfect markets, introduce measures to reduce acute inequalities and poverty and provide correctives to widespread information asymmetry." Budget as a major policy statement is to necessarily reflect the ongoing national and global macroeconomic changes to make it effective policy tool.

G. Karnam (✉)
Centre for Economic Studies and Policy, Institute for Social and Economic Change, Bengaluru, Karnataka, India
e-mail: gayithri@isec.ac.in

G. Karnam (ed.), *Public Budgeting in India*, India Studies in Business and Economics, https://doi.org/10.1007/978-81-322-3917-8_1

1.1 Economic Functions of the Government

There has been a general consensus on the allocation, distribution and stabilization functions of government. Government's role assumes importance in the provisioning of public goods due to the failure of markets. Public goods are characterised by "non-excludability" and "non-rivalry" of consumption. Non-excludability is a condition under which no individual can be excluded from consumption of a public good. These goods cannot be packaged and distributed to individuals separately (Hackbart and Ramsey 2002) Markets fail to provide such goods in an efficient manner as no one can be excluded from the consumption of a public good and the individuals can consume the same without having to pay for such goods resulting in free riding. Non-rival goods may be consumed by an individual without hindering the simultaneous consumption of others. Private goods on the contrary are rival and excludable. Hence, the market failure caused by the typical public goods characteristics necessitates public provisioning.

Distributive role has assumed enormous importance in the context of governments both at the national and the subnational levels in India given the large-scale presence of interpersonal, inter-regional inequalities. The economic growth focus with the public resources largely being allocated to physical resource development in the aftermath of independence leaned towards distributive justice by mid-1970s with the launch of "GaribiHatao" and the subsequent initiation of myriad poverty alleviation programs. The Eleventh and Twelfth plans are especially marked by inclusivity focus aiming at increased allocation of public resources to mainstream the marginalised sections of the society.

Stabilization role basically aims at addressing the macroeconomic issues relating to economic growth, inflation, unemployment, etc. Monetary and fiscal policies are the key instruments used in the process of stabilizing the economy. The macropolicy pronouncements such as promotion of economic growth, reduction in unemployment serve as the basis for framing the budgetary decisions. Government budgets are instrumental in achieving these objectives through their tax and expenditure policies. The current fiscal consolidation process with targets laid down for fiscal, revenue and debt level emphasised by the governments both at the Central and subnational levels are measures aimed at stabilization.

2 Issues in Public Budgeting in India

The expansion in the scope and nature of government intervention has been adding to the complexity of issues in public budgeting. With the rapid enhancement in the scale and scope of government intervention, budget planning for provisioning of public services, be it for new schemes or continuation of old schemes, is rarely based on a scientific financial need assessment. Financial allocations are based on resource availability, and given the political dominance in the budget-making process, schemes that gain popularity get preference. New schemes get conceived year on year with inadequate understanding of the physical and financial requirements. Introduction of capital projects with token allocations and not backed by scientific project appraisals have often resulted in issues such as time and cost overruns. The existing schemes are often guided by incrementalism subject to resource availability. There is little hesitation in axing the budgetary allocations towards the end of the financial year depending on the extent of adjustment required to fulfil the fiscal targets which are often ad hoc in nature. Government has made ill prepared and failed attempts to introduce performance orientation to budgets. It has very rarely used the performance information in the budget-making process, with the exception of may be a couple of plan programs, which would have enabled informed decision-making and substantially toned up the expenditure planning process.

Budgets also have had issues of poor fiscal marksmanship, wherein the actual budget figures deviated significantly from the planned figures.

There have been a number of issues with reference to the execution of schemes. There have been issues concerning a major mismatch between the budgetary allocations to releases and the final expenditure subjecting the formulated schemes to fund uncertainties and inadequacies. The target approach both with reference to the financial targets and physical targets is driving the effort in the direction of fulfilling the targets rather than ensuring efficient service delivery. In the process, there is either overprovisioning of services, an example being the excess social housing that has happened in Yadgir and Uttara Kannada districts in Karnataka (Gayithri 2014) or underprovisioning. A serious issue hampering the effectiveness of schemes relates to the bunching of expenditure towards the tail end of the financial year which has resulted in poor translation of outlays into outcomes.

Performance of the government on resource front comprising of tax and non-tax revenue too has been rid with serious issues. Commenting on tax performance in India, Rao (2015, 60) states "The tax system in India, despite several rounds reforms, has not been able to generate the required revenue. The revenue productivity of the tax system as measured by the ratio of tax revenue to GDP has virtually been stagnant over a long period of time". He further states that several exemptions and concessions given by the government tend to distort resource allocation in the country.

The present volume is an effort in providing an understanding of the budgets, unearthing the complexities of public budgeting and the issues associated with public budgeting in India. This effort is made to reach out to a large number of users who may not have a correct understanding of budget concepts, the procedures involved in the framing of budgets, budget considerations and budget implications written by scholars who have had a long involvement with the government budgetary processes and also researchers who have had an extensive experience in analysing government budgets. The volume in all has twelve papers.

3 Overview

V. S. Mallar in his paper entitled "Indian Constitutional framework for fiscal regime" has reviewed the fiscal provisions of the Constitution of India, their relevance, rationale and their likely implications for the economic system as a whole. The paper maps the Constitutional amendments effected from time to time to address the fiscal issues such as federal financial imbalances. The paper argues that even with Constitutional provisions compelling allocation of surplus Union resources to the states, the grant-in-aid power is not controlled altogether thus giving room for the Union to dominate states through the conditions attached to the grants. The paper also dwells on the roles and responsibilities of the Comptroller and Auditor General (CAG) and its requirement to uphold the Constitution of India in the financial administration.

"The Budget what it means and how it is prepared" by M. R. Srinivasa Murthy provides a lucid account of the budget preparation and the structure. The nitty-gritty of the budget making, the procedures involved, their sequencing, the roles and responsibilities of the officers concerned, the structure of the budgets and their economic significance are detailed very clearly, a job very well accomplished by the author, having steered these processes at the helm of affairs in the state of Karnataka. He also highlights the complexities associated with the budget making in collating and prioritising all the demands and the effort involved in negotiating with varied interests, conflicting demands and accommodating in the budgets.

"Public revenue: sources and growth" by Sreedevi is an attempt to discuss the sources of public revenue, its classification, tax reforms in India both at the Centre and the states. The paper analyses trends in revenue both at the Central and state governments and addresses a number of policy issues concerning revenue mobilisation. The paper observes that while the simplification and reforms have helped in the mobilisation of larger revenues both at the Central and state government, collection efficiency needs to be toned up.

"Managing government expenditure—Searching for lines of control" by Bhandary and Nagesha is a very detailed account of public expenditure both in terms of theory, practice and the changing contours of public expenditure over time. The paper documents the existing evidence on impacts of government expenditure on growth, regional development and the issues of public expenditure efficiency in India. Experiences with reference to reforms in expenditure planning and management and the fiscal rule approach in effecting control and the outcome approach are discussed. An important message that emerges from the discussion is the current trend, wherein there is lack of genuine effort, wherein targets are fixed only to miss them, road maps being prepared only to revise, transparency that conceals information. The paper reiterates the need to revisit the recommendations made by a number of committees and rectify the currents flaws prevailing in the system.

Gayithri in her paper on "Public expenditure: Issues and concerns" analyses the trends in key expenditure variables. Tracing the broad trends in the fiscal and revenue deficits, the paper argues that the uncontained share of revenue deficit which is diverting borrowed resources from capital investments to consumption purpose, caution immediate policy attention. Further, it is argued that this attains special importance in the context of the inadequate social and economic infrastructure and their poor quality. Growth and composition of expenditure by the accounting classification and economic classification are critically analysed. The paper addresses issues of quality of public spending that has not drawn any serious attention of the policy makers until now. The paper argues that despite the rhetoric in certain budget speeches to tone up quality of spending and constitution of committees to examine the quality of government spending, a number of issues remain unaddressed. Despite the recommendation of various Committees and Commissions from time to time to review of government expenditure and contain unproductive expenditure, nothing much has been achieved until today. The government till date continues to have multiple schemes that are duplicative in nature. The paper also examines issues of public accountability and the inadequacy of current frameworks.

With the 73 and 74 amendments of the Constitution in India, the local budgeting attains considerable importance and, in this background, Anantharamu's paper examines the budgeting practices of Panchayats in Karnataka and also draws the lessons to be learnt from the best practices across the world. The paper outlines the structure of rural local bodies (RLBs) in Karnataka and analyses the sources of revenue to the Panchayats and also the major expenditure items. Budgeting practices to be followed by RLBs in Karnataka as per Karnataka Panchayat Raj Act, 1993, and key lessons to be learnt from the international best practices with regard to local budgeting are outlined.

Gayithri in her paper on "Program Performance budgeting to enhance quality of public expenditure: Approach and challenges in Karnataka" presents a critical account of the budget reform initiatives adopted in a fiscally progressive state—Karnataka with a special focus on the Program Performance Budget attempted by the state with support from the United State Aid for International Development (USAID). The paper argues that sustenance of Karnataka state's fiscal recovery in the long run is subject to reforms in expenditure planning and management. The paper also addresses the current lapses such as experimentation with a number of frameworks both by the Central and subnational governments, and not getting close to a proper application of such frameworks. The PPB framework used in Karnataka too is discontinued. It is argued that a more important use of such frameworks is when the performance information is used in framing informed decisions which helps in toning up allocative efficiency. An essential requirement is to identify the relevant outcome indicators and generate data to verify progress in that direction. The paper suggests that there are a number of successful country cases that have put in place a meaningful performance orientation, India need not reinvent the wheel, and the best practices can be carefully studied and adapted to our requirements. Such an effort however cannot succeed sans strong political will.

S. K. Das in his discussion on accrual budgeting analyses the advantages and limitations of cash and accrual-based budgeting processes. It is argued that in the context of the new public management systems that emphasise on transparency, cost-effectiveness and managerial flexibility, there is a need to move away from cash-based budgeting to accrual-based budgeting. In the context of performance assessment, sustainability and accountability of government operations, the author argues that accrual-based budgeting is a better tool than cash-based budgeting in estimating the cost of services, asset and liability position of the government. The broad features of accrual-based budgeting and the experience of New Zealand and Australia are examined in the paper, and the prospects of introducing similar budgeting practices in India are discussed. Based on the pilot experience of Railways and Postal Department and some Indian states like Madhya Pradesh, Haryana, Gujarat and Rajasthan, it is cautioned that transition to accrual-based system would be expensive due to the substantial investments required in the IT infrastructure and also not very easy. However, learning from the successful experiences of countries like New Zealand and Australia, the author feels would be helpful in the Indian efforts to move to accrual-based budgeting.

Public accountability has been a subject of growing importance, and there has been a growing public demand to make the governments accountable to the resources garnered by the government through taxes and other levies. Premchand in his chapter on "Revisiting financial accountability" outlines the evolution of the concept of public accountability. The author engages in a captivating narration of changing concept of public financial accountability over time in general and Indian context in particular and the growing demand for greater public accountability. It is observed that in practice it always ended up as a compromise between the demands of the people and what the ruling powers were willing to concede. The author highlights the growing importance of performance audit that did not traditionally form a part of the appropriation and accountancy audit of the audit departments. The long persistent structural limitations in the form of excluded items from the realm of Public Accounts Committee such as Contingent liabilities, tax expenditures or the taxes foregone by the governments in the form of tax concessions announced from time to time, the ad hoc nature of the audit of grant aided private partnerships and the limited commercial audit of the commercial banks, the growing non-performing assets and the ultimate burden on the shareholders are issues observed to be continuing in the public accountability arena. The author raises a key concern emerging from the current practices of constituting committees that are not effectively ensuring accountability which needs to be addressed by designing effective means of control and accountability.

Financial reporting and audit standards in terms of timeliness, adequacy and reliability are critical inputs for effective public financial management. Vijaya Kumar presents an account of the principles underlying government accounting and auditing, the structures, the roles of treasury, Accountant General and the government accounting reform initiatives of Government of Karnataka in his paper on "Government Accounting and Auditing". The paper argues that the government accounts need to be classified and reported both in their aggregate and disaggregated forms. The need to track and record government financial operations in as detailed, systematic and accurate manner as possible to enable reliable and efficient management of public finances is emphasised in the framing of informed financial decisions that ultimately help in efficient public financial management. The structure of accounts under the Consolidated Fund and the coding pattern of revenue and expenditure is discussed.

Major roles and responsibilities of the Comptroller and Auditor General (CAG) and the major checks undertaken are critically evaluated. Major reform initiatives under treasury system initiated in Karnataka and its limitations are discussed. The paper also addresses the issues of effectiveness of public financial accountability.

In the context of the changing strategies adopted by governments across the globe in general and India in particular in the building of infrastructure, Nagesha has made an effort to unearth the pros and cons of Public Private Partnerships (PPPs) and India's experience this far in meeting the unmet infra needs of the economy and their level of efficiency. The paper brings to light the fact that PPPs are concentrated in sectors like transport largely limited to National highways (NHs), airports and urban infra projects even while areas such as the health and education and rural infra projects remain unattractive despite their huge inadequacy. However, select case studies of PPPs discussed in the paper have proven advantages of cost effectiveness and savings to the government based on the Value for Money analysis. The paper also has observed that the users in particular of the PPP National Highways have experienced time and fuel efficiency. These are important insights in the context of huge infrastructure inadequacies prevailing in the country for alternative financing options and regulatory policies.

In all, the collection of essays presented in this volume have made an attempt to address some of the current Indian public budgeting issues and is hoped to cater to the needs of student and research community at large. The initial idea underlying this venture was to provide a non-technical and basic understanding of public budgeting, the principles underlying the preparation and practices to the general public and student community. In doing so, we thought the most appropriate way to accomplish this is to have both a theoretical and practical understanding of public budgeting by having a mix of contributions from both practitioners having rich experience in government service and academicians with public finance expertise. While it has been quite challenging to capture all the current issues of public budgeting and their ramifications for Indian economy in a single volume, given the vast changes in the global and Indian budgetary practices, we hope a beginning has been made and there may be future additions to this exercise.

References

Gayithri (2014). Housing subsidies in Karnataka. In K. Gayithri (Ed.), *Government Subsidies in Karnataka, ISEC Monograph*, 2014, Monograph, 34.

Hackbart, M., & Ramsey, J. R. (2002). The theory of the public-sector budget: An economic perspective. In A. Khan, & W. B. Hildreth (Eds.), *Budget theory in the public sector*. Quorum Books.

Rao, M. G. (2015). Political economy of government finance in India. *India Review, 14*(1), 58–72.

Chapter 2
Indian Constitutional Framework for Fiscal Regime

V. S. Mallar

1 Introduction

Constitutional law is fundamental law of superior obligations. It is the fulcrum on which entire polity revolves and economic system operates. Generally, the Constitution of India like any other Constitutions of the world is, first and foremost, a political document, setting down a legal framework, but in substance, it is a socio-economic document spelling out and specifying a constitutionally desired socio-economic order. Art. 38(1) of the Constitution categorically envisages and contemplates that the State shall strive to promote the welfare of the people by securing and protecting as effectively as it may a social order in which justice, social, economic and political shall inform all the institutions of the national life.

Since the Constitution of India is a legal document which embodies chosen values, the Fundamental Rights along with the Directive Principles of State Policy constitute the life force of the Constitution, and both of them must be quickened into effective action by meaningful and purposive interpretation. The aforesaid opinion of Chief Justice Chandrachud fortifies the belief that Constitution of India is not merely a politico-legal document; it is equally a socio-economic document which lays down the commitment of the people of this country towards realization of social equality and elimination of economic inequality. This in turn results in the significance of the perception that Part Ill and Part IV (Fundamental Rights and Directive Principles of State Policy) together constitute the core of the commitment to social revolution and economic emancipation and they are the conscience of the Constitution.

At the time of framing of the Constitution of India, doubts relating to fiscal prudence and canons of financial propriety were obviously uppermost in the minds of the founding fathers of the Constitution. Article 39(b) read with Art. 266 (3) and Art. 37 were considered adequate. They never thought profligacy would become a

V. S. Mallar (✉)
National Law School of India University, Nagarbhavi, Bengaluru 560242, India
e-mail: vsmallar@nls.ac.in

G. Karnam (ed.), *Public Budgeting in India*, India Studies in Business and Economics, https://doi.org/10.1007/978-81-322-3917-8_2

reality in the Indian Republic. But later events have proved otherwise. With the above jurisprudential background of the Constitution of India in view, an attempt is made in this article to delve into and to review the fiscal provisions of the Constitution of India, their relevance and rationale the appropriate constitutional authorities, their powers and functions and the impact and influence of these provisions on the Indian economic system as a whole.

2 Constitutional Imperatives

A review of the fiscal regime embodied in the Indian Constitution reveals several significant provisions pertaining to the Indian financial matters Procedure to be followed by Parliament and the State Legislature are detailed in Art. 112 to Art. 116 and Art. 202 to Art. 206; borrowing powers and procedure of the Union and States are set down in Art. 292 and Art. 293; to correct federal financial imbalances, provisions for distribution of the revenues between Union and States (Art. 268 to 272) conferment of Grants-in-aid by the Union (Art. 275) role and status Finance Commission (A. 280); the Constitution of State Finance Commissions for recommendation in respect of devolution to local bodies as a well as powers to impose taxes (Art. 243-I for Panchayats and Art. 243 Y for Municipalities), in addition to the original provisions in the Constitution in Art. 265 which adumbrates the Doctrine of Taxation which has wide ramifications for the fiscal realm. Art. 265 and Art. 266 stand as sentinel on qui vive of legislation along with Art. 245 rightly securing limits for the power play. Art. 360 speaks about the imposition of Financial Emergency. During the pendency of Proclamation of Financial emergency, Union of India in the exercise of executive power has been empowered to issue directions to any state to observe such canons of financial propriety as a may be specified in the direction which will include also reduction of salaries and allowances of persons serving in connection with the affairs of State. A similar provision also exists with respect to persons serving in connection with affairs of the Union. It is also pertinent to note that salaries and allowances of the judges of the Supreme Court of India and the High Courts may also be reduced notwithstanding what is said expressly in proviso to Art. 125 (2) and proviso to Art. 221(2) if Art. 148 envisages a Comptroller and Auditor General of India, whose powers and functions are clearly indicated in Arts. 149 to 151. Some of these Articles have undergone Constitutional amendments in 1976 and 1979. While the foregoing provisions of the Constitution of India are broad in their scope, the VII Schedule of the Constitution specifies the relevant entries in the Union

- List, State List and Concurrent List, which can have a deep impact and significance on the sufficiency of the finances to discharge the functions constitutionally required of the Union and the States. The founding fathers of the Constitution felt that the mechanism of devolution of taxes, revenues and grants-in-aid would have lasting effect on the balance between functions and finances. One of the perennial problems of a democratic federal polity is the asymmetry between functions and finances. The centralization of taxation for levy and collection of taxes in a comprehensive economy with concomitant macro-economic administration and management under Constitution of India leads to the arousal and accrual of enhanced resources for the Union which has much of the variety of functions that are required to be discharged for the welfare of the common man, although the Constitution of India fixes the primary responsibility directly on States in general and local bodies in particular after 73rd and 74th Constitutional Amendments for ensuring compliance with existing laws.

One of the major Constitutional Amendments which has deep repercussions for the financial system of the country is in the form of Art. 366 (29 A) "Deemed Sale" vide the Constitutional 46th Amendment 1982 which widened the concept of sale and brought within its purview of sale six transactions giving the power to the States, units of Indian Federation to exclusive competence to impose taxes under Entry 54 List II of the VII Schedule. This has resulted in the enhancement of financial resources to States than hitherto before passing of the 46th Constitutional Amendment Act.

Art. 280 also underwent basic change by insertion of Clause (bb) © and (d) by the Constitution 73rd Amendment Act of 1992. The Finance Commission is a constitutional authority under Art. 220 to make recommendation to correct federal financial imbalances in the interest of sound finance. Notwithstanding its constitutional status, the Planning Commission which has been established by an executive decision of the Government of India, has been exercising some overlapping functions in the field of Centre–State fiscal relations and consequently strategies are required to be devised to coordinate activities of both Finance Commission and Planning Commission.

The Finance Commission makes recommendations once in every 5 years, and it is an ad hoc body. It becomes *functus officio* as soon as report is submitted to the President. It basically deals with tax sharing and fiscal need grants. In contradistinction with Finance Commission, the Planning Commission is a continuous body and deals with large-scale resources by way of Grants under A. 282 and loans to the States for planning purposes. In view of the same, the Planning Commission has come to exert and extend a profound influence on the Indian Federalism more than the Finance Commission. The Finance Commission is not required to take into account the Centre–State fiscal relations under the plan. The Planning Commission steps in after recommendations are made by the Finance Commission in the realm of tax sharing and grants and plan programs both for the Centre and States taking into their needs and resources and finally decided the quantum of money to be given to each state by way of loans and grants under Art. 282. Thus, the funds which flow from the Planning Commission recommendation is more massive and substantial than the resources distributed through Finance Commission. This development has given new dimensions to the Constitutional provisions and made a paradigm shift in the area of Centre–State fiscal relationships, Of course, it must be admitted that a certain degree of coordination has been achieved between Planning Commission and Finance Commission over a period of time. The five-year time schedule for which Finance Commission gives its recommendations now more or less coincides with the time frame of five-year plan, and consequently, it enables the Planning Commission to make necessary adjustments in the plan grants in the context of the recommendations of the Finance Commission. Moreover, a member of the Planning Commission is now nominated to the Finance Commission. There has been a proposal that Finance Commission should not be just an ad hoc body and a standing mechanism be created to maintain vertical transfers. It must also be said to the credit of the Eleventh Finance Commission that it recommended a small permanent secretariat to maintain and sustain continuity in the working of Finance Commissions.

3 Controller and Auditor General (CAG)

Under the Controller and Auditor General (duties, powers and conditions of service) Act, 1971, Parliament has stipulated two types of functions for CAG. In the capacity of an accountant, he is required to compile the accounts of the Union and the States. These accounts are required to be kept in such form as the president may prescribe on the advice of CAG (Art. 150). As an auditor, CAG is required to audit all the receipts and expenditure of the Union and States and to ascertain whether money disbursed was legally available for and applicable to the service or purposes to which the same has been applied and whether expenditure is inconformity with the authority which governs it.

It is needless to mention that audit plays a pivotal role in the sphere of legislative financial control. The Legislature appropriates specific sums for specific "purposes of the Constitution" as Art. 266 (3) contemplates. Audit ensures that both the sum allotted and the purposes authorized are in conformity with the law. The scrutiny and check of such figures and purposes should be done by independent person so as not to deviate or depart from 'legislative intention. If this is not done, legislative control over appropriation may be frustrated. CAG is required to satisfy on behalf of the Legislature as to the economy and efficiency of the expenditure. Hence, audit is meant for ascertaining whether there are waste and extravagance. CAG is authorised to refuse to permit any expenditure in contravention of the provisions of the constitution and any law made there under. Therefore, CAG is required to uphold the Constitution of India as by law established to the best of ability, knowledge and judgment (III Schedule) in the field of financial administration. In this way, it is incumbent upon CAG to verify any improper exercise of discretion, and the propriety of sanction and expenditure. CAG strengthens the accountability of the administration in the financial sphere. The legislative control of the executive is made more effective by retrospective, ex post facto examination of the expenditure. In view of the above function, CAG has been given the status similar to that of the Judge of the Supreme Court.

Combining such functions of accounting and auditing in the same authority has invited consistently criticism from some quarters. No doubt, accounting is essentially an executive function, whereas auditing is quasi-judicial function, namely checking of financial transaction against the permissions and prohibitions of the Constitution and of the laws.

A combination of two essentially distinct functions inevitably involves some kind of contradictions. Economy and experience have been responsible to create such systems before the commencement of the Constitution. It will be in the interest of constitutional values to disassociate the two functions so as to ensure transparency and accountability in the arena of financial administration. Presently, the disassociation is through separate authority for accounts and audit, but both come under the CAG.

4 Public Finance and Legislative Control

Art. 112 to Art. 116 pertains to the fundamental procedure for the grant of money which the Parliament is required to follow. Art. 202 to Art. 206 prescribes the procedure for the grant of money with the State Legislatures is required to adhere to. The aforesaid Constitutional provisions assure and ensure effective control by elected representative over the financial matters, and President and Governors, respectively, are required to lay down before the Parliament and State Legislature, respectively, an annual financial statement popularly called the budget. This document gives out the estimated income and expenditure for the financial year. The estimates of expenditure show distinctly the sums charged on the Consolidated Fund of India and the sums required to meet other expenditure out of the Consolidated Fund. The expenditure 'charged' on the Consolidated Fund is not submitted to 'vote', it is open to Central Legislature/State Legislature to deliberate upon these non-votable items of expenditure. 'Other expenditure' is required to be submitted in the form of demands for grant to the House of People/Legislative Assembly which has the power to assent/refuse to assent to any demand to reduction of the amount specified therein. Private members have no power to propose new items of expenditure or to increase the amount specified in the statement for any head of expenditure. Thus, no proposal for the expenditure of public revenue can be made except on the recommendations of the executive.

The Legislature thus controls public finance through the grant of money to the administration for expenses in respect of public services, levy of taxes and authorization of loans. The Indian Constitution has envisaged an effective and elaborate mechanism for securing legislative control over public finance, keeping in view the following cardinal principles.

1. The first and foremost principle regulation of Constitutional relations between Government and the Legislature in the matter of finance. The executive cannot raise money by taxation, borrowing or otherwise, without authority of Legislature.
2. The second principle emphasizes the regulation of relations between two branches of Legislature in financial matters. The authority of raising money through the means of taxes or loans or authorizing the same belongs constitutionally exclusively to the popular house viz. Lok Sabha. Rajya Sabha merely

assents to it. It cannot initiate, reverse or alter a grant. Rajya Sabha in relation to the Union or as the case may be Legislative Council in relations to the States does not have authority in this regard. Lok Sabha/Legislative Assembly has the real control over the same. Hence, financial powers are concentrated in the hands of the popular representatives of the people assembled in the Lok Sabha/Legislative Assembly. Rajya Sabha/Legislative Council (wherever there is a bicameral Legislature) has a subsidiary and subordinate role in this regard.

3. There is a restriction on the power of the Legislature to authorize expenditure. Parliament cannot vote money for any purpose whatsoever except on demand made by the ministers. Also, it can allocate monies from the Consolidated Funds only 'for the purposes of the Constitution' as specified in Art. 266 (3).
4. There is also a limitation on the power of the Legislature to impose taxation on its own motion. The Legislature cannot impose any tax except upon the recommendation of the Executive.

5 Constitutional Procedure for Adoption of Bill

Legislation, inter alia includes imposition of tax and appropriation of money. A legislative proposal is made in either of the house in the form of bill. An elaborate procedure pertaining to the passage of bill in a House is laid down in the Rules of Procedures which each House has made (Art. 118 and Art. 208).

The Constitution of India lays down solely the fundamental rules of procedures which are detailed below, all bills except Money bill or financial bill may be introduced in either House of the Parliament. Financial or money bills relate to fiscal matters such as bills authorizing expenditure out of the Consolidated Fund of India or imposition of tax, etc., can be introduced only in the House of Capital. Every bill generally needs the agreement of both Houses of Parliament. If there is disagreement between houses over any provision or provisions as proposed in the bill or over amendments, the bill cannot be said to have passed by both Houses of Parliament. There are two exceptions to the above proposition

a. It pertains to money bill as defined in Art. 109. Money Bill is regulated by a special procedure with which dispenses the necessity of the concurrence of Council of State as regards the provisions mentioned therein.
b. Passing of a Bill at joint sitting of the two Houses. The bill must be other than the Money Bill. In short, the Constitution of India does not provide for the equal powers to both Houses. The Powers of Council of States are limited in two ways.

    i. It has no power to initiate money or financial bill.
    ii. Its consent is dispensed with in the case of money bills.

Other bills despite the absence of consent by the Council of State may become law if they are passed by at a joint sitting in which members of the House of People are numerically more. According to Art. 110, Money Bill contains only provisions dealing with all or any of the following matters namely, Art. 110 (a) to (g).

a. The imposition, abolition, remission, alteration or regulation of any tax;
b. The regulation of the borrowing of money or the giving of any guarantee by the Government of India, or the amendment of law with respect to any financial obligations undertaken by the Government of India;
c. The custody of the Consolidated Fund or the Contingency Fund of India, the payment of money into or the withdrawal of moneys from any such Fund;
d. The appropriation of moneys cut of the Consolidated Fund of India;
e. The declaring of any expenditure charged on the Consolidated Fund of India or the increasing of the amount of any such expenditure;
f. The receipt of money on account of the Consolidated Fund of India or the public account of India or the custody or issue of such money or the audit of the accounts of the Union or of a State; or
g. Any matter incidental to any of the matters specified in sub-clauses (a) to (f).

It is also provided that a bill cannot be considered as Money Bill if it only deals with

i. Imposition of fine or other pecuniary liabilities.
ii. Payment of fees for licenses are fees for services rendered.
iii. Imposition, abolition, remission, alteration and regulation of any tax by any local authority or body for local purposes. If any question arises a whether a bill is a Money Bill or not, the decision of the speaker of the House there on is final.

In short, from the point of view of the procedure of the Parliament, there are three types of Legislative Bills,

1. Money Bill
2. Financial Bill
3. An Ordinary Bill

A Money Bill is a Bill which contains only provisions relating to Art. 110 (1) (a) to (g). A Bill which makes provisions for the items mentioned in Art. 110 (a) to (g) and additionally with any other provision is called a Financial Bill (Art. 117 (1)). A Bill which is neither a Money Bill nor Financial Bill is an Ordinary Bill.

Under Art. 265, which embodies the doctrine of taxation, there are certain constitutional pre-requisites

1. The levy and collection of taxes should only be done under the authority of law. It cannot be done under executive fiat or a unanimous resolution passed by the Legislature or by judicial decision.

Chapter 3
The Budget: What It Means and How It Is Prepared

M. R. Sreenivasa Murthy

1 Introduction

The presentation of Government of India's annual budget in the parliament, as also a state's budget in the legislature, attracts widespread media attention for several days before and after the event. The media coverage of the budget mainly focuses on the highlights of the Finance Minister's budget speech and the critical comments by political parties and business interests. Very rarely is any attempt made to analyse the actual budget documents other than a summary of what is called the Annual Financial Statement and a few highlights of taxation proposals. Also, the process of preparing a government's budget is seldom the subject of public curiosity. The general public therefore remain largely uninformed about the details of the budget proposals relating to how most activities of government are proposed to be financed during the relevant year. According to one critic, '...the budget is always locked in a Black Box to be opened only on the day of its presentation to disseminate the fragrance of its promises, accompanied by long winding speeches of finance ministers often interspersed with couplets embodying the wisdom of sages and carrying very little meaning for the common man; even the bulky documents that the exercise produces are incomprehensible to most'.

In a democracy, taxpaying citizens must have knowledge of the manner in which public funds are being allocated for different purposes and how these funds are being utilised. Informed criticism of the government's financial management can make a significant contribution to efficiency in the functioning of a government. This in turn calls for not only an understanding of the economic and fiscal policies as outlined in the budget speech but also the essential structure of the budget and the terminology used in the budget documents. The present paper is an attempt to

M. R. Sreenivasa Murthy (✉)
Bangalore, India
e-mail: mrsmurthy1976@gmail.com

G. Karnam (ed.), *Public Budgeting in India*, India Studies in Business and Economics, https://doi.org/10.1007/978-81-322-3917-8_3

outline the structure of government's budgets in the Indian context and to explain the more important concepts used in fiscal management.

The budget is essentially a financial statement setting out estimates of a government's anticipated revenues and proposed expenditure for the budget period, usually a year. Unlike many other government documents, the budget has implications of a far-reaching nature affecting the lives of citizens in several ways. The multitude of a government's functions include a variety of activities ranging from the defence of the country to the maintenance of law and order, provision of economic infrastructures like roads and railways to social services like primary and higher education and medical facilities, and promotion of economic activities like agriculture, industries and mining. The effective performance of these functions critically depends upon the funds made available in the budget for meeting the required expenditure. The fiscal strategy adopted by the government is expressed in terms of higher or lower taxes and borrowings proposed to meet the expenditure of the government. The annual budget of a government, and particularly the budget speech of the Finance Minister, depicts a road map for the government's performance for the financial year. The budget speech, along with the Economic Review usually presented on the eve of the presentation of the budget, also provides a review of the main issues facing the economy and the polity, and the approach of the government in addressing those issues. All these aspects of the budget have their impact on the economy and are of vital importance to citizens who seek to have an understanding of the economic environment in which they work and pursue their individual interests.

As is well known to all, the 'presentation of the budget' in the Parliament or a state's legislature involves the reading of the budget speech on the appointed day and tabling of the 'Annual Financial Statement' (the 'budget') and a number of accompanying documents, many of them of a somewhat complex nature. The information provided in these documents mainly includes the detailed estimates of revenue receipts and other funds from a variety of taxes and other sources and expenditure of various departments. Some of these documents are required by law to be presented with the budget, while others are meant to supplement the information contained in the budget. The official Budget Manual of Government of India lists the following as the documents to be presented in the Parliament along with the budget.

1. Finance Minister's Speech (the budget speech)
2. The Annual Financial Statement
3. Key to Budget Documents
4. Demands for Grants
5. Expenditure Budget Volume-1
6. Expenditure Budget Volume-2
7. Receipts Budget
8. Budget at a Glance
9. Key Features of Budget
10. FRBM Statements (As required under the Fiscal Responsibility and Budget Management Act):

a. The Medium-Term Fiscal Policy Statement
b. Fiscal Policy Strategy Statement
c. Macroeconomic Framework Statement.

The following paragraphs attempt a brief description of these documents which should be helpful in understanding the overall structure of the budget and gaining an insight into the terminology used in these documents. The budget process and the formats used both by the Government of India and the state governments being very similar, one can easily make sense of the budget documents of any state with knowledge of the documents of the central budget. We may, however, deal with aspects of a state's budget which are significantly different from the central budget.

2 The Budget Speech

As already mentioned, it is the budget speech of the Finance Minister which attracts the maximum public attention and media scrutiny. Typically, the budget speech begins with a brief review of the prevailing economic situation in the country/state. This has been a tradition both at the Centre and in the States. For example, in the very first budget speech delivered in Parliament after the adoption of the Indian Constitution, the then finance minister John Mathai said on 28 February 1950 that 'I want at this stage to take the House back to the main economic events that occurred during the year 1949…', and to '…survey the principal economic trends…since the last budget was presented'. He then went on to deal with the problems that the country was facing including the situation of inflation caused in the aftermath of the Second World War, the problem of the low level of production in certain sectors, the balance of payments situation and a few other issues. In subsequent years, notably from 1958 to 59, it has been the practice to present a separate Economic Review a day or two before the presentation of the budget, to describe the economic situation in the country/state in some detail. This is intended to serve as a background to an appreciation of the general economic policies of the government as also the proposals that may be included in the budget. Thus the budget speech usually begins with a mention of the main trends in the economic situation, and even major political factors which have a bearing on the budget proposals.

The budget speech of the finance minister is also used by the government as an opportunity to spell out its economic and social philosophy and the strategy adopted to achieve certain specified objectives. An outstanding example of the budget speech laying out an entire range of reforms is to be found in the budget speech of Dr. Manmohan Singh in July 1991. Dr. Singh had then outlined an entire scheme of the liberalisation of the various aspects of the Indian Economy including the move to opening up the economy for foreign direct investment. In more recent times also, finance ministers continue to give expression to various lofty aspirations or policy objectives to preface their budget speeches. For example, in his budget speech of 2015–16, the Union Finance Minister Mr. Arun Jaitley claimed that 'my proposals… lay out the roadmap for accelerating growth, enhancing investment and passing on the benefit of the growth process to the common man, woman, youth and child: those, whose quality of life needs to be improved'. In his budget speech for the following year (2016–17), the Minister also announced what he described as a 'Transform India' agenda based on a set of 'nine pillars' of policy initiatives.

Apart from expressing the policy objectives of the government, the first part of the budget speech typically contains a number of 'budget announcements' of popular interest. These relate to various new programmes and schemes (or changes proposed in the existing programmes) to be implemented during the following financial year giving a brief description of the intended outcomes of these measures. In this part, government often includes measures affecting the day-to-day lives of people, like provision of free or subsidised services, appointment of a new pay commission for government employees, or waiver of outstanding loans of farmers.

The first part of the budget speech also contains a summary of the financial proposals in the budget including the total estimated expenditure for the financial year, the resources proposed to be mobilised from taxes and non-tax revenues, as also the borrowings to be mobilised to cover any excess of estimated expenditure over the total revenues ('the fiscal deficit').

The second half of the budget speech, which is also of great interest to most people who follow the presentation of the budget, typically focuses on taxation proposals, not only those relating to the levy of new taxes but also any increase or restructuring of the existing taxes with concessions or reliefs in those levies. The rationale behind the tax proposals is also set out in the budget speech along with an estimate of the financial impact of the proposals. Details of individual tax proposals are given in the Annexure to the budget speech. The impact of these proposals relating to taxation may often be immediate and dramatic as any tax relief may make an immediate and significant difference to people's incomes or the prices of certain commodities. It is to be noted that by an existing Act of Parliament, the tax proposals relating to indirect taxes (e.g. excise duty) are made effective on the day of the presentation of the budget when the Government also introduces the Finance Bill containing the legal provisions relating to taxation.

3 The Annual Financial Statement

The most important of the budget documents is called 'the Annual Financial Statement' which is 'the budget' in terms of the Constitution. The Constitution describes the budget (the Annual Financial Statement) as a statement of the estimated receipts and expenditure of the Government of India or a State for a financial year (Articles 112 and 202). Being an extremely brief and consolidated summary of all receipts and payments detailed in various accompanying budget documents, the Annual Financial Statement of even Government of India barely exceeds a dozen pages in print. Only the major categories of 'receipts' or the sources of funds and expenditure of government are shown in this document. The document gives these figures, as is customary in most budget documents, in four sets. The actual figures of revenue or expenditure of the previous financial year are given first. These figures are followed by the budget estimates (as approved) and the revised estimates (as likely) for the current year, i.e. the year in which the budget is being presented. The last column shows the figures relating to receipts or expenditure of the budget year, the forthcoming financial year to which the budget relates. The Annual Financial Statement also presents the summary of the total estimated receipts and expenditure in three main parts, i.e. the Consolidated Fund, the Contingency Fund and the Public Account.

4 One Budget, Many 'Funds'

'The Consolidated Fund' consists of all monies which 'belong to the government', i.e. the monies collected as taxes, duties, fees and other charges and all loans raised by government as also any repayment receipts of loans advanced by it. In the case of Government of India, the Consolidated Fund does not include the portion of the central taxes which are assigned to the states as only the centre's share of such revenues is deemed to be at the disposal of the Government of India (Article 266 of the Constitution). Any expenditure out of the Consolidated Fund of India can be incurred only as authorised by the Parliament, and in the case of the Consolidated Fund of a State, as authorised by its legislature, with the exception of items of expenditure classified as 'charged expenditure' (explained later) which is part of the budget but is not subject to vote by the parliament or the state legislature.

Article 267 of the Constitution also provides for the creation of a Contingency Fund of India, and a similar fund for each of the States, as may be approved by the Parliament or the concerned state legislature. This is an imprest amount, placed at the disposal of the government. It is in the nature of an adhoc authorisation to incur unforeseen expenditure up to a specified limit, a lump sum provision in the budget without any specific item of expenditure indicated. Using this provision, the government can incur expenditure with funds to be drawn out of the consolidated fund on any item of expenditure not included in the budget. Such expenditure can be approved by the legislature at a later date as part of a budget, or supplementary proposals for grants. On the legislature granting its approval for such proposals, the expenditure is transferred to the consolidated fund account and the amount drawn from the contingency fund is restored to enable further expenditure of a similar nature if necessary. The size of the contingency fund of government of India in 2016–17 was Rs. 500 crores. In the states, this limit is much smaller, with a state like Karnataka keeping it at a mere Rs. 5 crores.

Monies which do not 'belong' to government but which are received by it only as deposits form the 'Public Account'. The public account of the centre or a state typically includes funds received as contributions to the public provident fund, small savings, earnest money deposits for public works, and deposits made under orders of various courts. Temporary account entries at the time of transfer of cash from or to Pay and Accounts Officers or Treasuries within the government account and amounts yet to be classified to the appropriate source of revenues and therefore held as 'suspense account' are also included in this account. The receipts into the public account and payments made out of it are generally not subject to vote by the Parliament or the legislature of the state.

The budget also classifies the various items of receipts of government into 'revenue' and 'capital' receipts, and payments into 'revenue' and 'capital' disbursements. Generally, receipts of government which are non-redeemable (which do not involve an obligation to repay) and which are not received as sale proceeds of an asset are called revenue receipts. These include monies received from various taxes (both direct and indirect taxes), fees and charges relating to any services, seigniorage, royalties, and rents charged for the use of any resources or assets, fines and penalties collected under various laws, interest on loans advanced by government, as also any profits or dividends earned on investments made. The revenue receipts are generally of a recurring nature. The second category 'capital receipts' consist of monies borrowed from various sources, and proceeds of any sale of physical, financial or other assets like disinvestment of governments shares in public enterprises or sale of broadband spectrum. Typically, capital receipts of a government add to its liabilities or result in a reduction of its assets. Payments covering expenditure on items of a routine and recurring nature like salaries and maintenance of public assets are treated as 'revenue expenditure', while monies spent on construction or creation of various public assets, advancing of loans or repayment of loans borrowed by government are treated as 'capital expenditure'. The revenue and capital parts of the budget are also often described as 'above the line' and 'below the line' items, respectively.

5 The Revenue Budget

The first part of the Annual Financial Statement (AFS) typically depicts a summary of the 'revenue' side of the budget under the Consolidated Fund account. Three categories of revenue receipts depicted include (a) tax revenue, (b) non-tax revenue and (c) grants-in-aid and contributions. The central budget's AFS shows four categories of tax revenue, i.e. taxes on income and expenditure (income tax, corporate tax, etc.), taxes on property and capital transactions (securities transactions tax, estate duty, etc.), taxes on commodities and services (excise duty, customs duty, etc.) and taxes of Union territories without legislature. For example, the estimated revenue from all these taxes as shown in the central budget for the year 2016–17 was Rs. 16.31 lakh crores. After excluding the share of central taxes allocated to states of Rs. 5.70 lakh crores, the tax revenue of the Central government is shown as Rs. 10.61 lakh crores. Similarly, the estimated non-tax revenue for the year is shown under the categories of interest receipts, coinage and mint charges, revenue from railways, postal and communication services, and fees and charges received from myriad central departments. The total of non-tax revenue for the year 2016–17 in the Central budget is estimated at about Rs. 5.72 lakh crores. The last category of revenue receipts includes grants (not loans) and other contributions (including value of materials and equipment) received from external sources. The total revenue receipts of the central government for 2016–17, including tax and non-tax revenues, are thus estimated at about Rs. 16.33 lakh crores.

It is thus obvious that tax revenues comprise the predominant part of the revenue receipts of the Central government. This is also true in the case of most state governments in the country. In the AFS of a state government, its revenue receipts are depicted in the same format as in the central budget, mentioning items of the state's own sources of revenue like land revenue, stamps and registration, sales tax (VAT), state excise and sundry other sources.

Just as the revenue of the government is classified according to the nature of its source, the expenditure is shown under four broad categories depending upon the main objective for which it is being incurred. These are (1) General Services, (2) Social Services, (3) Economic Services and (4) Grants-in-Aid. The expenditure category of General services includes the establishments of the President of India, the Parliament, the Council of Ministers, tax collection Departments, the defence services and interest payments on government debt. Social Services cover the areas of education, health services, SC/ST and Backward Classes Welfare, etc. The category of Economic Services includes the activities relating to Ministries of Agriculture, rural development, irrigation, energy, transport, etc. Central grants to state governments and union Territories (other than grants given as part of central sector schemes, etc.) as also grants given to foreign countries are included in the last category. A similar grouping of expenditure categories is also followed in the budget of the state governments. These expenditure categories are meant to broadly indicate the relative shares of expenditure incurred by government on its functions of various kinds.

In the Central government's budget for 2016–17, the total estimated revenue expenditure on these four categories which includes the entire gamut of Central government services including the grants given to states and union territories for various purposes is estimated at about Rs. 19.87 lakh crores. Thus, the revenue expenditure of the Central government for the year 2016–17 is in excess of the revenue receipts shown above by about Rs. 3.55 lakh crores. This amount being the shortfall in the government's revenue receipts to cover the revenue expenditure is considered the 'revenue deficit' for the year. This implies that the government cannot meet all the projected expenditure on revenue account with its tax and non-tax revenues. Therefore, to meet this shortfall in revenue, the government will resort to borrowings or other 'capital receipts'. If on the other hand, there is a happy situation of the government's revenue receipts amounting to more than the projected revenue expenditure, then the budget is said to have a 'revenue surplus' which can be used to meet the government's non-revenue or capital expenditure.

It may be noted that during the recent years, most state governments in the country are able to show a revenue surplus in their budgets, as their revenue receipts are in excess of their revenue expenditure while the Central government continues to run a revenue deficit. Maintaining a revenue surplus is also a requirement of fiscal consolidation mandated by law under the Fiscal Responsibility Legislation adopted by the Government of India and the states.

6 The Capital Budget

The capital expenditure of the Central government and the states is also grouped into four main categories of general services, social services, economic services and loans and advances depending upon the sector or the purpose for which the expenditure is being incurred. Capital expenditure is incurred not only for building economic infrastructure projects like national highways, railway networks and nuclear power plants, but also infrastructure needed for social services like educational and scientific establishments, general administration and defence services. Proposed repayment of the principal portion of loans borrowed earlier is capital expenditure while payment of interest on such loans is revenue expenditure. Loans to be advanced to state governments, government companies or foreign countries and any investments in public sector banks and other undertakings also form part of capital expenditure.

Generally, governments finance their capital expenditure with capital receipts, which include borrowings from internal or external sources. The quantum of borrowings is reduced if the government's revenue receipts exceed the amount needed to cover their revenue expenditure, leaving a revenue surplus which will partly finance the capital expenditure. Where the revenues are inadequate to cover the entire revenue expenditure (reflecting a revenue deficit situation), the Central government, as also the states have to resort to borrowings to meet part of the revenue expenditure (the revenue deficit), and also the amount needed to finance the capital expenditure part of their budget. In the present situation (2017–18), the Central government borrows both for financing part of its revenue expenditure as well as its capital expenditure. Many of the states are able to generate a revenue surplus and therefore their borrowings are meant for financing their capital expenditure.

Borrowings by government (public debt) generally constitute the main form of capital receipts in the budget of both the Central and State governments in India. A variety of debt instruments like treasury bills of short duration (less than one year) and government bonds of medium and longterm maturity enable governments to raise funds from the domestic money market. Governments, both Central and State, also avail of temporary ways and means advances from the central bank, i.e. the Reserve Bank of India. Borrowing from external agencies like the World Bank and the IMF is resorted to when it is necessary to finance long-term development projects or to meet emergent financial situations. The budget documents generally show borrowings of government on net basis, depicting the amount borrowed over and above the repayments during the year. For example, if the government proposes to raise Rs. 1 lakh crores as fresh loans in a year and repay Rs. 50,000 crores of the principal of the existing loans, the budget will mention the net borrowing of Rs. 50,000 crores as capital receipts.

Repayment of loans received from states, public sector companies or other governments of any loans obtained by them, and sale proceeds of assets like shares in Government companies also form part of a Government's capital receipts and are called non-debt capital receipts.

The total capital expenditure of Government of India as shown in the budget for 2016–17 was about Rs. 2.47 lakh crores which together with the revenue deficit of Rs. 3.54 lakh crores necessitated mobilising capital receipts of about Rs. 6.01 lakh crores during the year. Taking into account about Rs. 0.67 lakh crores of non-debt capital receipts by way of recoveries of loans and other sources (like disinvestment of government shares in public undertakings/sale of other assets), the budget shows a net borrowings target of Rs. 5.33 lakh crores. This represents the overall deficit of the budget described as the ‘fiscal deficit’ which is the amount of government expenditure to be financed entirely by borrowings during the year.

7 The Public Account

As mentioned earlier, the public account consists of monies received by government other than revenue receipts and capital receipts. The government receives these monies merely as a banker, and refunds/repays these amounts to the concerned, often with interest, in accordance with the terms and conditions governing such deposits. The amounts in the public account are available to government as its cash balances (with the Reserve Bank). The government typically invests these cash balances in short-term instruments to earn some interest. Also, these cash balances often provide the liquidity needed to meet government expenditure when there is a temporary mismatch between the government’s own receipts and expenditure commitments.

In the budget of the Government of India, the public account is shown in six major categories. The National Small Savings Fund (NSSF), which accounts for the bulk of the public account (about Rs. 5.20 lakh crores out of about Rs. 9.61 lakh crores in 2016–17), consists of monies deposited by people in National Savings Certificates and post office savings bank accounts. The State Provident Fund deposits and postal insurance contributions constitute another substantial part of the public account. Reserve Funds set apart by government out of the Consolidated fund for various purposes (e.g. Central Road Fund, NREGA Fund, National Disaster Response Fund) are set apart and deposited in public account for being used as and when necessary by the concerned agencies. Deposits made by the public in respect of court cases, etc., are another component of the public account. Finally, suspense accounts of government (amounts received pending classification/reconciliation), money orders and other remittances account for a small portion of the public account. The public account balances are of considerable help to government in the day-to-day cash management and meeting its liquidity needs even though receipts and payments of public account funds are not subject to vote by the Parliament or the state legislature. Public account balances can also be used by government as part of their borrowings (capital receipts) to the extent such funds are available over a significant period. Typically, National Savings Scheme Funds are used for advancing loans to state governments as these deposits are available for comparatively long periods. But such borrowings from the public account are also subject to the approval of parliament/legislature as part of the budget.

8 Voted and Charged Expenditure

As mentioned above, any expenditure out of the Consolidated Fund of India can be incurred only as authorised by the parliament, and in the case of the consolidated fund of a state, as authorised by its legislature. Under the Constitution, an exception is, however, made to this rule in the case of specified items of expenditure categorised as 'charged'. These items include expenditure on the establishments of certain functionaries like the President of India and Governors of states, institutions like the Supreme Court of India and the high courts and repayment of loans borrowed by Government. These items are treated as 'charged' on the Consolidated Fund and are not subject to vote by parliament or the state legislature even though they are subject to discussion. The Annual Financial Statement and the budget documents show the 'charged' items separately from the other items of expenditure which are 'voted'.

9 Receipts Budget

From the point of understanding the financial position of the government, one of the most informative documents presented with the budget is the 'Receipts Budget'. This is a document which provides a source-wise estimate of the monies that the government proposes to mobilise during the financial year, to meet the entire expenditure as set out in the budget. It provides details of the estimated tax and non-tax revenue receipts and capital receipts. In respect of each source of receipts, the amount actually received during the previous year, the amount estimated in the budget and the revised estimate for the current year, and the estimated receipts for the forthcoming (budget) year are shown in this document. These estimates are also accompanied by brief but helpful explanatory notes about the nature of the source and the reasons for any major variation in the trend of receipts. For example, in the central budget, details of tax revenue under each of the individual levies in the categories of taxes on income, customs and excise duties, service tax and taxes of union territories are shown along with the various components like surcharges and cesses. The share of central taxes to be apportioned to the states and the net amount to be retained with the Central government are clearly indicated. As per the Eightieth Constitutional Amendment, only the Centre's share of the central taxes forms part of the consolidated fund of the Central government.

Similar detailed analysis is given in this document in respect of all the sources of non-tax revenues like the revenue from railways and postal services, dividends earned on investments made in public sector enterprises, royalties earned on oil exploration licences, interest received on loans advanced by government to various companies, fees charged for various administrative services like issue of passports or user charges collected in government-run hospitals.

The 'Receipts Budget' is most remarkable for the amount of detailed information it contains on the government's debt which is listed under the category of 'capital receipts'. This section of the document first lists the non-debt capital receipts in two categories: recoveries of loans and advances from states, foreign governments, public sector enterprises and others, and from proceeds of divestment of government's shares in various companies. This is followed by a source-wise listing of borrowings proposed both from internal and external sources. The internal sources include a variety of financial instruments like treasury bills of 14–364 days duration, ways and means advances representing temporary borrowings from the RBI, and government bonds of different periods of maturity and rates of interest sold to the public. Borrowings from internal sources also include amounts of public account deposits like Provident fund and small savings which the Central government may itself utilise or invest in the market by issue of bonds. A part of the small savings deposits is earmarked for being lent to the states. Any amount remaining in the public account uninvested will be added to the government's cash balances. If the cash balances are utilised for funding the government's expenditure, it is shown as 'drawdown of cash balances', which is another expression for borrowings.

The 'external debt' section of the document lists the foreign sources from which the government proposes to receive funds during the year. These may include loans from the World Bank or other international organisations or governments of other countries. Investments made by foreign countries and organisations in Central government securities are also shown as capital receipts. The sum total of the capital receipts listed in the Receipts Budget thus reflects the extent to which the government's expenditure is to be financed by funds other than its revenues and its dependence on borrowed funds.

Several Annexes to the Receipts Budget include further valuable information regarding the financial position of the government. These statements indicate trends in the collection of revenues and the level of borrowings during the last ten years, as also trends in plan and non-plan expenditure. The total debt owed by government to both internal and external sources is listed source wise with a summary of the overall liabilities and assets of the government (excluding assets relating to defence and certain other items of sensitive nature). Thus, the Receipts Budget represents a veritable mine of information regarding the financial position of the government.

The Receipts Budget of a state government also contains a detailed presentation of all the sources of revenues and capital receipts even though it is usually less elaborate in the explanatory notes provided.

10 Demands for Grants

Just as the Receipts Budget gives an overview of all the sources of government's revenues and capital receipts, the document called 'Demands for Grants' lists out all the categories of government's expenditure for the budget year. As already mentioned above, any expenditure out of the consolidated fund can be incurred only after obtaining the approval of the Parliament or the state's legislature concerned. This approval for expenditure is given through an Appropriation Bill passed for the purpose. The legislature thus ‘grants’ approval for expenditure after considering the ‘demands’ of the government for authorisation to incur expenditure. The Demands for Grants is therefore a key to understanding the expenditure side of the budget.

The funds required for expenditure by different Ministries/Departments of government are listed under separate ‘demands’ which represent a group of activities to be funded by the budget, with each group bearing a demand number. Sometimes, the same Ministry or Department has its activities classified under different demands. For example, the Ministry of Agriculture and Farmers’ Welfare has its demands categorised under three separate demands, i.e. Demand No. (1) Department of Agriculture, Cooperation and Farmer’s Welfare, (2) Department of Agricultural Research and Education and (3) Department of Animal Husbandry, Dairying and Fisheries. In all, Government of India’s 2016–17 budget has ninety-eight separate ‘Demands’ including a demand for the expenditure required to be approved for each of the Union Territories without legislature.

Each of the demands in the document contains a statement with break-up of ‘charged’ and ‘voted’ expenditure for each of the items of expenditure. The expenditure is then given under broad itemisation called ‘Major Heads’. The major heads of account of each ministry/department are numbered according to a unique number code which helps in classification of expenditure in the government accounts. The brief nomenclature of the head of account also gives an indication of the purpose for which the proposed expenditure is to be incurred. For example, the Government of India’s budget for 2016–17 lists the following Major heads in the Revenue Section of the demand no. 1 relating to Agriculture:

> 3451 Secretariat-Economic Services; 2070 Other Administrative Services; 2401 Crop Husbandry; 2402 Soil and Water Conservation; 2416 Agricultural Financial Institutions; 2425 Co-operation; 2435 Other Agricultural Programmes; 2552 North-East Areas; 3601 Grants-in-Aid to State Governments; and 3602 Grants-in-Aid to Union Territories Governments.

Similarly, the following major heads are listed under the Capital Section of the same Demand:

> 4070 Capital Outlay on Administrative Services; 4401 Capital Outlay on Crop Husbandry, 4402 Capital Outlay on Soil and Water Conservation; 4435 Capital Outlay on Other Agricultural Programmes; 4552 Capital Outlay on North Eastern Areas; and 6425 Loans for Cooperation.

Each of the major heads of account usually has a number of minor and detailed heads of account grouped under it, and the budgeted expenditure is to be further classified into these minor and detailed heads. The details of the minor and detailed heads are given in the budget documents called the Expenditure Budget and Detailed Demands for Grants.

11 The Expenditure Budget

The 'Expenditure Budget' of Government of India is presented in two volumes, which cover the entire expenditure proposed in the budget analysed in different ways. It is interesting to see that the same data relating to the budget provisions for expenditure of different ministries and departments of government can be presented in more than a dozen ways, each representing a different perspective. Thus, the Expenditure Budget begins with a simple table giving the total expenditure of the government by all its branches, classified into revenue and capital expenditure separately for plan and non-plan categories. The Expenditure Budget for 2016–17, for example, shows the total expenditure of Rs. 19.77 lakh crores divided into revenue expenditure of Rs. 17.30 lakh crores, and capital expenditure of 2.46 lakh crores. The revenue expenditure is further classified into non-plan expenditure of Rs. 13.27 lakh crores and plan expenditure of 4.03 lakh crores. (This practice of making a distinction between plan and non-plan expenditure is proposed to be discontinued with effect from the budget of 2017–18.) Similarly, the capital expenditure includes non-plan expenditure of Rs. 1.00 lakh crores and plan expenditure of Rs. 1.46 lakh crores. The table also goes on to give a further break-up of the proposed plan expenditure into the amounts to be given to states and union territories as central assistance for their plans and the amounts to be spent by the Central government itself as plan expenditure. In addition, the plan expenditure proposed to be incurred by the central public enterprises is also shown separately. A subsequent statement in the document gives the revenue and capital expenditure proposed for each ministry or department and the five union territories without legislatures under non-plan and plan categories. These statements are followed by brief notes explaining the reasons for increase or decrease in the proposed provisions over the provisions made/expenditure incurred in the previous year.

The Expenditure Budget further analyses the non-plan expenditure into interest payments and debt servicing, subsidies on food, petroleum products, etc., and grants and loans to be given to states, union territories, public enterprises, and foreign governments. The Central government's own non-plan expenditure is also classified into expenditure on General Services, Social Services and Economic Services. The grants and loans given to States, Union Territories, etc., are also listed individually in separate statements. The plan expenditure in the budget is similarly depicted in different statements giving the amounts of expenditure by different ministries, union territories and public enterprises.

12 Benefits to Special Categories

The Expenditure Budget includes a Gender Budget showing the quantum of public expenditure earmarked in the budget for women under various programmes and activities of the Central government. This section is followed by statements showing the budgeted expenditure on various schemes under the Scheduled Castes Subplan, the Tribal Subplan, and for the welfare of children. The expenditure proposed to be incurred by various ministries for the benefit of the north-eastern states is also separately depicted. Other useful statements included in the volume provide information on trends in plan and non-plan expenditure over the past ten years, grants for creation of capital assets and for meeting the salary expenditure of various organisations, and the establishment expenditure of various ministries of the Central government itself.

While the first volume of the Expenditure Budget presents the government's expenditure proposals in terms of various parameters like capital or revenue expenditure or plan or non-plan expenditure and the sections of society likely to be impacted by it etc., it does not give details of the item-wise expenditure to be incurred by each of the ministries and departments of the Government. That information is provided in volume 2 of the Expenditure Budget in a more or less straightforward manner. This volume (called the Notes on Demands for Grants) gives details of the expenditure proposals for each Ministry and Demand, under all major heads of account with break-up of allocations for the subheads as well. This is perhaps the document which the ministries and departments refer to ascertain the allocations for their programmes and to cite the budget heads indicated there in order to sanction expenditure for their activities. Even the information in this volume of the Expenditure Budget is not sufficiently detailed to cover allocations meant to be used for the detailed items of expenditure like salaries, allowances, transport facilities, and building rents. Those minute details of allocations are prepared by each Ministry and Department separately and presented to Parliament as Detailed Demands for Grants. These detailed documents are not presented with the Budget but are made available to Parliament when the demands of the concerned Ministry are taken up for consideration during the detailed discussion of Demands.

The practice in the states, however, is to present a document called the Summary of Demands and Charged Appropriations along with documents containing the details of expenditure estimates with the budget.

13 FRBM Documents

The Fiscal Responsibility and Budget Management Act is a legislation passed by Parliament in 2003 to provide a legal framework for fiscal prudence in the management of the finances of the Central government. Among the States, Karnataka passed its Fiscal Responsibility Act in 2002, while almost all the other states passed their fiscal responsibility legislations after the Central Act came into force. Essentially, the fiscal responsibility legislations requires the Centre and the States to limit the fiscal deficit (the annual net borrowings by government) to a maximum of 3% of the Gross Domestic Product (GDP) in the case of the Central Government and 3% of the Gross

State Domestic Product (GSDP) in the case of a State Government. Further, both the Centre and the States were required to eliminate revenue deficits in their budgets by 2008–09, so that their borrowings represented by the fiscal deficit were to be used only for meeting capital expenditure. The FRBM law also imposes limits on extending government guarantees for loans borrowed by public sector undertakings and others.

The record of the Central government, as also some states, in complying with the fiscal consolidation regime envisaged by the FRBM legislation has fallen short of the initial expectations. The target year for limiting the fiscal deficit to less than 3% of GDP was shifted by Government of India from 2007 to 08 by an amendment to the FRBM law on the ground of fiscal expansion considered necessary in the wake of the global financial crisis in 2008. This date has further been extended by subsequent amendments. In the case of states, the target of lower than 3% fiscal deficit was achieved by most states by 2010, even though some states did have substantial borrowings through their public undertakings which were used for meeting the revenue expenditure responsibilities of the government (e.g. power sector subsidies). In the matter of limiting the overall debt burden of the government also, the record has been mixed. As against the optimum level of cumulative combined debt of state and Central governments at about 53% of GDP as estimated by the Twelfth Finance Commission, the actual debt level is in excess of 75% of GDP in 2017–18. As reflected in the 2016–17 budget documents of the Central Government, the total debt burden of the Central Government stood at Rs. 68.92 lakh crores as at the end of March 2016 representing about 50% of the estimated GDP for 2015–16. The combined debt burden of the States amounted to Rs. 31.04 lakh crores as per the budget estimates for the year 2015–16, according to the statistics published by the Reserve Bank of India. This represented about 24% of the combined GSDP of states.

An important aspect of the cumulative debt of the government is also the burden of interest payments it imposes on the budget. For example, the interest payments on the outstanding debt of the Central Government during 2016–17 are estimated at Rs. 4.93 lakh crores, which amount to 28% of the total revenue expenditure and 46.7% of the total revenue receipts of the Central government for the year. In the case of the States, their combined debt burden necessitated an estimated total of Rs. 2 lakh crores of interest payments during 2015–16 amounting to about 11.2% of their revenue receipts for the year as per the Review of States' Budgets published by the Reserve Bank of India. The recommended interest payments to revenue receipts ratio according to the Twelfth Finance Commission is 28% for the Central government and 15% for the State governments.

The FRBM Act also requires the government to present to the parliament three important statements which provide the analytical background for understanding the economic philosophy and the fiscal strategy underlying the budget proposals. In the Macroeconomic Framework Statement, the government gives its analysis of the prevailing economic situation in the country including the growth prospects of different sectors of the economy and the GDP, trends in wholesale and retail prices, the money supply and credit availability position, and the trends in the capital markets. The Medium-Term Fiscal Policy Statement and the Fiscal Policy Strategy

Statement outline the trends in important fiscal parameters like the revenue and fiscal deficits as well as the overall debt position of the government. The trends in the growth of different categories of revenue and expenditure as well as the policy and strategies of the government in these matters are explained in these documents. The FRBM documents require the government to spell out a coordinated approach to the management of its finances in keeping with the development needs of the country's economy. They also help in making the fiscal policies of the government transparent to the general public.

14 Other Supporting/Explanatory Documents

Budget documents presented to the Parliament include other explanatory documents like the Budget at a Glance, Key to Budget Documents and Highlights/Key Features of the Budget. The Budget at a Glance provides a summary of the Annual Financial Statement, the allocations proposed for various Central Government Plan programmes, and the total grants proposed to be given to states and union territories. The Key to Budget Documents describes in brief the nature of information available in each of the budget documents. The Highlights is a list of the major initiatives in the Budget, in terms of new measures for resource mobilisation, new welfare and development programmes and other aspects of the budget for which the government would like greater media attention.

15 Budget in the Making: The Process

While watching the presentation of the annual budget on television or reading about it in the newspapers is exciting to many people, few are really aware of the long-drawn process involved in preparing a government's budget, whether at the Centre or in the States. Also, the media coverage of the budget event perhaps masks two important aspects of the budget-making process. First, notwithstanding that the finance minister who presents the budget is depicted as the author of the budget, it is a document prepared with the active participation of most branches of government, including all the ministries, departments, and even companies and corporations owned by the government. Second, neither the finance minister nor the finance ministry/department of the government have a completely free hand in determining the size and shape of the budget. The finance minister may announce a number of welfare measures to benefit different classes of citizens, but such measures are usually formulated in consultation with different ministries beforehand. Any important economic policies, even if announced in the budget speech for the first time, are similarly formulated in consultation with a number of ministries and departments. Most expenditure proposals originate in different ministries and departments for the finance ministry to incorporate in the budget documents. Also, barring measures like imposing new taxes or restructuring existing taxes, the budget is largely determined by the ongoing activities of the government most of which are of a recurring or continuing nature.

Given the fact that the government's budget is a regular annual feature and most activities funded by the budget are of a continuing nature, it is inevitable that the process of budget preparation is highly standardised. Most of the work in preparing a budget is done in a routine manner according to set procedures and a predetermined calendar every year. However, the exercise is not completely lacking in tension and drama, particularly as the budget preparation approaches the final phases, days before its presentation in the Parliament or state legislature.

The various activities involved in the preparation of a government's annual budget are typically spread over a period of about five months. It has been the practice that the annual budget of the Central government for the financial year commencing on 1st April is presented on the last working day of February (it is now shifted to the end of January with effect from 2017). The work on the preparation of the budget generally begins towards the end of September of the previous calendar year. The Budget Division of the finance ministry kicks off the process by issuing a 'Budget Circular' containing detailed instructions to all the ministries and departments on the preparation of estimates of receipts and expenditure for the next financial year. The Budget Circular deals with the procedure to be followed in preparing the estimates, the formats in which the estimates are to be presented and the dates by which these estimates have to be submitted to different levels of scrutiny within each ministry/department, and finally, to the finance ministry.

As we have seen earlier, the Budget estimates deal with estimates of resources including tax revenues, non-tax revenues and capital receipts like borrowings. Estimates of tax revenues are furnished by the departments responsible for tax administration like the Central Board of Direct Taxes (CBDT) and the Central Board of Excise and Customs (CBEC) in the case of the Central government. In the States, it is the departments dealing with tax collection like the Commercial Taxes Department, the Department of State Excise, the Department of Stamps and Registration, the Motor Vehicles Department which have to provide the estimates of tax receipts for the budget year. Typically, the budget preparation procedure requires that the estimates are prepared first at the level of each district, circle or zone in each tax collection agency and then aggregated at the level of the heads of the respective departments. The estimates are to be prepared keeping in view the taxes collected by each level of the agency during the last two or three years, the trend of collection during the current year, and any change in the potential for collection due to increase or decline in the business or other activity taxed or due to revision in the rate of taxes applicable. Every department of government is urged to carefully consider every year the possibility of increasing the revenue by improving the efficiency in collection or by suitably enlarging the tax base. A similar procedure is followed in preparing estimates for non-tax revenue collected by many government agencics, like toll charges collected on highways, fee collected in educational institutions and hospitals run by government, or revenue obtained from sale of produce in government farms or forests. Dividends received by government on capital invested in public sector companies, and interest received on loans advanced by government to various organisations or persons are also included in the non-tax revenues of government estimated by the concerned departments.

In all these cases, estimates of revenue for the next year are furnished along with details of the revenue collected during the previous year, the revenue realised in the first half of the current year and the revised estimate of the likely revenue till the end of the current year as compared to the budget estimates. By following such detailed procedure, it is sought to avoid any unrealistic estimates being included in the budget, out of step with what is actually realised in the past, unless there are valid reasons for such changes, like a revision of the tax rates or a change in the tax enforcement measures.

The capital receipts of government consist mainly of borrowings which may be loans for specific projects like construction of airports, ports or other infrastructure projects implemented by different departments of government or borrowings from the market for meeting the budgetary gap—the fiscal deficit. In the case of project-related loans obtained from international or domestic sources, the receipts estimates are to be furnished for inclusion in the budget considering the likely drawings of such loans depending upon the actual progress in implementing such projects. Receipts of other loans obtained for meeting the fiscal deficit (including loans obtained for repayment of past loans) are generally estimated by the ministry of finance (finance department in a State). Estimates of other capital receipts accruing from disinvestment/sale of government's shares in public undertakings, repayment of government loans by various borrowers, etc., are prepared by the concerned ministries/departments as per guidelines given in the Budget Circular.

16 Expenditure Estimates

Every branch of government incurs expenditure on its activities and is therefore involved in estimating the expenditure side of the budget. The expenditure estimates prepared by government departments consist of revenue expenditure on items like salaries and other office expenses, including rents, maintenance of office equipment and sundry other items relating to a department's continued existence. The other category is expenditure on provision of various services and benefits to people like provision of medicines in hospitals, maintenance of roads and buildings, payments of pensions and scholarships and innumerable other services (including vital functions like defence, maintenance of law and order, internal security, administration of justice) involved in the process of governance.

The estimates relating to revenue expenditure are usually generated by officers at the district/circle level upwards and aggregated at the top level in each department. Instructions on preparation of revenue expenditure generally seek to ensure utmost economy in expenditure, particularly in the case of salaries and office expenses. It is for this purpose that departments are required to give very detailed estimates of establishment expenditure on each category of posts and every type of office expenditure. It is not uncommon that the finance ministry imposes specific limits on increase of revenue expenditure from year to year in its anxiety to ensure that the revenue expenditure of government does not greatly exceed the revenue receipts of government. Even though revenue expenditure involves some of the most vital functions of government, it is often mistakenly equated with unproductive, expenditure. The reason for such prejudice against revenue expenditure is perhaps the feeling that most of it relate to payment of salaries to government servants. As a result, revenue expenditure of most departments is usually subjected to 'economy orders' whenever the government faces a financial crunch.

The pressure on revenue expenditure is mainly on account of the growing burden of interest payments, as some recent studies have shown. Interest payments as a proportion of revenue receipts have increased close to half of the revenue receipts of the Central government and some states, leaving inadequate scope for funding important government functions like provision of educational and health services, welfare of weaker sections, and maintenance of law and order.

Most estimates of capital expenditure relate to creation of tangible assets like construction of infrastructure projects, office buildings or acquisition of heavy equipment for use on a long-term basis. Departments in charge of creating assets like airports, roads, buildings, irrigation works, and urban amenities are typical agencies accounting for capital expenditure. The finance ministry/department is in charge of preparing capital expenditure relating to repayment of loans or grant of loans to states and various other entities, and investments in the equity of public undertakings.

The expenditure estimates are prepared not only for revenue and capital expenditure separately, but they are further classified into plan and non-plan expenditure depending upon whether a certain activity or item of expenditure is undertaken as part of the ongoing Five-Year Plan or is a continuing activity from an earlier period. With the abolition of the Planning Commission of India by the Central Government, it is to be seen whether preparation of Five-Year Plans will be altogether discontinued by both the Centre and the States with effect from the end of the 12th Five-Year Plan in 2017. This would then see the end of this classification of expenditure in the budget.

The budget procedures require that all expenditure estimates must contain the actual expenditure incurred in the previous financial year and the revised estimate of likely expenditure during the current year as compared to the budget approved for the current year. Expenditure estimates for the ensuing financial year (the budget year) cannot vary substantially from the past expenditure and current year's estimates unless there is adequate justification furnished for any significant variation. Further, each department in government is required to examine internally if there is scope for discontinuing any existing item of expenditure, or significantly reducing the expenditure on any item, consistent with the present policy relating to the activity of that department. Finally, any new expenditure item can be included in the budget only after an exercise called 'pre-budget scrutiny' which involves the consideration of the need for the activity proposed to be undertaken and the reasonableness of the expenditure compared to its intended objectives. All expenditure proposals relating to ongoing as well as new expenditures, are reviewed in pre-budget consultations between the finance ministry and the estimating departments before they are finally accepted for inclusion in the budget estimates.

17 Pre-Budget Meetings

The budget estimates prepared by different levels in each ministry/department are consolidated at the level of the Heads of Departments for scrutiny by their respective Internal Financial Advisors (IFAs). These are senior functionaries who coordinate the budget preparation as well as expenditure monitoring for one or more ministries/departments. The consolidated budget proposals of each ministry are then sent to the finance ministry for being considered in the pre-budget meetings. The expenditure estimates of Departments are discussed in these meetings, usually conducted by the Secretary (Expenditure), to arrive at a decision on the overall size of a department's Expenditure Budget for the next year and the allocation of funds for different activities proposed. Keeping in view the limits communicated to a department after the pre-budget meeting, the budget proposals are recast as the final version of the 'Statement of Budget Estimates (SBEs)' which are then processed by the budget division for inclusion in the budget.

In the case of estimates relating to revenue receipts, the estimates prepared by the Central Board of Direct Taxes and the Central Board of Excise and Customs are discussed at the level of the Finance Secretary and the Secretary Revenue. Similarly, in the states, the heads of taxation departments have detailed discussions with the Finance Secretary. Needless to say that these pre-budget meetings often involve discussion of proposals for mobilising additional resources through fresh measures of taxation or restructuring of existing taxes. Given the importance of these measures, it is customary for the Finance Minister himself to chair some of these meetings. Also, the sensitivity attached to the proposals relating to taxation makes it necessary that these discussions are held in due secrecy.

Pre-budget meetings to prepare inputs for the budget take place not only at the official level in different ministries and departments, but also at the political level involving ministers, members of parliament/legislature and others interested in influencing the process of making the budget. Many of these meetings may be of an unstructured nature like the meetings that ministers may have with their supporters or constituents about specific policy measures or projects to be considered for the benefit of particular sections of citizens or business groups. These consultations, informal as they may be, are nevertheless of some importance as they could have a bearing on important policy pronouncements or major projects announced in the budget. Ministers also have detailed discussions with the officials of their ministries about the budget proposals before they are forwarded to the finance ministry. It is also customary for the finance minister to involve the ministers concerned while discussing budget proposals in the pre-budget meetings. Besides holding pre-budget meetings within the government, it is customary for the finance minister at the Centre, as also in most States, to have pre-budget discussions with a number of organisations representing trade, industry, labour and other important sections of the economy to elicit suggestions on measures required to improve the business environment in general and specific policy measures for promoting various economic activities. These pre-budget meetings often involve hard bargaining between various interest groups and the government and between various ministries in government and the finance ministry.

Apart from the pre-budget meetings as mentioned above, numerous informal consultations take place within the government on various aspects of the budget. To the extent the government decides to include major policy announcements in the budget, it is natural that the finance minister consults, and is briefed by, his political colleagues in government, including the Prime Minister/Chief Minister. It is also the practice that the cabinet meets to endorse the budget proposals at a formal meeting usually on the day of the budget presentation just before the finance minister presents the budget in parliament/legislature. This signifies the government's approval to the proposals contained in the budget even though the details of the proposals are not discussed in this meeting. The budget proposals thereafter become the proposals of the entire government with the very survival of the government depending upon the budget being approved by the parliament/legislature.

If the foregoing description of budget preparation has portrayed it as a prosaic number crunching bureaucratic exercise, it is only partly true. Budget preparation essentially involves allocation of scarce public resources between competing demands of government's numerous functions. In a democratic system, such demands are articulated often with great vehemence. Every year, most ministers and heads of departments in government see budget preparation as an opportunity to maximise the reach of activities of their departments and enlarge their own spheres of influence. In a developing country, there is no dearth of areas which need government's intervention in support of some section of the society or other and each such demand for a new intervention would entail additional expenditure, often on a sustained basis. During the preparation of the budget, not only ministers concerned but members of parliament and legislature, business leaders and community representatives, civil society activists, employee organisations and other groups actively lobby for inclusion of some of their proposals in the budget often supported by facts and figures in support of their demands. It is also not uncommon that some of these demands even relate to granting relief from the existing taxes, further making inroads into the resource base available to the government.

It is indeed a vexatious task for the finance minister and his team to collate and prioritise all the demands received. The task of negotiating with these various interests, reconciling their often conflicting demands, and accommodating them to the extent they are feasible, involves considerable effort on the part of those in charge of preparing the budget. Given the complexities of the situation, it is the courage, and often the cunning, of the finance minister and his team of officials which produces a budget accommodating some new demands, cutting down expenditure on some activities (often without appearing to do so) and daring to impose new taxes or to expand the base of existing levies. If, in the whole process, the budget manages to reflect a coherent approach to the management of government's finances and serves as an aid to the government's economic policy, the finance minister and his team would have every reason to feel satisfied about a job well done!

Chapter 4
Public Revenue: Sources and Growth

N. Sreedevi

1 Introduction

Every government needs funds to finance its activities. Its requirement of resources increases with the expansion of the scope of its activities.[1] So fundamental is money to the government that one might redefine the orthodox constituents of the State by saying that it consists of territory, people, sovereignty, organization and financial resources (Ayer 1961).

This paper makes an attempt to discuss (i) classification of public revenue in general; (ii) what the theory says about the public revenue and what is in practice; (iii) sources of public revenue and their growth at the Central as well as State governments. The data source is Handbook of Statistics on Indian Economy that is available in the website of Reserve Bank of India and union budget documents for various years particularly since 1991.

This paper comprises seven divisions. General classification of public receipts is discussed in Sect. 2, while Sect. 3 recapitulates the theoretical issues. Section 4 speaks about demarcation of revenue resources across Centre and States in India. Sections 5 and 6 deal with the reforms and the growth trends of taxes at the Central and State levels, respectively. Section 7 gives the summary and conclusions.

[1]The presence and active participation of State in economic activities of the economy is justified on the reasoning that an unregulated market mechanism suffers from several failures of its own and the State must step in to counteract them. Hence, certain activities, which logically should be in the hands of the State, are taken up by the State. In other words, a society should have a State for not only performing those activities but also for such additional non-economic activities which go with them.

N. Sreedevi (✉)
Centre for Economic and Social Studies, Hyderabad, Telangana, India
e-mail: nsreedevi@cess.ac.in

G. Karnam (ed.), *Public Budgeting in India*, India Studies in Business and Economics, https://doi.org/10.1007/978-81-322-3917-8_4

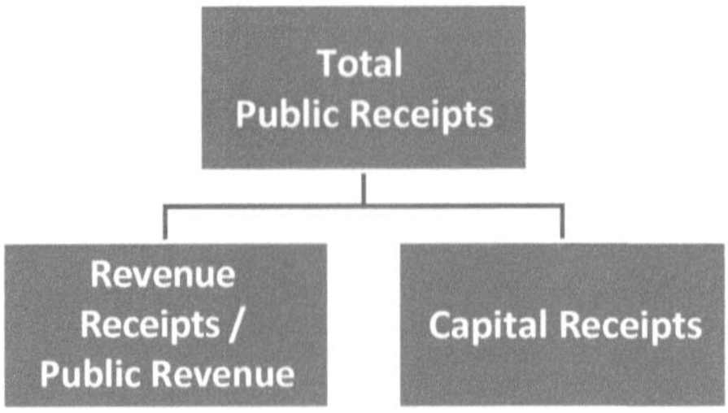

Fig. 1 Classification of government or public receipts

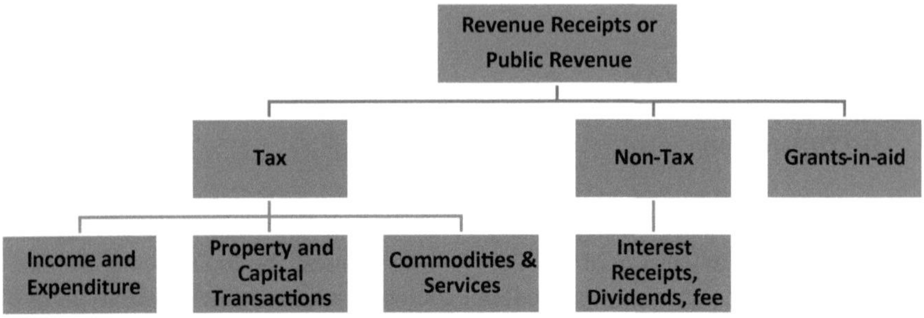

Fig. 2 Classification of public revenue receipts

2 Public Revenue: General Classification

It is customary to classify the government or public receipts into (i) revenue receipts or public revenue and (ii) capital receipts[2] (Fig. 1). Public revenue constitutes all revenue receipts received during the financial year. It is recurring in nature and consists of tax revenue, non-tax revenue and grants-in-aid. Further classification of tax and non-tax revenue is given in Fig. 2.

3 Tax Revenue: Theoretical Issues

The tax system is looked at, by the government authorities, as a means towards accomplishing one or more objectives and setting certain criteria or principles as guidelines for developing the tax system. Adam Smith put forward certain principles

[2]This paper is focused on public revenue only. However, capital receipts consist of loans raised by issue of treasury bills, open market loans, ways and means advances, other loans, loan recoveries, deposits and other receipts. The capital receipts, mostly borrowings, are meant for developmental activities taken up by the government shown under capital expenditure. In other words, capital expenditure is meant for acquisition of capital assets like land, buildings, machinery and equipment necessary for economic growth. Revenue expenditure is met out of revenue receipts, whereas capital expenditure is met out of capital receipts which are mostly borrowings.

and termed them as Canons of Taxation. They are equity, certainty, convenience and economy. Modern economists added other principles such as productivity (or adequacy), buoyancy, flexibility and simplicity.

Growth process of an economy is highly complex in nature, and during this process some growth-oriented organizations take an advantage, while the economy faces the challenges in promoting some other. Consequently, economy finds certain upcoming sectors very tax potential, while some other sources of revenue lose their entity. Hence, there arises a need for a periodical reformation of the tax system in all aspects to augment the revenue resources. The following sections discuss the demarcation of revenue resources among different levels of government particularly the Centre and the States, reformation of tax system and growth trends at each level.

4 Public Revenue in India—Demarcation Between Centre and States

Seventh Schedule of the Constitution of India (1950) has enumerated fiscal powers of the Union as well as State governments (Appendix Table 5) and the concurrent powers exercisable by both. Having realized the built-in vertical imbalance, the framers of the Constitution made a few statutory provisions for the resource devolution from the Centre to the States. Hence, public revenue of the State governments includes share in central taxes and grant-in-aid. Further break-up of revenue at both levels of government is given in Appendix Tables 6 and 7. Tax revenue may also be categorized into direct taxes (DT) and indirect taxes (INDT).

Though the set of principles intended for subnational governments or State governments in a federal system meet the core public finance principles,[3] the fundamental questions that arise are do the apportionment of revenue sources between the levels of governments meet these approved principles? Do individual sources of revenue are designed to meet accepted principles and also are collectively consistent with the same? How well the subnational revenue system is designed to implement on the ground? However, there has been a significant change in the Indian fiscal federalism over a period of time.

Various studies show that though our tax system, particularly direct taxes, is quite progressive but fails in terms of Canons of simplicity, certainty and efficiency. Hence, the initiation of reforms has become inevitable.

[3]Principle of adequacy, stability, efficiency, equity, autonomy, administrative feasibility, political feasibility and integration/consistency (see Smoke 2013).

5 Tax Reforms in Central Government—Revenue Growth Trends

The government embarked upon a series of reform measures[4] since 1991 through a wide spectrum of policy areas—industrial, trade, exchange rate, fiscal and financial sectors. The tax reforms were envisaged basing mainly on the *Tax Reforms Committee* recommendations.[5] The recommendations were implemented on both direct and indirect tax fronts. The objective of these reforms was to build a simple tax structure allowing a broad tax base and moderate tax rates, better execution and serving the aims of equity, progressivity as well as revenue augmentation. These reforms have changed the Indian tax structure ever since their implementation.

5.1 Direct Taxes: Reforms

Restructuring of personal income tax, one of the important direct taxes, was done by minimizing the slabs to three.[6] Tax rates were moderated in a phased manner. The peak rate, i.e. tax rate of the higher slab, was reduced from 50% in 1985–86 to 40% in 1995–96 and further down to 35 and 30% in 2000–01 and 2003–04, respectively. The entry rate, i.e. tax rate of the lower slab, was reduced from 25% in 1985–86 to 20% in 1990–92 and 10% in 1997–98. Measures were taken to broaden the tax base.[7] The income tax exemption limit was raised over a period. In order to simplify

[4]The growth rate of the GDP during the period of the 1980s registered an average of 5.81% much above the preceding decades' average growth rate of 2.95%. However, the year 1990–91 was characterized by a series of events that lead to a severe liquidity crisis in the economy. Macroeconomic imbalances, persistent expenditure overruns and revenue shortfalls, accentuated inflationary pressures in the economy coupled with strained balance of payment position led to rapid depletion of foreign reserves, and adding to these problems were the external oil shock, dislocations caused by the Gulf War and internal political instability. The combined impact of these factors led to rapid downturn in the capital inflows. The foreign exchange reserves finally reached a range of Rs. 2500 crores that would afford to pay for a fortnight.

[5]To focus on the tax rationalization, Government of India appointed 'Advisory Group on Tax Policy and Tax Administration for the Tenth Plan (2001), the Expert Committee to Review the System of Administered Interest Rates and Other Related Issues, 2001, Task Force on Direct Taxes and Indirect Taxes, 2002.

[6]In fact, reduction in the number of slabs was done earlier also from 11 in 1970–74 to 8 in 1980–81 to 4 in 1985–86.

[7]The income tax exemption with reference to the earnings from races was withdrawn. In 1992–93, a presumptive tax of Rs. 1400, on an optional basis, was introduced for shopkeepers/retail traders whose annual turnover was below Rs. 5 lakh. The scope of presumptive tax was extended to small road transport operators. A new estimated income scheme was introduced for retail traders engaged in the business of any goods or merchandise having a total turnover below Rs. 40 lakhs. At the same time, the existing presumptive tax scheme which did not yielded the desired results was discontinued. The residents of large metropolitan cities who satisfy any two of the following economic criteria, viz., ownership of a four-wheel vehicle, a telephone, occupation of immovable property, foreign travel in the previous year, were brought under the tax net. The scheme was extended to 35 cities.

the tax process, 'SARAL' (one-page tax return form) was introduced and this was made applicable to all individual taxpayers.

The corporate tax rates, in line with the personal income tax rate trends, were reduced over a period of time. The distinction between corporate tax rate, trading companies and investment companies was removed. Modifications were made in the treatment of depreciation and investment allowance. To widen the tax base, a minimum alternate tax was introduced in 1996–97. Capital market started developing during this period with the effect of liberalization.

5.2 *Indirect Taxes: Reforms*

On the indirect tax front also, the objective was to rationalize the system, bring down the rates, simplify the procedures to speed up the process, encourage indigenous industries and improve the competitiveness of the industrial sector.

Customs duty structure underwent significant changes. Prior to 1991, the rates were more than 20 with and peak rate of import tariff exceeded 300% ad valorem. In 1991–92, it was reduced from 300% to a maximum of 150%. In the following year, it was brought down to 110%. The peak rate was further brought down to 50% in 1995–96 and to 40% in 1997–98. Regarding non-agricultural products, the peak rate of customs duty was lowered from 15 to 12.5% in 2006–07 and further reduced to 10% in 2007–08. Thus, over years, the peak tariff decreased considerably. At present, there is no change in peak rate for non-agricultural products. It continues to remain at 10%.

The number of rates of custom duty was also reduced over a period. In 1999–2000, the ad valorem rates of customs duty were brought down from seven to five and in the following year to four. Measures were also taken to unify the custom duty rates for items in the same category to rationalize the system and simplify the procedures. Measures were also taken. Further, to arrange for a level playing field to the national industry, an additional levy of 8% on imports was levied.

Excise duty structure, another important source of indirect tax revenue, too underwent similar changes. The objective was to restructure the excise duty with broad base and low rates of duty, providing relief wherever necessary and raise receipts common to entire tax system, shifting to ad valorem rates to the extent possible, extending the range of MODVAT in the area of excise duty. Accordingly, in 1994–95, a major restructuring of the excise tax was undertaken. MODVAT was extended to capital goods and petroleum products. A modest beginning was

---

The net itself was widened to include two additional criteria, namely holding a credit card and membership of expensive clubs. If one fulfils one of the six criteria, one had to file his/her income tax return. The scheme was henceforth to be known as "One-by-Six". In the year 1999–2000, the scheme was further extended to cover another 19 cities. In 2005–06, mobile telephone was eliminated from the one-in-six criteria and instead inserted the item payment for electricity of more than Rs. 50,000. In 2006–07, the one-in six criteria were abolished and FBT introduced in 05–06 was continued.

made towards shifting from specific to ad valorem to ensure buoyancy. In the year 1999–2000, existing 11 rates were decreased to 3—a central rate of 16%, a merit rate of 8% and a demerit rate of 24%.[8] In 2008–09, the CENVAT rate on all goods reduced from 16 to 14%. At present, the attention is paid only on those items for which modifications in the duty rates are required. This policy is likely to pave the way for Goods and Service Tax (GST)—a comprehensive indirect tax on goods and services throughout India replacing the taxes levied by the central excise and service taxes and State VAT and a few other indirect taxes.

In order to extend the tax base, exemptions given under customs and excise duty have been reviewed and a large number of them were withdrawn. The services sector which accounts for a significant portion of the gross domestic product has been brought under the tax system by imposing service tax in 1994–95—a new indirect tax. A beginning was made with a tax rate of 5% charged on three services—telephone, non-life insurance and stock brokers. Over a period of time, the number of services taxed was increased gradually and so did the tax rate. At present, the service tax rate is at 14.5%.

Administrative reforms were also taken up. In order to simplify the process and ensure better compliance, a few administrative changes were made in terms of excise procedures such as *simple return* indicating the duty paid on self-assessment basis rather than furnishing copies of invoices along with monthly returns. A scheme of selective audit was introduced while expelling the routine examination and checking of returns and documents. Excise assesse was permitted to pay the excise duty in bimonthly payments. Monthly payment scheme, for the small-scale sector, continued. Simple, user-friendly valuation mechanism in commercially acceptable lines was made.

Measures were taken to increase the performance in the operation and implementation of excise laws through minimizing the number of contact points between the officials and assesse; restricting factory visits by the officials; respecting the orders of commissioner (appeals)/the tribunal; and simplifying the process in MODVAT cases for second appeal. A Citizens' Charter was made available to place the citizen's rights and the obligations with reference to customs and excise officials.

On the whole, with respect to checking tax evasions and to ensure better compliance and to unearth the black money a host of measures were introduced. A new scheme—Voluntary Disclosure Scheme—was introduced in order to bring out the black money in the system. Settlement Commission was set up, and necessary provisions were made to avoid delays in the clearance of certain types of disputes connected to customs and excise duties. For Advance Tax Rulings for Excise and Customs, an authority was set up keeping in view the need for foreign investors to be assured in advance of their likely indirect tax liability.

Apart from these measures, it was made compulsory to quote PAN or GIR number in high-value businesses such as purchase and sale of immovable property, motor

[8]To achieve this, the existing rates 5, 10 and 12% were merged to 8% rate; 13, 15 and 18% rates merged into 16%; and a new rate of 24% in the place of 25%.

vehicles. Anti-tax evasion measures were introduced by making the banks to report all the details of the deposits.

Other important measures were subcontracting the non-core activities of income tax department, for example allotment of PAN; for annual scrutiny of the returns, taking only 2% of the returns through computer-generated random selection; directly crediting all refunds to the taxpayer's bank account through electronic clearance system; reducing the number of forms from 422 to 22 for tax deduction/collection at source; introducing one page return form for salaried individual income taxpayers, house property interest; e-filing of returns and abolition of the procedure of obtaining tax clearance certificates from a person leaving India or a person tendering for a government contract. Further, a beginning was made towards modernization of tax administration. Income Tax, Customs and Central Excise departments underwent Business Process Reengineering (BPR) to have a nationwide network connection with their offices in cities, to create national databases; national data centres. BPR includes set-up of data warehousing facilities and disaster recovery sites, jurisdiction-free filing of returns. It also includes online tracking of status of accounts and refunds of income tax; introduction of a risk management system and Electronic Data Interchange (EDI) in the Customs Department to reduce waiting time for cargo; E-payments of customs and excise duties, etc. In short, total computerization and networking are done in both the departments—Central Board of Direct Taxes (CBDT) and Central Board of Excise and Customs (CBEC).

5.3 Goods and Services Tax (GST)

In India, in the arena of indirect taxes, the implementation of Goods and Services Tax with effect from 1 July 2017 was a very major step. The expedition in the direction of GST was initially proposed in the Union Budget for 2006–07 with an intention to introduce it with effect from 1 April 2010. Its objective was to lower the cascading effect or double taxation effect and direct a way towards a common national market. It continued with the Constitution of Empowered Committee consisting of State Finance Ministers (EC) to formulate a road map for the GST to go on board. In November 2009, first discussion paper on GST, after the deliberations within EC as well as with Central government, has brought out the features/structure of the envisioned GST.

With the introduction of GST, certain Central and State taxes were congregated into one tax.[9] With the implementation of GST, the central taxes which are replaced are: (i) Central Excise Duty; (ii) Duties of Excise (Medicinal and Toilet Preparations); (iii) Additional Duties of Excise (Goods of Special Importance); (iv) Additional Duties of Excise (Textiles and Textile Products); (v) Additional Duties of Customs (commonly known as CVD); (vi) Special Additional Duty of Customs

[9]Before GST, we find constitutional demarcation of fiscal powers between the Centre and the States clearly. See Table 5.

(SAD); (vii) service tax; (viii) cesses and surcharges insofar as they relate to supply of goods or services.

Similarly, State taxes that are included within the GST are: (i) State VAT; (ii) Central Sales Tax; (iii) Purchase Tax; (iv) Luxury Tax; (v) Entry Tax (all forms); (vi) Entertainment Tax (except those levied by the local bodies); (vii) taxes on advertisements; (viii) taxes on lotteries, betting and gambling; (ix) State cesses and surcharges insofar as they relate to supply of goods or services. However, GST will not be applicable to alcohol for human consumption. It will not be applicable to five specified petroleum products (crude, petrol, diesel, ATF and natural gas) till recommended by the GSTC.

On 12 April 2017, four laws, namely CGST Act, UTGST Act, IGST Act and GST (Compensation to States) Act have been passed by the parliament. By 8th July 2017 all states and Union territories with legislature have passed their respective SGST Acts. With this the economic integration of India was completed. Notifications have been issued under each of the Acts of CGST, IGST, UTGST and GST (Compensation to States). States have followed the same under their respective SGST Acts.

The following are the most important aspects of GST:

i. GST is based on 'supply' of goods or services, while the earlier tax(s) levied on manufacture of goods/sale of goods/provision of services.
ii. The principle of GST is destination-based consumption taxation, whereas earlier was on origin-based taxation.
iii. GST is dual in nature allowing the Centre (CGST or GSTC) and the States[10] (SGST) to levy tax on a common base at the same time. Union territories without legislature would levy union territory GST (UTGST).

An Integrated GST (IGST) levied on interState supply (including stock transfers) of goods/services will be collected by the centre in order to maintain the credit chain undisrupted. Import of goods is also considered as interState supplies and kept under IGST besides the applicable customs duties. Similarly, import of services is treated as interState supplies and hence is subject to IGST.

The rates under CGST, SGST/UTGST and IGST are based on mutual agreement between Centre and the States under the aegis of the GSTC. Transfer of funds/accounts is settled periodically on the basis of returns filed by the taxpayers.

Studies related to other countries, which have implemented GST, revealed a positive impact of GST on their economic growth. As GST was implemented in India recently, i.e. in July 2017, only revised and budget estimates for the years 2017–18 and 2018–19, respectively, are available under GST, and accounts will give a better picture on GST.

---

[10]Including union territories with legislature.

5.4 Public Revenue of the Central Government: Growth Trends

Of the total receipts, while the total revenue receipts showed an increasing trend, the capital receipts declined gradually (Fig. 3). The total revenue receipts (capital receipts) increased (decreased) over a period of time with marginal ups and downs throughout the study period, barring a consistent increase (decline) during 2003–04 to 2007–08.

Effect of reforms on the direct and indirect tax regimes is glaringly visible. Of the total tax revenue, the direct tax revenue which was less than 20% gradually increased constituted about 80% and reverse is the case with indirect tax revenue (Table 1 and Fig. 4). Both converged in 2006–07, and thereafter the revenue from direct taxes exceeded its counterpart, indirect tax revenue. This is quite evident in the proportions of total tax revenue and also in the proportions of GDP (Table 1 and Fig. 5). It is noteworthy to highlight that during the 4-year period 2003–04 to 2007–08, the gross tax GDP ratio went up by over three percentage points. This has been attributed to the high economic growth and better tax administration (*Report of the Thirteenth Finance Commission* (2010–15), Volume 1). The impact of global slowdown is quite evident in the year 2008–09 and thereafter. Neither the total revenue nor the tax revenue (direct or indirect) has not revived the earlier situation of 2007–08 again. The non-tax revenue showed a declining trend (Table 1 and Fig. 5).

But the impact of reforms on direct and indirect taxes varied. The former exhibited an uptrend, while the latter showed a decline (Figs. 6 and 7). The economy which was highly dependent on indirect taxes before the implementation of reforms shows

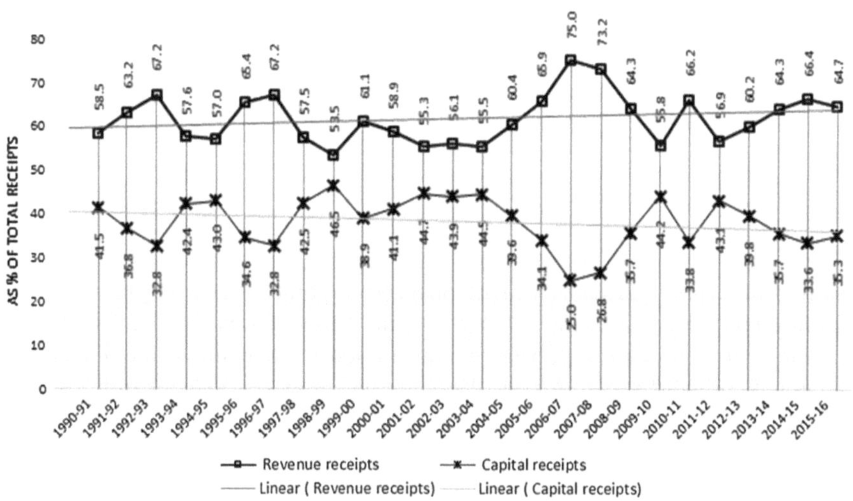

Fig. 3 Composition of total receipts—Union government. *Source* Calculated from the data using Handbook of Statistics on Indian Economy, 2014–15 Reserve Bank of India (2015)

Table 1 Trends in revenue receipts of Central government (as % of GDP)

	Year	1990–2000	2000–2010	2010–2016
I	**Revenue receipts (A + B)**	**8.85**	**9.50**	**9.15**
A	**Tax revenue (a + b)**	**6.43**	**7.33**	**7.26**
a	**Direct tax**	**1.73**	**3.59**	**3.85**
i	Personal income tax	0.31	1.35	1.42
ii	Corporation tax	1.30	2.23	2.43
b	**Indirect tax**	**4.69**	**3.73**	**3.41**
i	Excise duties	1.83	1.98	1.54
ii	Customs duties	2.69	1.27	1.15
B	**Non-tax revenue**	**2.42**	**2.17**	**1.89**
	Interest receipts	1.60	0.75	0.40
II	**Capital receipts**	**5.85**	**5.66**	**5.46**
III	**Total receipts (I + II)**	**14.69**	**15.16**	**14.61**

Source Calculated from the data using Handbook of Statistics on Indian Economy, 2014–15, Reserve Bank of India (2015)

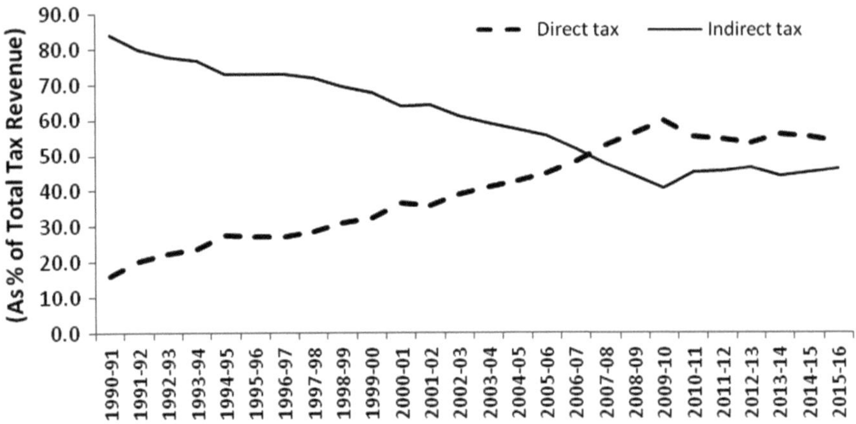

Fig. 4 Trends in direct and indirect taxes: Central government

a shift to direct taxes particularly to personal and corporate taxes which have shown a significant improvement/increase in the revenue. This shift is mainly attributed to the simplification of tax structure, better administration and liberalizing the economy in the case of corporate sector. Among the major indirect taxes, revenue from customs duty was higher than the union excise duties till 1999–2000 and declined drastically in the proportion of GDP, whereas revenue from union excise duties increased since then till the occurrence of economic slowdown. Both the resources are nearer to the convergence after the economic slowdown.

In brief, in the 1990s, the Central government has taken up a series of measures to rationalize the tax rates and structure. In the early 2000s changes such as the

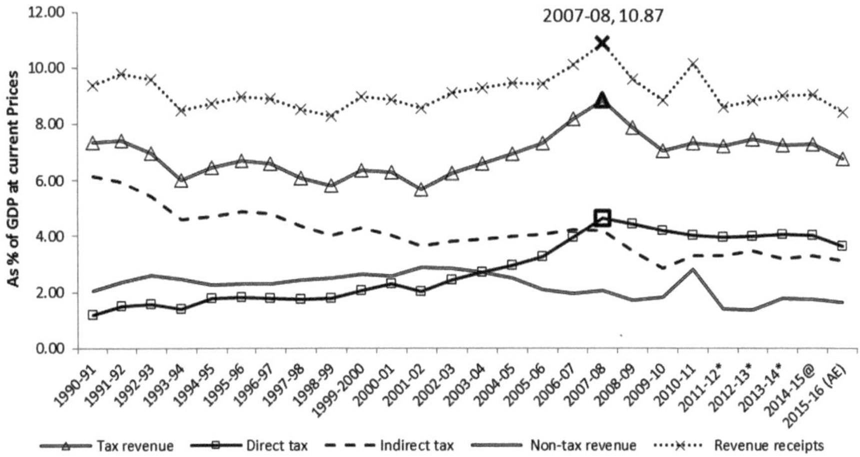

Fig. 5 Trends in revenue receipts: Central government

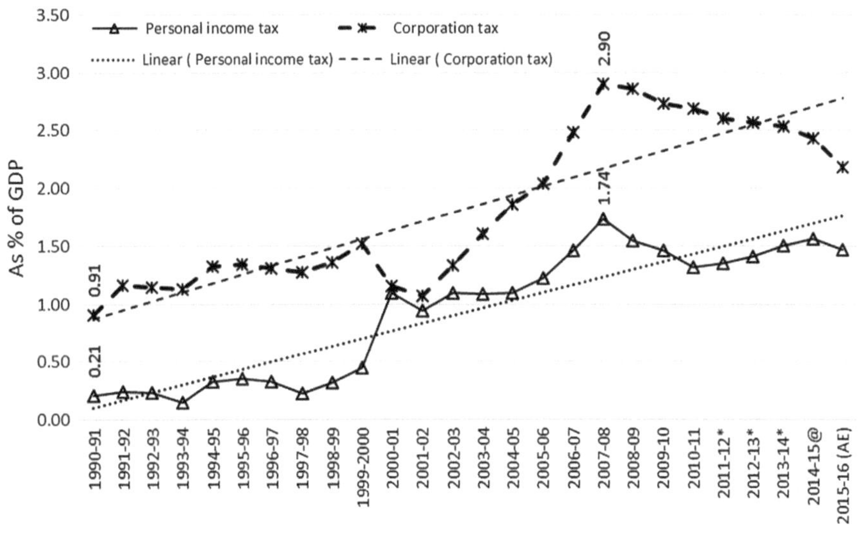

Fig. 6 Trends in major direct tax revenues

introduction to rule based fiscal management and administrative changes and the implementation of the Tax Information Network have significantly transformed the Fiscal scenario.[11] It is noteworthy to highlight that during the 4-year period 2003–04 to 2007–08, the gross tax GDP ratio went up by over three percentage points. This has

---

[11]Significant rise in the tax compliance has been realized, and for the first time in the history of Indian Public Finance, tax collections from direct taxes exceeded that of the indirect taxes in the year 2007–08 as stated in the Report of the Thirteenth Finance Commission. Volume 1, 2010–15, p. 45.

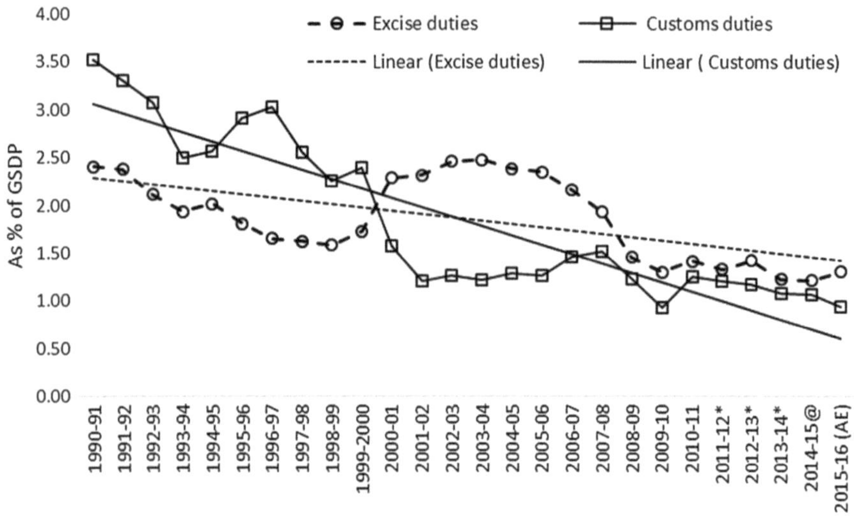

Fig. 7 Trends in major indirect tax revenues

been attributed to the high economic growth and better tax administration. However, the impact of global slowdown is evident in the revenue of the government.

6 Tax Reforms in State Governments—Revenue Growth Trends

Many States also had portrayed medium-term reforms with specific fiscal targets, even earlier to the initiation of rule-based fiscal legislations. With the general fiscal stress at the State level, a number of States had commenced many policy initiatives to augment revenues and also the efficiency of tax mobilization. Computerization of revenue-earning departments is one among them. The States have focused on efficient utilization of existing resources, better enforcement and tax compliance through simplification/rationalization of tax structure of States' major tax sources—sales tax, motor vehicle tax, land revenue. Implementation of value-added tax (VAT) is a milestone in this process. Under the non-tax revenue system, States reviewed the user charges for power, water, transport, etc.

The States took proactive measures also, in the backdrop of overall economic slowdown in 2008–09 and thereafter, such as streamlining the revenue generation, simplification of procedures such as rules, inspections, registrations and opening of single-window system for industries and businesses to carry on their activities. Among the fiscal stimulus measures adopted by some States include decrease in the stamp duty and registration fee on land/property transactions. Most of the States, in order to uphold the tax compliance, have reduced the VAT rates.

Table 2 Receipts of the State governments: patterns (as % of GDP)

		1990–2000	2000–2010	2010–15
I	Total revenue receipts	10.74	11.71	13.22
II	Total capital receipts	4.03	4.34	3.04
III	Total receipts (I+II)	14.77	16.04	16.26

Source Calculated from the data using Handbook of Statistics on Indian Economy, 2014–15, Reserve Bank of India (2015)

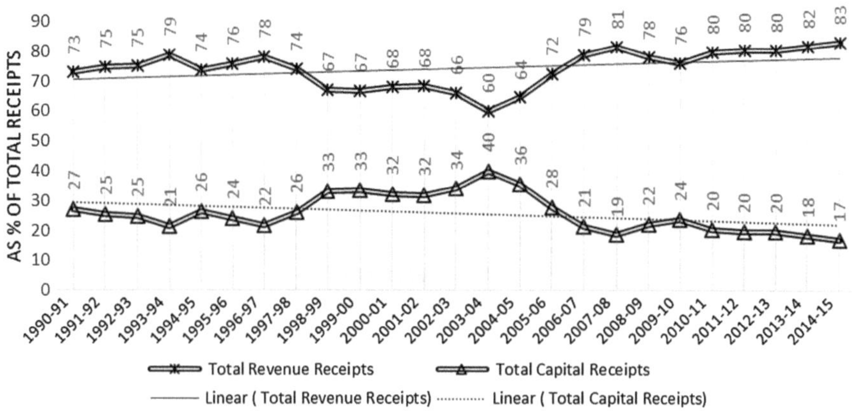

Fig. 8 Total receipts of State governments: composition (%)

6.1 *Public Revenue of State Governments: Growth Trends*

Decade after decade, the average proportion of total receipts in GDP showed an increasing trend (Table 2) mainly because of the total revenue receipts. The composition of total receipts shows that, while the total revenue receipts declined in the first half of the study period indicating a higher dependency on capital receipts (mostly borrowings) reversed the situation in the second half of the study period (Fig. 8). The total revenue receipts (capital receipts) increased (decreased) over a period of time with marginal ups and downs throughout the study period, barring a consistent increase (decline) during 2003–04 to 2007–08. Till 2003–04, the dependency on capital receipts, which are mostly borrowings, was increasing mainly because of inadequate upsurge in the proportion of revenue component.

Of the total revenue of the State governments, though States' own revenue constitutes a bulk share, its average share declined decade after decade, hence a corresponding increase in the Central transfers, particularly grants-in-aid (Table 3). Year-wise composition is given in Fig. 9 showing fluctuations in both the components throughout.

Table 3 Composition of States' revenue receipts (%)

	Year	1990–2000	2000–2010	2010–15
I	**Total revenue receipts (A + B)**	**100.0**	**100.0**	**100.0**
A	***Total tax revenue***	***68.7***	***70.2***	***71.5***
(i)	State own tax revenue	46.5	47.9	49.2
(ii)	Share in central taxes	22.2	22.3	22.4
B	***Non-tax Receipts***	***31.3***	***29.8***	***28.5***
(i)	State own non-tax revenue	15.2	12.1	9.0
(ii)	Grants from the centre	16.1	17.7	19.5
C	***State own revenue (Ai + Bi)***	***61.6***	***60.0***	***58.2***
D	***Central transfers (Aii + Bii)***	***38.4***	***40.0***	***41.8***

Source Calculated from the data using Handbook of Statistics on Indian Economy, 2014–15, Reserve Bank of India (2015)

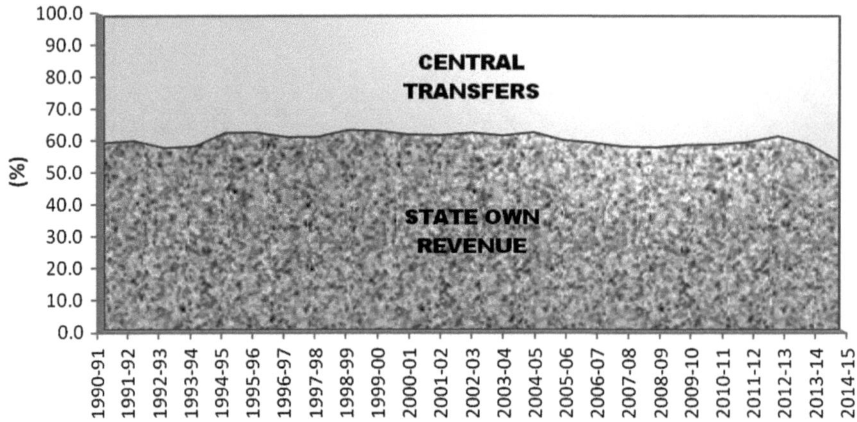

Fig. 9 Composition of total revenue of State governments

6.2 *Tax Revenue Trends in State Governments*

Pattern of revenue receipts during the study period shows that States' total revenue (also its components excepting own non-tax revenue) showed a consistent increase in the decadal averages of the 1990s, 2000s and first half of the present decade (Table 4). But year-wise details show a different picture.

Experiencing the fiscal stress, the proportion of all States' own tax revenues to GDP decreased from 5.20% in 1990–91 to 5.03% in 1995–96 and further declined to 4.90% in 1999–00. However, as most of the States reached a decision to apply floor rates in sales tax and also to moderate several exemptions, there was a considerable increase in 2000–01. In 2000–01, the proportion of States' own tax revenues to GDP had progressed and restored to 5.2% and then consistently increased till 2006–07.

Table 4 State governments' receipts (as % of GDP)

		1990–2000	2000–2010	2010–15
I	**Total revenue receipts (A + B)**	**10.74**	**11.71**	**13.22**
A	*Total tax revenue*	*7.38*	*8.22*	*9.46*
(i)	State own tax revenue	4.99	5.61	6.50
(ii)	Share in central taxes	2.39	2.61	2.95
B	*Non-tax receipts*	*3.36*	*3.49*	*3.77*
(i)	State own non-tax revenue	1.63	1.41	1.19
(ii)	**Grants from the centre**	1.73	2.07	2.58
II	**Total capital receipts**	**4.03**	**4.34**	**3.04**
III	**Total receipts (I + II)**	**14.77**	**16.04**	**16.26**
C	*State own revenue (Ai + Bi)*	*6.62*	*7.03*	*7.69*
D	*Central transfers (Aii + Bii)*	*4.12*	*4.68*	*5.53*

Source Calculated from the data using Reserve Bank of India (2015), Handbook of Statistics on Indian Economy, 2014–15

With regard to own non-tax revenues, there has been a downward trend—in the total revenue composition as well as in relation to GDP—both in decadal averages and annual series, barring 1 or 2 years. The share in central taxes relative to GDP also declined from 2.43% in 1990–91 to 2.19% in 1998–99 and further down to 2.18% in 1999–2000. Following decade showed an increase in Central transfers which may be attributed to the impact of economic reforms at the national level, Finance Commission's recommendations and also the economic boom—continued till the impact of global slowdown in 2008–09 and subsequent 2 years. During the present decade too, the Central transfers (share in Central taxes as well as grants-in-aid) have increased. On the whole, the proportion of States' aggregate revenue receipts in GDP turned down from 11.3% (1990–91) to 9.6% (1998–99)—lowest in the decade—and thereafter it has increased in the decade of the 2000s and till 2014–15 (Figs. 10, 11, 12 and 13).

In brief, the rise in the percentage of revenue receipts in relation to GDP, after experience the fiscal stress till the mid-1990s, may be attributed to

a. Better rate of growth in own tax revenue.
b. Higher rate of growth in the economy.
c. Higher economic growth and fiscal reforms at the national level contributed to higher rate of growth in States' share in Central transfers. Its percentage in GSDP exhibited an uninterrupted up turn up to 2007–08 mostly.

The reason for the decline in the revenue/GDP ratios during 2008–09 attributed to the impact of global slowdown on the Indian economy/State economy and thus

1. Decreased growth rate of States' own tax revenue as well as share in central taxes.
2. Fluctuations/fall of grants-in-aid.

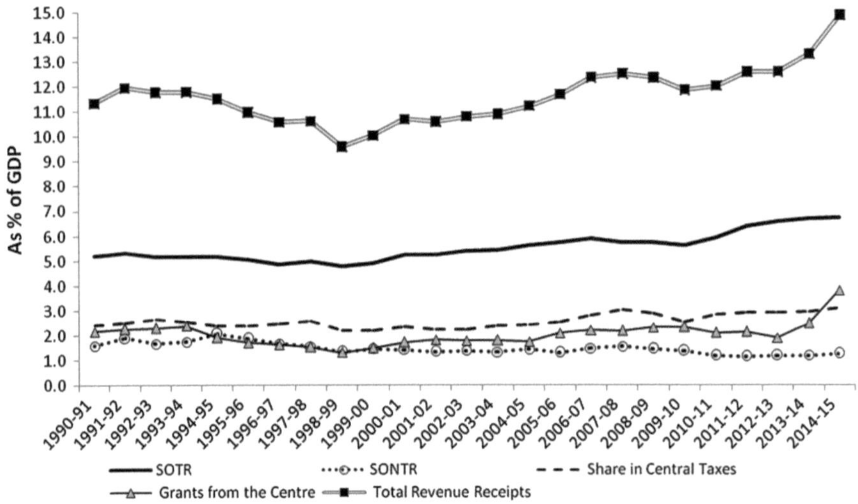

Fig. 10 Pattern of receipts of the State governments

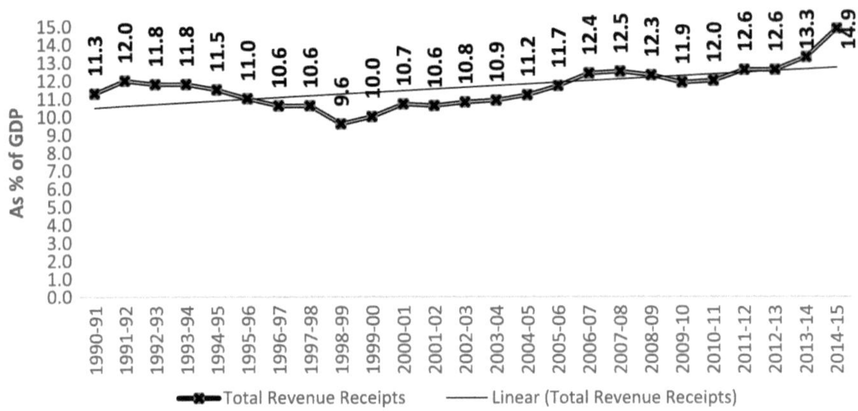

Fig. 11 Trends in total revenue—State governments

3. Fluctuations/fall in the own non-tax revenue.
4. Relatively lower economic growth rate.

In short, receipts of state governments revealed varied trends during the study period—steady/fluctuating downward trend during 1996-2004 and then a rising trend for the period of 2004-05–2007-08. In the remaining period, though faced an economic downturn, showed an uptrend the first half of the present decade and continued in the higher plane.

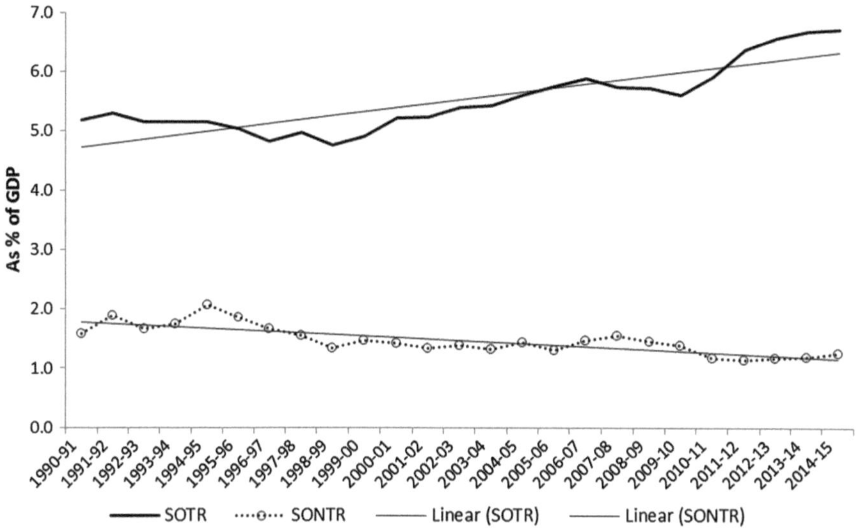

Fig. 12 Pattern of own revenue—State governments

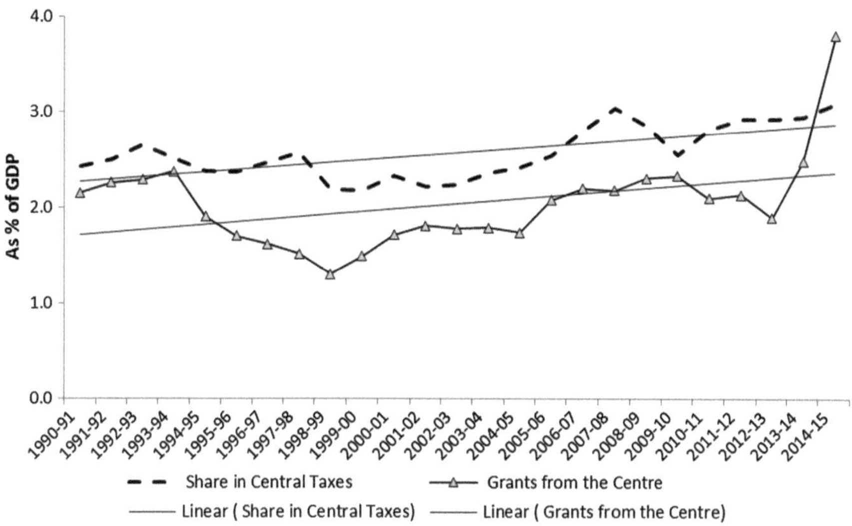

Fig. 13 Pattern of Central transfers to the State governments

7 Summary and Conclusions

To conclude, the gap between theory and practice is quite evident. Realizing the fact that Indian tax system—tax rate and tax base—is cumbersome, initiation of simplification/rationalization of tax system has been started which in turn has reflected in the revenue growth. Similarly, the State governments also followed the reform path, implemented various measures in consonance with the Central government and achieved the results too. However, much is to be done with regard to cannon of efficiency. This is only revenue side of the fiscal policy.

Appendix

See Tables 5, 6 and 7.

Table 5 Fiscal powers under Union and State lists: seventh schedule, the Constitution of India (1950)

The Union List enumerates twelve main sources of tax revenue
1. Taxes on incomes other than agricultural income
2. Duties of customs including export duties
3. Duties of Excise on tobacco and other goods manufactured or produced in India except (a) alcoholic liquors for human consumption (b) opium, Indian hemp and other narcotic drugs and narcotics
4. Corporation tax
5. Taxes on capital value of assets, exclusive of agricultural land, or individuals and companies, taxes on capital of companies
6. Estate duty in respect of property other than agricultural land
7. Duties in respect of succession to property other than agricultural land
8. Terminal taxes on goods or passengers, carried by railway, sea or air, taxes on railway fares and freights
9. Taxes other than stamp duties on transactions in stock exchange and future markets
10. Rates of stamp duty in respect of bills of exchange, cheques promissory notes, bills of lading, letters of credit, policies of insurance, debentures, transfers of shares, proxies and receipts
11. Taxes on the sale or purchase of newspapers and on advertisements published therein
12. Taxes on the sale or purchase of goods other than newspapers, where such sale or purchase takes place in the course of interstate trade or commerce
The State List enumerates nineteen sources of tax revenue which belong exclusively to the States
1. Land revenue
2. Tax on agricultural income
3. Duties in respect of agricultural land
4. Estate duty in respect of agricultural land
5. Taxes on land and buildings
6. Taxes on mineral rights, subject to any limitation imposed by parliament by law relating to mineral development

(continued)

Table 5 (continued)

7. Duties of Excise on the following goods manufactured or produced in the States and countervailing duties at the same or lower rates on similar goods manufactured elsewhere in India
(a) Alcoholic liquors for human consumption
(b) Opium, Indian hemp and other narcotic drugs and narcotics
8. Taxes on the entry of goods into a local area for consumption, use and sale therein
9. Taxes on the consumption or sale of electricity
10. Taxes on the sale or purchase of goods other than newspapers
11. Taxes on goods and passengers carried by road or inland waterways
12. Taxes on vehicles, whether mechanically propelled or not, suitable for use on roads including tram-cars
13. Taxes on animals and boats
14. Tolls
15. Taxes on professions, trades, callings and employments
16. Capitation taxes
17. Taxes on luxuries including taxes on entertainments, amusements, betting and gambling
18. Rates of stamp duty in respect of documents other than those specified in the Union List with regard to stamp duty
19. Fees in respect of any of the matters in List II but not including fees taken in any court

Table 6 Source of revenue of the Central government

A.	**Tax revenue**
(a)	**Taxes on income and expenditure**
	Corporation tax (DT)
	Taxes on income other than corporation tax (DT)
	Hotel receipts tax (DT)
	Interest tax (DT)
	Fringe benefit tax
	Other taxes on income and expenditure (DT)
(b)	**Taxes on property and capital transactions**
	Estate duty (DT)
	Taxes on wealth (DT)
	Gift tax (DT)
	Securities transaction tax
	Banking cash transaction tax
(c)	**Taxes on commodities and services**
	Customs (INDT)
	Union excise duties (INDT)
	Sales tax (INDT)
	Service tax (INDT)
	Other taxes and duties on commodities and services

(continued)

Table 6 (continued)

(d)	**Taxes of union territories without legislature**
	Gross tax revenue
	State's share excluded from the consolidated fund
	Tax revenue of the Central government
B.	**Non-tax revenue**
(a)	Fiscal services
	Currency, coinage and mint
	Other fiscal services
(b)	Interest receipts, dividends and profits
	Interest receipts
	Interest from State and union territory governments
(c)	Other non-tax revenue
	General services
	Social and community services
	Economic services
	Non-tax revenue of union territories
C.	**Grants-in-aid and contributions**
	External grant assistance aid material and equipment
	Total—non-tax revenue
	Total—revenue receipts

DT direct taxes; *IDT* indirect taxes

Table 7 Source of revenue of the State governments

	Total revenue (I + II)
I	**Tax revenue (A + B)**
A.	**Revenue from States' taxes (i–iii)**
(i)	***Taxes on income (a + b)***
(a)	Agricultural income tax (DT)
(b)	Tax on professions, trades, callings and employment (DT)
(ii)	***Taxes on property and capital transactions (a–c)***
(a)	Stamps and registration fees (INDT)
(b)	Land revenue (DT)
(c)	Urban immovable property tax (DT)
(iii)	***Taxes on commodities and services (a–g)***
(a)	Sales tax[a] (INDT)
(b)	State excise duties (INDT)
(c)	Taxes on vehicles (IDT)

(continued)

Table 7 (continued)

	Total revenue (I + II)
(d)	Taxes on passengers and goods (INDT)
(e)	Electricity duties (INDT)
(f)	Entertainment Tax (INDT)
(g)	Other taxes and duties (INDT)
B.	**Share in central taxes[b] (DT & IDT)**
II.	**Non-tax revenue (C + D)**
C.	**Grants from the centre**
D.	**States' own non-tax revenue (a–f)**
(a)	Interest receipts
(b)	Dividends and profits
(c)	General services
	of which:
	State lotteries
(d)	Social services
(e)	Economic service
(f)	Fiscal services

[a]Comprises General Sales Tax/VAT, Central Sales Tax, Sales Tax on Motor Spirit and Purchase Tax on Sugarcane, etc.
[b]With the eightieth amendment of the Constitution (80th Amendment) Act, 2000, all the central taxes are pooled and shared between the Centre and the States
DT direct taxes; *INDT* indirect taxes

References

Ayer, S. P. (1961). *Federalism and Social Change*. Bombay: Asia Publishing House.
Government of India. (2001). Advisory Group on Tax Policy and Tax Administration for the Tenth Plan.
Government of India. (2001). The Expert Committee to Review the System of Administered Interest Rates and other related issues.
Government of India. (2002). Task Force on Direct Taxes and Indirect Taxes.
Government of India. (2009). Thirteenth Finance Commission, 2010–15 Volume 1.
Government of India. Union Budget Documents for various years.
Reserve Bank of India. (2015). Handbook of Statistics on Indian Economy, 2014–15.
Smoke, P. (2013). Why theory and practice are different: The gap between principles and reality in sub national revenue systems. International Center for Public Policy, Working Paper 13-13, April, Department of Economics, Georgia State University. http://ScholarWorks.gsu.edu/icepp.

Chapter 5
Managing Government Expenditure: Searching for Lines of Control

B. S. Bhandary and Gopalkrishniah Nagesha

1 Introduction

Public expenditure is a subject of great importance. It embraces almost all subjects of human interest—economics, politics, administration, public policy, management, law, science, sociology, anthropology to name some. Debates and discussions on ideologies and important concepts such as equality, efficiency, justice, and fairness continue to engage the attention of policy makers. It is a crowded place, and its study involves complex issues. It would be useful to have some glimpse at the history of public expenditure and a bit of theory so that we can have a better perspective on the subject .

Public expenditure involves making choices, at almost every stage. Resources are scarce. People have to decide how much resources the States should acquire and how much it should leave for the market. What must be the magnitude of the public sector? Government should decide which are the priorities for expenditure, and also priorities within priorities. How much for growth and how much for distribution? What is the level of fiscal deficit and how much is size of debt. How much for growth and how much for consumption and how much for investment? How to mobilise the resources for expenditure and what should be the method of financing the expenditure? What should be the role of Union government and what should be the role of States and of local governments. How much is the trust and how many rules for auditing and how

---

The first author Bhandary was formarly associated with Vijaya Bank (presently he is no more).

G. Nagesha (✉)
Post Graduate Department of Economics, Government First Grade College,
Yelahanka, Bengaluru, India
e-mail: nageconomics@gmail.com

B. S. Bhandary
Vijaya Bank, Bangalore, India

G. Karnam (ed.), *Public Budgeting in India*, India Studies in Business and Economics, https://doi.org/10.1007/978-81-322-3917-8_5

many control statements. It is a continuous search for choices and fixing appropriate dividing lines, which keep shifting (for details read Bagchi 2005).

1.1 Growth in Public Spending: A Historical Perspective

Research evidence revealed that government expenditure and its composition have been largely guided by the role of State from time to time. Government expenditure increased substantially particularly in industrialised countries in the latter part of the nineteenth century. According to Bagchi (2005) the size of the government measured by the proportion of government expenditure to gross domestic product (GDP) which stood on the average at not more than 10% at the beginning of the last century and only 18% even at the time of Second World War and increased to over 40% by 1980 in advanced countries. This phenomenal increase in government expenditure naturally gives room for asking the reasons for the same.

Some of the important debates and developments taken place in the book have relevance for countries like India. "The philosophy of the economists and society's views of the role of the State in the economy have changed remarkably over the past two centuries. Because of this, public institutions and the government's involvement in the economy have changed as well. Since 1870, government expenditure has raised considerably in all of today's industrialised countries. Although this increase has not been equal in all countries, it is nevertheless remarkable that the growth in public spending has been a general phenomenon despite the considerable differences and geographic and language barriers that have existed among industrialised countries" Tanzi and Ludger Schuknecht (2000).

In the historical account of growth in government spending and the underlying philosophy, Tanzi analyses the growth by important phases like the period up to First World War, the effects of war, the interwar period and the growth effects of Keynesianism in the 1980's. The minimal economic role advocated by the classical economists and the "Laissez Faire" preference limiting the role of government largely to the national defence, police and administration had translated into a public expenditure constituting a very small share in the gross domestic product (GDP). Around 1870, unweighted average public expenditure was accounted to only about 10% of gross domestic product. In the USA, government expenditure was about 7% of GDP.

In the latter part of the nineteenth century, however classical economists started to be challenged by Marxian thinking, which strongly influenced the socialist movement in Europe. By the end of the century, the German economists Schmollar and Wagner had added redistribution of wealth to the legitimate and normal government functions.

First World War resulted in a considerable increase in spending in particular among the countries that were more affected by the War. On an average public expenditure had increased to 18.27% by 1920, and in France, Germany, Italy and UK, the countries were most affected where expenditure has increased more than

25% of GDP. The Great Depression completely changed the thinking owing to the failed private sector investment and its theory, Supply creates its own demand.

Ashford and Kelley's (1986) study reveals that many of the "European countries had introduced rudimentary social security systems and the Depression resulted in a wave of expansionary government expenditure policies including social programmes by late 1920s. The Depression was seen by many as a monumental failure of the market economy and of laissez faire, a failure that justified the government intervention and made many intellectuals look with varying degrees of admiration at the economic experiments going on in Russia, Germany and Italy". Owing to the changed thinking and to address the changing societal requirements public expenditure on an average increased to 22.8% of GDP by 1937. Governments across the globe assumed considerable importance during the period 1960–1980, with their active participation in allocation, distribution, stabilisation and growth functions, alongside was a rapid increase in the share of government expenditure in GDP to 40% and in some cases even more. Governmental activity in India expanded considerably with its active participation in every sector in the post-independence era with government lead planning until the launch of major structural reforms in 1991. Government expenditure which was barely 9% of GDP at the time of independence increased to 25% in 1980's (Bagchi 2005) hovered around 30% of GDP by late 1980's.

2 Theory

2.1 State and the Market

The professional thinking on the role of State and market has been changing from time to time and conflicting. While there are convincing arguments in favour of governments assuming many responsibilities, there are equally strong arguments in favour of private sector triggered by the inefficient public-sector performance. This has largely been the basis for the "Structural adjustments and Stabilisation" measures initiated by a number of countries following the neoliberal thinking. According to Samuelson, 2004, one of the principal problems of political economy is deciding on the appropriate boundary between the State and the market.

Bagchi (2005) study reveals that "Finances of the government, how much of country resource the government should acquire for its own use, how and what makes for their efficient spending—'public finance' in short—have been a subject of perennial interest to thinkers since ancient times. Kautilya's Arthashastra written some two thousand years ego devotes a substantial part of the work to 'Treasury, Source of revenue, Accounts and Audit'. Public Finance has however come in for special attention in the last fifty years, primarily because of phenomenal expansion of the public sector since the Second World War".

In advanced countries as observed in the previous sections, the size of the government measured by the proportion of government expenditure to gross domestic product (GDP) which was about 10% at the beginning of last century increased to about 40% (in some cases even more) by 1980. In the Indian context, it has increased from 9% at the time of independence to almost 20% in late 1980's. It has increased; now, it is around 12.74% in FY 2017. In this context, a number of questions have been raised in the literature such as Why this enormous increase in public expenditure? These developments raise some important issue—what should be the size of public sector? How it should be financed? How preferences of the people get articulated? Why does the economy require a public sector at all when the private sector which claims to function efficiently without the intervention of the government can meet the demands of society by providing required goods and services? These questions get further complicated when regional dimensions are factored in a vast country like India characterised by huge imbalances in development. While there is fiscal decentralisation in place, in reality the policy priorities get framed at the national or the subnational levels. How to have the regional needs reflected in the expenditure allocated? Given the recent emphasis on tracking of results of government expenditure, there are issues such as how effectively the "outlays" have got translated into "outcomes" and whether performance information gets used in the framing expenditure allocations in the ensuing budgets, popularly known as informed decision-making. There are differences amongst economists in responding to these important questions.

We require a defence force to defend the country, a police force to maintain law and order in the society, a legal system to facilitate transactions as per contracts, a judiciary to provide justice to the people. These services cannot be provided by the private sector. Even with regard to economic activities by the State, we have noted how economists have argued in support of the need for active interference of the government. According to Bagchi, emergence of public finance has its origin in the recognition that economic activity in a community cannot meet all the needs of the people constituting it if left entirely to market. "In every human community there are certain wants felt in common by all members—'public goods' as they have come to be known—which because of their very nature the market will not provide at all, or in adequate measure."

These are goods and services that can be provided by the government.

1. Economic activity occurring in the market cannot yield socially optimal outcome without at least some regulations.
2. Where private economic activities generate externalities, i.e. when private and social cost and/or benefits diverge and the market cannot take care of them as a result of which competitive outcomes turn out to be inefficient.
3. Market can fail also because of imperfect competition and inadequacies in information needed for efficient functioning.
4. There are reasons why competition may fail such as barriers to entry of new firms into an industry, increasing returns to scale, natural monopolies.
5. Social welfare as perceived by society can be increased through programmes of income redistribution undertaken by the State through transfers or through State provision of education, health and social security. These are functions that

belong properly to government. In essence, institution like government is needed to take collective action for meeting the collective wants because of the fact that individuals may not cooperate in their enforcement and non-cooperative behaviour is often preferred individual strategy.

Once it is accepted that the government intervention in the activities of the State is important for the welfare of the people, questions that need to be responded are: what is the role and appropriate size of public sector? What is the basis on which it is determined? What are the implications for raising resources by way of taxes and borrowing for meeting the expenditure of the public sector?

The basic question to be considered here is the allocation of resources and their efficient uses. Some of the theories evolved by economists to address these issues are analysed in brief here. According to AB, the advent of the marginal analysis helped to demonstrate how efficient use of resources could be achieved in both private and public sectors by matching the preferences of consumers for goods with the cost of production/provisions. "Although a beginning was made by Knut Wicksell, a great Swedish economist in 1980s, the rigorous formulation of conditions for optimal provision of public goods or the optimal size of public expenditure by equalising cost and benefits at the margin—had to wait till the publication of Nobel Laureate Paul Samuelson's celebrated three-page article 'Pure Theory of Public Expenditure' in 1954. The marginal conditions that ensure what is known in economics as 'Pareto optimality' after the great Italian economist Villfred Pareto evolved out of Samuelson's formulation". It can be noted that the requirement for the outcome of economic activity in a community to be regarded as Pareto optimal is that no one can be made better off without making someone worse off. Regarding preference revelation for public good, Wicksell postulated an approach that originated the theory of public choice as an integral part of fiscal process. He postulated a political process of voting as a substitute for bidding in the market.

According to Samuelson (2010), governments commonly have three main economic functions in a market economy. These functions are increasing efficiency, promoting equity and fostering macroeconomic stability and growth:

1. Governments have increased their efficiency by supporting competition, cutting externalities, like pollution and providing public goods.
2. Governments have promoted equity by promoting tax and expenditure programme to redistribute income towards particular groups.
3. Governments have foster macroeconomic stability and growth in addressing unemployment and inflation through encouraging economic growth through fiscal and monetary policy regulations.

2.2 Externalities

The vital externalities mainly include unregulated factories that do tend to pollute the air, water and land. Often communicable diseases break out, and private market has little incentives to develop effective public health programmes. Consumers are sometimes poorly informed about the characteristics of goods they buy. The markets are not perfect to address the problem; hence, it results in market failures.

2.3 Distribution of Income

Income distribution is often accompanied by government taxation and expenditure policies. Many advanced economies presently frame a regulation that the children must not go hungry because of economic conditions of their parents and the poor and vulnerable people should not die because of insufficient money for needed medical care. The governments also promote that the young population in the country must attain free quality public education. The middle- and old-age people shall be able to live out their years with their minimum level of income.

2.4 Public Choice Theory

2.4.1 Economics in Politics

"Basically the theory of public choice explores how expenditures on public goods and the modus of financing them are determined through the political process, applying, wherever possible and appropriate, principles and techniques of economics." (Bagchi 2005).

The motivation for employing methodologies of economics to political process stems from the problem of ascertaining the preferences of public for public goods. In the case of private goods, households/individuals reveal their preferences through their demand in response to which firms undertake production of the goods demanded, both operating in the goods market. In the case of public goods, no such mechanism is available, and so, governments are faced with the problem of how to act according to citizens' choices.

According to Samuelson and Nordhaus (2010), "public choice theory examines the way different voting mechanisms can function and shows that there are no ideal mechanisms to sum up individual preferences into social choices. This approach also analyses government failures which arise when State's actions fail to improve efficiency" (p. 384).

The emergences of public choice economics reflect also dissatisfaction with the implicit assumption that government effectively corrects market failures of the public sector in increasing the efficiency of the economy and welfare of the people. There are economists who claim that government intervention can also lead to waste of resources and redistribution of income in undesirable fashion. Governments can make bad decisions or carry out good ideas badly. Indeed just as market failures, so as government failures.

Samuelson and Nordhaus (2010), "These are the domain of Public Choice Theory examines the way different voting mechanism can function and shows that there are no ideal mechanism to sum up individual preference into the social choices. These approaches also analyses government failures which arise when State action fail to improve economic efficiency" (p. 288).

3 Functions of the Fiscal State

According to Richard A Musgrave for whom the State is a "contractarian venture" based on and reflecting the shared concerns of its individual members, "fiscal resources are needed to execute State functions and way in which they are tendered shapes how individuals and the States are related". He further adds that State and public sectors form an integral part of a multifaceted socio-economic order. "Visible hand of budgetary processes, in short, is no less natural than the invisible hand of the market. A variety of needs are to be met and tasks to be undertaken, some better served by the former and the others by the latter more. Failure arise and need to be dealt with under both with both rendering essential and complementary contributions". This order includes not only Pareto efficient use of resources, but also distributive justice. A weave of fiscal economics, which holds that "all is well" if only Pareto optimality prevails, bypasses other essential components of social coexistence.

Musgrave et al. (2004) is known for assigning three major functions to the public sector. "(1) The provision for social goods or the process by which total resource use is divided between private and social goods and by which mix of social goods is chosen. This provision may be termed the allocation function of budget policy. (2) Adjusting of distribution of income and wealth to ensure conformance with what society considers as a fair or just State of distribution, here referred to as distribution function. (3) The use of budget policy as a means of maintaining high employment, a reasonable degree of price level stability and an appropriate rate of economic growth, with allowances for effect on trade and on the balance of payments" (p. 6). These objectives are a part of the stabilisation functions.

First step in Samuelson's formulations of a pure theory of public expenditure consists of defining "public goods" analytically to isolate characteristics that distinguish them from private goods. Samuelson (1954) defines public goods "as those of which consumption is 'non-rival',[1] Unlike private goods, public goods cannot be parcelled out or rationed amongst individuals. On the other hand total consumption of private goods can be derived by adding each individual's consumption."

In the case of public goods, the total amount consumed is the same for all the individuals. This is the essence of non-rivalry in consumption. Commonly cited example is the defence of the nation.

---

[1]Non rival goods are those goods, which all enjoy in common in the sense that one individual's consumption leads to no diminution from any other individual's consumption of those goods.

Another important characteristic of a public good is that if provided to one individual, another individual cannot be excluded from its benefits easily or, if at all, only at a prohibitive cost. Whereas one can avail of a private good by paying a price for it, in contrast, no one can be assigned exclusively the right to enjoy a public good against a price. As a result, there is no apparent incentive for anyone to reveal his or her preference. Everyone can expect to gain access to the benefit of public good once it is provided without paying a price that is, ride free, for the simple reason that exclusion is not possible, at least not simple to enforce. Of course, if everyone rides free the public goods will not be supplied at all and that provides the rationale for government intervention.

Joseph Stiglitz (2005) assigned following six functions for the government.

Establishing Infrastructure:

1 Governments role in establishing the infrastructure is very crucial. Akhtar Ali (1997) "In a broader sense, much of the role of the government can be viewed as establishing infrastructure in its broadest sense—educational, technological, financial, physical, environmental, and social infrastructure of the economy". Market cannot operate in a vacuum, and infrastructure is necessary if markets are to fulfil their role. Because constructing the broad infrastructure is beyond the capacity or interest of any single firm, it must be primarily the responsibility of the government" (p. 1) (Akhtar Ali 1997).

2 "Promote technology; the second role of government is in promoting technology. Progress of science is very important. "Over more than one fifty years during which it has supported research, US government has had impressive record of success." East Asian governments have also played a central role in the promotion of technology.

3 Supporting the financial sector: Third role of the government is to support the financial sector "sometimes, depicted as a brain of the economy, financial sector is responsible for deploying capital resources in the most efficient way". In 1863, The US recognised the need to create a national financial system and passed the national banking act. East Asian governments also played an active role in ensuring the safety and soundness of financial institutions.

4 Investing in infrastructure. Fourth role of government is investing in infrastructure including institutions, and in roads and communication systems. In this context he has drawn our attention to the importance of institutional infrastructure, which includes property rights, contract and bankruptcy laws and policies to promote competition, where it is viable and to regulate markets where it is not.

5 Preventing Environmental Degradation: we should not confuse increases in GDP with increases in standard of living. Recent attempt at building 'green' GDP accounts recognises the importance of environmental protection. It will take generations to undo the environmental damage that has been wrought in many countries.

6 Creating and Maintaining a Social Safety Net: The sixth role of the government is in creating and maintaining a social safety net including access to basic health services. In some cases, these activities can be justified in utilitarian terms;

they increase the productivity of the labour force and foster political stability by reducing opposition to change. They may also be justified in terms of basic values. Standard of living embraces more than the variables captured in GDP statistics. Improved health conditions represent improvement in living standards, even if such an improvement not reflected in GDP."

There is a need for "balancing of the strengths and limitations of market and governments and the determination of how they can best complement each other. It does not begin with two columns labelled 'activities to be carried out by government' and 'activities to be carried out by the private sector'. This careful balancing puts greater emphasis on how the government does what it does and it interacts with the private sector".

"Making government perform better is an important concern everywhere. Good policies on education, health, and environment are not luxuries to be postponed to a later date. Making government focus more on customer orientation, performance, competition is also essential. Indeed scarcity of resources and the tightness of fiscal constraints facing the developing countries today make it imperative that the resources to be spent efficiently" (p. 69).

4 Government Expenditure and Economic Growth

One of the key objectives of public expenditure is promotion of growth and development. The theoretical and empirical literature has hinted at the need to have well-designed and well-implemented public spending to improve resource allocation by supplying critical public goods, thereby boosting longer run growth prospects. Ramon and Lopez (2010) "on the development role of fiscal policy provides a multidimensional perspective on development combining income growth, equity and development quality. Issues addressed relate to the core of development policy debate. The discussion revolves around how fiscal policies affect the "key dimensions of quality" and is argued that sustainability of development results is fundamentally affected by the nature of the growth and fiscal policies have an especially important effect on the quality aspects of the growth" (p. v). The study reiterates the fact that quality of growth is important as growth itself.

However, in reality, political economy prevails over rational economic decisions that fetch long-term economic gains to expenditure decisions that gain short-term popular support to the governments leading to poor expenditure planning and execution. The enormous potential that the government has in promoting quality growth gets thwarted by irrational expenditure decisions causing greater damage to the economy. In order to achieve a balanced and sustained growth, the study of Ramon and Lopez (2010) states that "at least 3 types of assets matter for production and welfare: physical capital, human capital and natural capital. Technological progress and the policy environment affecting the use of these assets matter as well. It has been argued that traditionally greater attention has been given to the accumulation of physical capital and financial capital. In the context of poverty reduction, the study argues that greater attention to areas such as human (and social) capital and natural (and environmental) capital should be given as these are the primary assets that the poor possess" (p. 7).

"Accumulation of all three types of capital is crucial for balanced and sustainable growth. Market failures usually lead to under investment in human capital and over exploitation of natural capital. Such results affect the lower-income segments of the population disproportionably and tend to benefit a minority of the population. Market failures are therefore a source of structural inequality, which in turn, is detrimental to efficiency and growth." (The World Bank 2010, p. 7).

The term "public goods is broadly defined here to include spending on education, health, social security transport, communication, public order and safety, and housing and community amenities. Other public goods include resource management, pollution control and abatement, and the adaptation of low emission technologies. There is a need to scale up standards of public goods and enhanced provision with increased revenue base. Emphasis is to be laid on increasing the efficiency of government expenditures, which in turn, would allow for raising the quality of education, health care, social protection, crime prevention and infrastructure services" (p. xii).

Empirical evidence bears testimony to the benefits of quality spending "for the quantity and quality aspects for economic growth. Government spending on public goods is strongly associated with faster economic growth as well with greater poverty reduction" (Ibid, p. xiii). The literature argues in favour of quality of public spending rather than the quantity that is poorly planned.

Government spending on public goods in India by Houqi Hong and Sadiq Ahmed, World Bank, (2010) has used panel data from 14 Indian States between 1990 and 2002; this paper empirically examines how "the share of government spending on public goods such as health, education and basic infrastructure affects gross domestic product growth and poverty reduction at the State level. The study observes that the share of public goods expenditures in total State government expenditures has a large positive and significant impact on per capita GDP growth. The study highlights that reallocation of funds to increase the share of public goods expenditures could on an average lead per capita GDP growth rate to increase by up to 2.7% points. Another equally important finding is that as State fiscal policies also have significant impact on poverty reduction, allocation of funds to increase the share of social public goods expenditures could on average reduce the poverty head count index up to 6.6% points". In the Indian context, yet another study (Panagariya et al. 2014) analysing the State-level reforms, growth and development in Indian States observe that generally the States with higher per capita GSDP also had high per capita expenditures on developmental heads. This indicates according to the authors that the States with higher per capita GSDP are in a position to raise large volume of revenues providing greater fiscal space for spending more on developmental services. With reference to growth rates of per capita expenditure on developmental services it is stated that in the aggregate, there has been a significant acceleration in the growth rates during the second period (2004–2012) in keeping with the trend in the growth rate of GSDP in the State. With the real per capita GSDP growth rate accelerating from 3% in the first period to 7.4% in the second, additional fiscal space was created. Their analysis shows that accelerating economic growth is a critical factor in creating fiscal space for the states to spend on social and physical services.

4.1 State's Development Expenditures and Implications for Regional Development

Both Central and State governments have important roles in providing physical and social infrastructures, and the role of public expenditure is very crucial in this process. The constitution assigns a predominant role to the States in the provision of social services like education, health care, water supply and sanitation and urban development and a co-equal role with Central government in providing physical infrastructures like power and road transport. Therefore, State government spending on them is an important factor determining the pattern of growth in the country.

In this connection, it may also be noted that Panagariya, Chakraborty and Rao in their book highlighted the States' Development Expenditures in India (Table 1).

Further, it may be recalled that the centre incurs expenditures on many public services that are important for the States, directly or indirectly, for implementing various programmes by the States. Cumulatively, all these factors may have an impact on the performance of States.

Panagariya and Rao (2014) have analysed the State government expenditures on "developmental heads comprising social and economic services" which include both capital and revenue expenditures. Social services mainly include education, medical and public health, water supply and sanitation, housing and urban development. Economic services include promotion of agriculture and allied activities, industry, road and transport, and communications. Public expenditure plays an important role in determining the size and quality of physical and social infrastructures required to be created in the economy.

Table 1 Annual average growth rate of expenditures

Development services	1994–2003	2004–2012	1994–2012
Education	10.2	14.7	10.1
Medical and public health[a]	8.8	17.9	10.5
Total social services	10.5	17.5	11.8
Total economic services	7.2	15.4	11.7
Total developmental services	8.9	16.8	11.9

[a]Medical and public expenditure includes medical and public health, family welfare, and water supply and sanitation
Source Panagariya et al. (2014)

Table 2 Trends in social sector expenditure (Centre and States)

Years	(Revenue + Capital) in Rs.		
	As % of GDP	As % of aggregate public expenditure (Revenue + Capital)	Per capita expenditure
2002–03	6.44	22.53	1441
2003–04	6.41	21.80	1581
2004–05	6.35	22.61	1746
2005–06	6.67	24.01	2059
2006–07	6.83	24.65	2419
2007–08	6.65	24.39	2687
2008–09	7.68	26.71	3536
2009–10	7.99	26.78	4167
2010–11	7.96	27.34	4860
2011–12 RE	8.29	27.97	5724
2012–13 BE	8.49	28.32	6532

RE revised estimate; *BE* budget estimate
Source Gayithri and Raju (2014)

According to the authors, the analysis of per capita expenditure on major social and economic services brings out several interesting points. All States' average per capita aggregate expenditure in 2011/12 was Rs. 7412 or about 10% of per capita GSDP (Table 2).

Per capita expenditure on social services was Rs. 4159 and on economic services Rs. 3276 which constituted only 5.7 and 4.5% of per capita GSDP, respectively. All States' per capita expenditure on education was Rs. 1934 and on health care a mere Rs. 485. As a ratio of per capita GSDP, these translated to a mere 2.6 and 0.7%, respectively.

Gayithri and Raju (2014) study reveals that aggregate social sector expenditure inclusive of the spending by both Central and State governments, as a percentage of GDP increased from 6.44% in 2002 to 2003 to 8.49 in 2012–13. Aggregate expenditure which had dropped 6.4% in 1995–96 has picked up in the recent decade, and the increase in social sector spending as a per cent of GDP has been significant, which is a welcome development given the Human Development challenges faced by India. The share of social sector in the total expenditure has experienced an increase from 22.53% in 2002–03 to 28.32% in 2012–13. There has been a 350% increase approximately in the per capita social sector expenditure from Rs. 1441 in 2002–03 to Rs. 6532 in 2012–13 (Table 3).

Table 3 Share of expenditure allotted to social sector (as % of total expenditure)

Years	Social service expenditure of Centre and State	Social service expenditure of Centre	Social service expenditure of State
2002–03	22.53	10.77	31.56
2003–04	21.80	11.91	29.73
2004–05	22.61	11.78	30.91
2005–06	24.01	12.64	31.69
2006–07	24.65	13.03	32.00
2007–08	24.39	13.04	32.95
2008–09	26.71	15.60	35.32
2009–10	26.78	14.57	36.01
2010–11	27.34	14.95	37.47
2011–12 RE	27.97	13.52	38.78
2012–13 BE	28.32	13.75	39.02

RE revised estimate; *BE* budget estimate
Source Gayithri and Raju (2014)

5 Economic and Functional Classification of Expenditure

There is another method of looking at the impact of expenditures on the economy. Ministry of Finance has been preparing an economic-cum-functional classification of budgetary transactions. Table 4 provides the details of total expenditures and details of budgetary outlays into functional categories. Such functional classification helps in analysing how much the Central government is allocating to different functions or purposes (Tables 5, 6, 7 and 8).

5.1 Fiscal Developments in India: Major Trends and Issues

The vital fiscal issues addressed from the Ninth Finance commission to 14FC is been analysed in this section.

The most persistent "deterioration is observed in the ratio of revenue deficit to fiscal deficit, which, by indicating the extent to which borrowed resources are used for current expenditures, shows the 'quality' of fiscal deficit. In 1991, this ratio was about 50%. It increased steadily to 75% in 1998–99. Thereafter, there was some improvement, but the ratio again increased back to the level of 75.6% in 2003–04, indicating that 3/4th of the borrowing has been used for current consumptions in some years" (Finance Ministry, GoI).

Trends in "fiscal deficit of the centre revealed that first it declined from 6.6% in 1990–91 to 4.1% in 1996–97. A similar profile is observed in the case of revenue deficit, which, after declining from 3.3% GDP in 1990–91 to 2.4% in 1996–97, rose

Table 4 Expenditure by economic classification (in Rs. Crore)

		2012–13 accounts	2103–14 revised	2014–15 budget
1.	**Total expenditure**	**1,374,746**	**1,543,832**	**1,726,250**
	(i) Gross capital formation	230,791	265,260	315,211
	(ii) Consumption expenditure	271,119	308,269	345,835
	(iii) Current transfers	851,208	955,795	1,050,427
	(iv) Others	21,628	14,509	14,778
2.	**Total expenditure (growth rate)**	**8.8**	**12.3**	**11.8**
	(i) Gross capital formation	(−)1.8	14.9	18.8
	(ii) Consumption expenditure	6.1	13.7	12.2
	(iii) Current transfers	12.5	12.3	9.9
	(iv) Others	36.3	(−)32.9	1.9
3.	**Total expenditure (point contribution)**	**8.8**	**12.3**	**11.8**
	(i) Gross capital formation	(−)0.3	2.5	3.2
	(ii) Consumption expenditure	1.2	2.7	2.4
	(iii) Current transfers	7.5	7.6	6.1
	(iv) Others	0.5	(−)0.5	0.00

Note Point contribution refers to contribution of individual component to total growth
Source GoI (2015)

steadily to 4.4% in 2001–02. The year 2002–03 witnessed an improvement in fiscal deficit to 5.9% of the GDP due to reduction in primary deficit, although the revenue deficit continued almost at the same level as 2001–02" (Finance Ministry, GoI).

Raising growth of revenue expenditure which is more than the revenue expenditure resulted in revenue deficit of the Central government and some of the State governments.

Revenue expenditure is treated as consumption expenditure, and when it exceeds the revenue receipts, it results in revenue deficit. This difference is usually met from borrowed funds which are supposed to be used for investment purposes. This results in adverse impacts such as enhanced interest payment burden on the revenue account, and since the borrowed funds are used up, even if partially for maintenance and consumption purpose, to that extent the funds cannot be contributing to either income generation or asset formation which otherwise would have occurred if used for capital investments. It results in borrowing to cover the gap between the revenue receipts and revenue expenditure.

In the context of increasing the revenue deficit, the Finance Commission has observed that "the resources which the governments need for providing essential

Table 5 Expenditure by functional head (in Rs. Crore)

		2012–13 Accounts	2103–14 Revised	2014–15 Budget
1.	**Total expenditure**	**1,374,746**	**1,543,832**	**1,726,250**
	(i) Social services	181,924	205,831	274,908
	(ii) Economic services	396,075	412,358	398,297
	(iii) General services	293,769	337,479	378,493
	(iv) Unallocable	502,978	588,165	674,551
2.	**Total expenditure (growth rate)**	**8.8**	**12.3**	**11.8**
	(i) Social services	1.7	13.1	33.6
	(ii) Economic services	3.1	4.1	(−)3.4
	(iii) General services	13.4	14.9	12.2
	(iv) Unallocable	14.0	16.9	14.7
3.	**Total Expenditure (point contribution)**	**8.8**	**12.3**	**11.8**
	(i) Social services	0.2	1.7	4.5
	(ii) Economic services	0.9	1.2	(−)0.9
	(iii) General services	2.7	3.2	2.7
	(iv) Unallocable	4.9	6.2	5.6

Note Point contribution refers to contribution of individual component to total growth
Source GoI (2015)

public services and for performing other functions expected of them are large and rising. The problem of scarcity of resources however cannot be solved by increasing revenue deficits, which is tantamount to living beyond ones means. The fiscal scenario in the country has gradually worsened to an alarming extent and corrective steps are required now to reverse the deteriorating trend and to create conditions for the restoration of health to the financial system" (Ninth Finance Commission, GoI).

Rule-based fiscal correction mechanism had become the order of the day in a number of countries. Mainly, "such reforms relate to formal deficit and debt rules, specification of expenditure rules and fiscal transparency. As per the Maastricht Treaty rule desirability for fiscal deficit is 3% of GDP. It is important to note that in the UK a "golden rule" of limiting borrowing only to finance capital expenditure has been followed since 1997 as a sustainable investment rule. In other countries, "Fiscal transparency implies being open to public regarding the structure and functions of government. Transparency requires that any policy changes must be introduced with a clear statement of relevance and objectives. Strategies of fiscal consolidation require a long term focus and the need to promote growth." (Finance Ministry, GoI, p. 25).

The Union government achieved this target in 2007–8 with the fiscal deficit declining to 2.5% of GDP. However in 2008–9 the Union government under took several fiscal expansionary measures such as revision of pay scales based on the Recom-

Table 6 FRBM and fiscal sustainability

Year	Fiscal deficit	Revenue deficit	Primary deficit	Ratio of revenue to fiscal deficit (%)
1990–91	6.61	3.26	2.83	49.36
1991–92	4.72	2.49	0.65	52.72
1992–93	5.33	2.76	0.72	51.73
1993–94	6.43	3.81	2.15	59.21
1994–95	4.74	3.06	0.39	64.60
1995–96	4.23	2.50	0.02	59.16
1996–97	4.11	2.38	0.24	58.01
1997–98	4.81	3.05	0.50	63.45
1998–99	5.14	3.85	0.67	74.78
1999–00	5.41	3.49	0.75	64.55
2000–01	5.69	4.08	0.93	71.74
2001–02	6.18	4.39	1.47	71.06
2002–03	5.87	4.37	1.10	74.36
2003–04 RE	4.77	3.60	0.27	75.59

Source Central budget documents and Indian public finance statistics, 2002–03
Notes Figures for 2003–04 are revised estimates
Fiscal deficit figures exclude States' share against small savings
Primary deficit is derived by netting interest payments from fiscal deficit

Table 7 Fiscal consolidation path for the Centre (per cent of GDP)

	2009–10	2010–11	2011–12	2012–13	2013–14	2014–15
Revenue deficit	4.8	3.2	2.3	1.2	0.0	−0.5
Non-debt capital records	0.1	0.5	0.6	0.8	0.9	1.0
Capital expenditure	2.1	3.0	3.1	3.8	3.9	4.5
Fiscal deficit	6.8	5.7	4.8	4.2	3.0	3.0
Outstanding debt (adjusted)	54.2	53.9	52.5	50.5	47.5	44.8

Table 8 Consolidated fiscal reform path of Centre and States (per cent of GDP)

	2009–10	2010–11	2011–12	2012–13	2013–14	2014–15
Fiscal deficit—States	2.8	2.6	2.5	2.5	2.4	2.4
Fiscal deficit—Centre	6.8	5.7	4.8	4.2	3.0	3.0
Net central loans to States	0.1	0.0	0.0	0.0	0.0	0.0
Fiscal deficit—consolidated	9.5	8.3	7.3	6.7	5.4	5.4
Debt stock—States	27.1	26.6	26.1	25.5	24.8	24.3
Debt stock—Centre	54.2	53.9	52.5	50.5	47.5	44.8
Outstanding central loans to States	2.5	2.2	2.0	1.7	1.5	1.3
Consolidated debt	78.8	78.3	76.6	74.3	70.8	67.8

mendation of The Sixth pay commission, waiver of farm loans and the expansion of the Mahatma Gandhi National Rural Employment Guarantee (MGNREGA) to all districts from the 200 district it was original is slated to cover. In addition oil prices escalated sharply, leading to arise in subsidy. As a consequence of all this as well as a global crisis, the fiscal deficit of the Union government increased to 6% in 2008–09 and 6.5% in 2009–10" (Finance Ministry, GoI).

"Elimination of revenue deficit was considered as the long term permanent target for both the Centre and the States. The fiscal consolidation path for the Central government envisaged a decline in the revenue deficit of 4.8% of GDP as projected for the fiscal year 2009–10 to a revenue surplus 0.5% of GDP by 2014–15" (Finance Ministry, GoI). It was expected that this would allow capital expenditure to increase to 3.5% of GDP.

5.1.1 Increasing Trends in Public Debt

The Finance Commissions has warned that another cause for serious concern is the rapid increase in public debt.

Thirdly, the FC ascribes the macroeconomic vulnerability of the economy "to the secular deterioration in its fiscal balance and highlights the need to restore fiscal equilibrium.

TFC states that the "Changes in the fiscal regime in 1982–83 from revenue surplus to revenue deficit has meant that what was earlier a non-debt creating source of financing has become a source of rising internal indebtedness. In other words, while revenue receipts used to cover a part of the capital expenditure, now an increasing part of the capital rcceipts are used to finance revenue expenditure. The consequent build-up of public debt and the interest burden, which is the now the largest and fastest growing item of expenditure, further fuel led the growth of revenue expenditure. This led to a spiral of growing deficits, rising debt, escalating interest costs, and further expansion of deficit" GoI (2005).

With respect to States the FCs observed that "almost all States have gone through three phase deterioration in the revenue account balance. In the first phase up to 1986–87, the non-plan account surplus was larger than the plan deficit and to that extent it was yielding an overall revenue surplus. Between 1986–87 and 1991–92, the magnitude of plan revenue deficit increased sharply and it became larger than the non-plan surplus, which itself has been declining. The third and final phase started in 1991–92, when the non-plan revenue account went into deficit. TFC refers to systemic factors underlining the deterioration rather than state specific reasons as all States have had almost identical turning points" GoI (2005).

"Stabilisation and structural adjustment programme of the centre was initiated in response to situation of "fiscal disequilibrium" which reached crisis proportions in 1991. Vital components of the reforms, includes to government finances are the policies relating to tax reform and reduction in fiscal deficit. "It was aimed to reduce in fiscal deficit both through improved receipts and reduced revenue expenditure. However, owing to the inflexibility of revenue expenditure in the short run and shortfalls in revenue caused by reduction in rates of taxes fiscal deficit reduction was attempted by reducing the capital expenditure" GoI (2005).

In the case of States, the TFC observes rising revenue deficit also resulted in the reduction of maintenance expenditure. "In order to accommodate rising interest payments and growth of wages and salaries, which have come to be regarded as committed expenditure, maintenance expenditure has been treated as a "residual item" GoI (2005). The telling adverse effects in the form of increased committed expenditure have had a visible impact on infrastructure. TFC states "The deteriorating conditions of roads poorly maintained hospitals, neglected schools and administrative buildings have together become a formidable supply side constraint on growth. Most assets like power stations, irrigation systems, highways are operating at levels well below their capacity on account of poor maintenance and continued neglect" Kapila (1996) (p. 232).

The EFC in its vital recommendations suggested that "The measures for restructuring of finances added a new dimension to the task of Commission, reflecting a twofold concern viz., the persistence of unsustainable large deficits in budgets at both levels and the deterioration of composition of government expenditure with a disproportionately large share of receipts getting pre-empted by interest payments and unproductive expenditures, leaving too little for the social sector and much needed investment. Commenting on the fiscal situation characterised by increasing revenue deficits over two decade period, the Eleventh Finance Commission observed that revenue deficits are only visible manifestations of multiple and deep seated imbalances in government finances calling for basic restructuring. With revenue deficit accounting for large part of fiscal deficit, it is not surprising that the Central government capital expenditure as a proportion of GDP has declined from over 6% in 1980s to an average of about 4.6% in the first half of 1990s and 2.6% as of now 1999–00" (Finance Ministry, GoI).

The sharp increase in salary intensity in social services in all States reduced the scope for efficient delivery of services in vital areas like health and education that are growth enhancing" (Finance Ministry, GoI).

Further, the vital issues in fiscal situation in Central and States are "Decline in the tax—GDP ratio, large pre-emptive claims of interest payments relative to revenue receipts, high revenue-deficit to GDP ratio, large and unsustainable fiscal deficit to GDP ratio, and falling levels of capital expenditure relative to GDP" (Finance Ministry, GoI).

5.1.2 Changing Structure of Expenditures of Central and States Expenditures

The quality of expenditure has also witnessed deterioration over the years as the share of capital expenditures declined from 5.6% of GDP in 1990–91 to 3% in 2002–03. (Finance Ministry, GoI).

Under the approach to the fiscal consolidation, the 13th Finance Commission has observed as under:

During 2005–2010 period, the closing debt–GDP ratio for 2009–2010 is estimated at 82% well above the FC-XII target of 75%. Our starting point was to determine the feasible target for the debt–GDP ratio, consolidated across the Centre and the States by 2014–15 (Table 9).

Twelfth FC has proposed the "target of 68% for a combined Centre and State debt–GDP ratio to be achieved by the year 2014–15 and 45% for the Central Government debt–GDP ratio" (Finance Ministry, GoI).

Table 9 Relative shares of Centre and States in revenue and total expenditures

Arrange for finance commission periods	Relative shares			
	Total expenditure		Revenue expenditure	
	Centre	States	Centre	States
FC-I	43.83	56.17	40.77	59.23
FC-II	49.47	50.53	41.83	58.17
FC-III	50.51	49.49	46.10	53.90
FC-IV	47.69	52.31	41.77	58.23
FC-V	43.14	56.86	40.00	60.00
FC-VI	47.35	52.65	44.19	55.81
FC-VII	44.79	55.21	41.98	58.02
FC-VIII	47.86	52.14	44.22	55.78
FC-IX	45.58	54.42	43.45	56.55
FC-X	43.35	56.65	43.18	56.82
FC-XI	43.77	56.23	44.03	55.97
FC-XII[a]	43.74	56.26	44.45	55.55
Overall average	45.92	54.08	43.00	57.00

Note [a]Average of three years (2005–08)
Source Basic data from Indian public finance statistics (various years)

Thirteen FC laid down the vision of not only balancing the "receipts and expenditure on revenue account of all the States and the Union, but also generating surplus for a capital investment was reiterated" (Finance Ministry, GoI).

Further to address the deteriorating fiscal situation of government, the 13th FC has suggested to bring the "liabilities of Central government on account of oil, food and fertilizer bonds into the fiscal accounting, and the impact of various other obligations of the Central governments on the deficit target. Overall approach of the Commission was to foster 'inclusive and green growth' promoting fiscal federalism" (Finance Ministry, GoI).

Further, in the fiscal policy of the governments both the Centre and States are moved towards achieving inclusive growth was the cornerstone of India's development project inclusivity was to serve as the base for recommendations in every sphere.

5.1.3 Fiscal Consolidation and Good Governance

There has been a significant "fall from 17.11% of GDP in 2003–04 to 14.13% of GDP in 2006–07. Further is declined to 12.74% of GDP during 2017–18. The fall in the ratio of total expenditure to GDP came mostly from a reduction in capital expenditure. Capital expenditure of centre which declined from 3.96% of GDP in 2003–04 to 1.67% of GDP in 2006–07, rose to 2.50% of GDP in 2007–08." (Finance Ministry, GoI). Expenditure on interest payments, defence, pay and allowances, and subsidies are the main components of the centre revenue expenditure, accounted for 63% of the total.

Mohanty and Banumurthy (2018) study on public expenditure efficiency in 28 Indian States reveals that "Good governance plays the more vital role than economic growth in improving the efficiency of public spending" (p. 4). Increase in the efficiency in public expenditure will not only enhance the fiscal sustainability but also increase tendency of reaching the objectives of SDGs across the Indian States. Further, the study finds that "there is wide variation in the public expenditure efficiency across the States. This variation could be due to the extent of good governance in the States as well as on the economic growth. It implies that higher budgetary allocations on social sector alone might not necessarily translate into an improvement in their social outcomes" (p. 30).

5.1.4 Role of Subsides in Fiscal Deterioration of Central and State Governments

Subsidies are yet another issue in the areas of fiscal developments. The "main subsidies provided by the centre are food and fertilizer subsidies. Food subsidies had grown sharply from a level of 4.8% of centres revenue receipts in 1996–97 to 10.4% in 2002–03." (Finance Ministry, GoI).

Expenditure on explicit subsidies is the third largest item expenditure after interest payment. The "explicit subsidies reported in the budget of the Central government do not include off budget bonds issued to oil marketing and fertilizer companies. Though the administrative price mechanism for petroleum products was discontinued, there is still no deregulation of petroleum product prices. Internal price of crude increased from an average of $38 per barrel in 2004 to $54 per barrel in 2005 and further to $70 per barrel in April–June 2006. This was followed by a sharp increase in the price of crude to $147 per barrel in July 2008. Linked with this increase in crude prices there was also a significant increase in prices of fertilizer imports. In order to partly compensate the oil marketing companies, selling petroleum products at government determined prices, the centre has started issuing bonds to oil companies. Taking into account off budget bonds, issued to all oil marketing and fertilizer companies and to other institutions, the augmented and revenue and fiscal deficit would work out to 6.34% and 7.99% of GDP, respectively, in 2008–09" (Finance Ministry, GoI).

A study sponsored by the commission and carried out by National Institute of Public Finance and Policy (NIPFP) shows that "the regressive nature of all major explicit subsidies on food, fertilizer and petroleum products. Despite inherent defects in subsidy regime, reforms have remained as a major policy challenge. Subsidies differ from other component of public expenditure which target provision of public goods like defence. Subsidies variously support private consumption and/or production inputs in a manner such that their incidence is difficult to quantify. Unless subsidies are pruned and better targeted, investment in public infrastructure will suffer" (Finance Ministry, GoI).

In the context of much debated subsidies, we have forgotten to include, "Revenue Forgone", item as an expenditure in total; majority of such items, especially at the subnational level, have not been tracked let alone the revenue losses being reported. In many countries, part of the government fiscal activity may go unnoticed because it is hidden in the form of revenue foregone and does not appear explicitly as spending. Such activity is known as *tax expenditure.*

5.1.5 Review of Union Finances-Fiscal Deficit

The "fiscal deficit of the Union government relative to the GDP declined steadily from 6.1% in 2001–2 to 4.5% in 2003–4. The FRBM Act mandated reducing the fiscal deficit to 3% by 2008–2009.

Another consequence was that the total "expenditure as a ratio of GDP increased by 1.5% points from 14.3% in 2007–8 to 15.8% in 2009–10. At the same time the gross tax revenues declined by more than 2% points from a peak of 11.9% of GDP in 2007–08 to 9. 6% in 2009–10." (Finance Ministry, GoI).

The various "tax concessions and exemptions given by the Union government reduces the revenue collections and adversely affects our resources accruing to both Union and State governments. Revenue foregone as estimated by the Union government reached the peak of 8.1% of GDP in 2009 as a percentage of gross tax revenues, it was highest (77.3%) in 2009–10. Since 2004–05 revenue foregone has always been in excess of 5% of GDP. In nominal terms the estimated revenue foregone for 2013–14 stands at rupees 572,923 Crore. This accounts for a little over 5% of estimated GDP of 2013–14 and about half of the total tax collection estimated during the year" (Finance Ministry, GoI).

5.1.6 Fiscal Developments in State Finances

Ahluwalia (2000) finds that despite the progressive fiscal transfers from centre, the poor States received much higher per capita transfers than richer regions. The respective transfers are intended to offset the revenue imbalances of the States; these results in less capital investment infrastructure sector in low-income States. The 1991 LPG reforms resulted in large private investment in economically rich States, which resulted in further increase of inequality between leading and lagging States.

Lekha Chakraborty and Pinaki Chakraborty (2018) study reveals that the health and education convergence is existed in Indian States. The study included 28 States of India for the period 2001–2014. For the health, IMR and education, literacy rate is used as proxy indicator. The rate of decline in IMR is much faster in less developed States compared to more developed States. With respect to economic indicators (per capita state GDP) that there is an absence of unconditional convergence among Indian States, i.e. with lower initial level of income are not catching up the advanced States.

GoI (2017) in the Economic Survey 2016–17 noted that "there continued to be divergence within India or an aggravation of regional inequality. From this inference, one could conclude that income may correspond to a conditional convergence, which we will analyse next, incorporating a few control variables. These estimations are highly relevant from the perspective of widening regional inequality among States in various economic outcomes (divergence)" (p. 23).

The 14th FC Commission found that "the predominant feature of State finances between 2004–5 and 2014–15 is overall improvement in fiscal indicators. This came about mainly due to an increase in the aggregate revenue receipts accompanied by compression of revenue expenditure relative to Gross Domestic Product (GDP). The process of Fiscal consolidation in the States has been reinforced by the enactment of Fiscal responsibility and budget management (FRBM) legislation." (Finance Ministry, GoI 2014).

The 14 FC reiterated the importance of linking outlays with outcomes. However, the need "to spell out key indicators for outputs and to monitor this within an already defined accountability framework was stressed. As a step towards improving the system the FC recommended the formulation of appropriate indicators for measurement of outputs, specification of standards and cost and establishing a suitable accountability framework. It was suggested that primary responsibility for the preparation of outcome budget should be at the level of spending to be consolidated at the relevant level of government (Finance Ministry, GoI).

Fixing the targets, only to miss them, and preparing the fiscal roadmaps, only to revise and re-revise it, does not reflect the genuine effort required for achieving the goal of fiscal consolidation, which is fundamentally required for a healthy and growing economy.

Transparency is another very important area, where we have not been credited with any glory as there have been attempts, not to present the pictures correctly, particularly where fiscal deficit figures and total liabilities of the government were reported.

5.1.7 Issues in Expenditure Reforms

Mohanty and Bhanumurthy (2018) "Public expenditure is efficient when the government, using its given resources, produces a maximum possible benefit for the country's population. Ceteris paribus, Governments that produce more outputs while spending less on inputs can be viewed as more efficient than governments that produce fewer outputs and use more inputs. Public expenditure not being efficient would mean either that the expenditure outcome could be increased without spending more, or else that expenditure could be reduced without affecting the output" (p. 3).

Expenditure reforms were given considerable emphasis on the fiscal consolidation process. Expenditure reforms aimed at improving the supply of public goods even while untargeted and regressive subsidies were reduced. It was considered important to improve the "productivity of public expenditure. Measures suggested included: (i) performance linked incentives to State and local bodies; (ii) measures to improve transparency and accountability, e.g. stricter audit procedures; (iii) institutional deepening for better expenditure management, e.g. creation of the local body ombudsman, fiscal council and independent evaluation organisation; (iv) promotion of innovations and diffusion so as to reduce the cost as well as to improve public services; and (v) larger fiscal transfer to local bodies, to encourage speedier implementation of 73rd and 74th Constitutional amendments regarding transfer of functions and functionaries in consonance with subsidiary principle" (Finance Ministry, GoI).

Rangarajan and Subbarao (2007) state that the Centre and States have enacted fiscal responsibility legislations after considerably long deliberations; hence, it is important to remain committed to the FRBM targets. These targets need not necessarily come in the way of meeting necessary and desirable expenditure. Rangarajan argues that strong growth enables meeting of the deficit targets and still leaves enough resources for meeting the expenditure needs. Remaining committed to fiscal responsibility will strengthen the present growth momentum. Hitherto "Union government has appointed several commissions and Committees to review the PEM systems and make suggestions for improvement. These include Expenditure Reforms Commission (2000) the Second Administrative Reforms Commission (2005) HLEC Committee (2010) lLMMHA Committee (2010) and Expenditure Management Commission to review the major areas of its Expenditure Management in 2014" (GoI 2014).

In this connection, it may also be noted that there are also such Committees set up at the subnational level like that of Expenditure Reforms Commission by the Government of Karnataka had appointed 2009 under the chairmanship of BK Bhattacharya. The commission had submitted four reports covering important areas such as project management, public works department, water resources department, education, health, urban development, irrigation, industry and other departments.

The report contains recommendations regarding certain prudential principles governing management of government expenditure, including intersectoral prioritisation, formulation and implementation of project/schemes. Unfortunately, there is no information in the public domain about the action taken by the government on the recommendations so far, in spite of the fact that the report indicated that the contents of the report should be available in the public domain. The 4th Report on the Expenditure reforms was submitted in June 2011.

The 14th FC has focussed the aspects of "Public Expenditure Management (PEM), namely budgeting and accounting standards, classification of receipts and expenditure and linking outlays to outcomes. Considering the demands on the accounting personnel needed to make the transition to the accrual-based accounting system the 12th Finance Commission recommended the setting up of National Institute of public Financial Accountants." (Finance Ministry, GoI 2014).

5.1.8 Tax Reforms in Context to Fiscal Improvements

Implementation of Goods and Service tax in 01 July 2017 is one of the vital measures to address the tax evasion, tax avoidance and complexity of tax system in the country. The present GST enhances the tax compliance, increase of interstate commodity and service transactions due to one tax one nation.

5.1.9 Abolition of Plan and Non-plan Expenditure

Government of India since FY 2017–18 removed the concept of plan and non-plan expenditure way of classification of expenditure. It is one of the rational measures in bringing the effectiveness of public expenditure.

5.1.10 Enhanced Fiscal Autonomy of States

14 FC recommended for enhancement of 32–42% of Central tax devolution to States. This is yet another measure in giving fiscal autonomy to States. From this measure, States themselves can spend based on their own requirements.

5.1.11 Best Practices for Fiscal Sustainability

Over the last few years, there has been increase in the recognition that the traditional focus on financial allocation and expenditure may have weakened the incentive for outcomes that actually benefit the poor and less well off, who are the presumed beneficiaries of this expenditure. As such, it is evident that improvement in delivery mechanisms can have a dramatic effect on the lives of the poor.

Total amount of money a government spends should be closely aligned to what is affordable over the medium, and in turn, with the annual budget: spending should be appropriately allocated to match policy priorities, and spending should produce intended results with least costs.

5.2 *Enhancing Effectiveness of Public Spending*

The importance of performance measurement is discussed in a number of studies, and also Commissions and Committees set up by the government from time to time. The vital studies are explained in the following.

World Bank (1998) has highlighted a number of factors as responsible for poor performance of government programmes. Practices like "Poor planning; No link between policy making, planning and budgeting; Poor expenditure control; Inadequate funding of operations and maintenance; Little relationship between budget as formulated and as executed; Inadequate accounting systems; Unreliability in flow of budgeted funds to agencies and to lower levels of governments; Poor management of external aid; Poor cash management; Inadequate reporting of financial performance; and poorly motivated staff".

Key elements of expenditure management reforms with a focus on performance highlight the need for the following elements.

1. Results achieved with expenditure.
2. Adequate links between policy making, planning and budgeting.
3. Well-functioning accounting and management systems.
4. Attention to the links between budgeting and managing systems and other service-wide systems and processes of government—for decision-making, for organising government, for personnel management.

The Second Administrative Reforms Commission, 2009, stresses on the need to tone up public finance management that includes resource mobilisation, prioritisation of programs, budgetary process, efficient management of resources and exercising controls" (GoI 2014).

1. Improving the collection of revenue is critical.
2. "Debt and cash must be managed efficiently. In particular, sound principles for deficit funding should be established, efficiencies sought as per proper risk management procedures introduced. Proper management of government borrowing programme will reduce the cost of funding.
3. Effective planning and allocation of resources is key and government should develop and institutionalise planning processes at all levels of government. Budgeting process must be transparent and inclusive. There should be focus on output rather than mere expenditure and related inputs, with strong accounting procedures.

4. Effective oversight and monitoring are crucial to sound governance and PFM reforms. A well-functioning PFM system must have clear rules on transparency and reporting, as well as enforceable sanction for failure. Oversight should be established by internal mechanisms in the national treasury as well as external oversight by bodies like independent parliamentary Committees, a public ombudsman a free media and civil society, and independent Auditor General (GoI 2009, 4).

Many good attempts are continuously being made to overcome as many of the short comings as possible. A Good example is the trend in OECD countries. Common elements of the budgetary reforms in OECD countries are:

1. Medium term budget frameworks;
2. Prudent economic assumptions;
3. Top down budgeting techniques;
4. Relaxing central input controls;
5. Focus on results;
6. Budgetary transparency and modern financial management practices;
7. Although they are identified as seven separate features, they do impact build on each other and must be seen as a package." (GoI 2014).

Medium-term budget frameworks aid in "achieving fiscal consolidation. Governments need to clearly state the government medium-term fiscal objectives in terms of high-level targets such as level of aggregate revenue, expenditure, deficit/surplus, and debt" (GoI 2014). These targets should be extended to all the departments and their programmes, and a strict adherence to the targets is very essential in achieving the goals. While these frameworks are used at the subnational level, however, there is a need to strengthen the application of these frameworks.

Gayithri (2011) states "Karnataka is a pioneer in the framing of the fiscal responsibility legislation and the preparation of MTFP year on year. However, the projections with reference to some expenditure items need to be toned up as the actual expenditures have deviated in a significant way from the projections presented in the MTFP" (p. 137).

Professionally developed MTFP frameworks tend to improve public financial management in a significant way. However, the current tendencies both at the Central and State government levels are to announce new schemes or at times the supposedly new schemes but in reality, old schemes with new nomenclature, on special days such as 15 August—Independence Day, 26 January—the Republic Day. Such announcements without adequately taking into consideration the short- and long-term fiscal implications can certainly jeopardise the MTFP efforts.

Following Schick, 1997 (as quoted in the World Bank 1998, 8), caution to have the basics right serves well in getting the reforms through to a success.

- Foster an environment that supports and demands performance before introducing performance or outcome budgeting;
- Control inputs before seeking to control outputs;
- Account for cash before accounting for accruals;

- Establish exterior controls before introducing internal control;
- Establish internal controls before introducing managerial accountability;
- Operate a reliable accounting system before installing an integrated financial management system;
- Budget for work to be done before budgeting for results to be achieved;
- Enforce formal contracts in the market sector before introducing performance contracts in the public sector;
- Have an effective financial auditing before moving to performance auditing;
- Adopt and implement predictable budget before insisting that managers efficiently use resources entrusted to them. (GoI 2014)

Virmani (2006) dwells at length on issues of expenditure planning aspects in the Indian context stressing on the importance of defining objectives and goals in a clear and precise manner and the need to effectively monitor and evaluate the programmes. A number of India-specific examples are provided in the context of public expenditure planning and management. Emphasis is also laid on toning up public accountability, and the author proposes a Web-enabled public information system using a smart card recording the benefits to the groups entitled to varied government programmes.

Madheswaran (2016) states that the "performance measurement allows policy makers, managers and citizens to evaluate the quality and effectiveness of government services. Performance measures include inputs (resources used), outputs (program activities), efficiency measures (ratio of input to outputs) and outcome (actual results of program and services). Many performance measurement systems are limited to measuring program input and outputs. Ideally, however, performance measurement efforts should also generate information about program results and outcomes" (GoI 2014). The study further adds performance measurement is a critical component of performance management which systematically uses measurement and data analysis and other tools that facilitate learning and improvement and strengthen the focus on results.

The "Government of India introduced the performance monitoring and evaluation systems (PMES) in 2009–10 to enable departments to transit from an input driven approach to result/outcome orientation. A generic results framework was developed and working guidelines prepared to enable Central ministries/departments to prepare their result framework document" (GoI, RFD).

RFD is based on relatively simple concept—'what gets measured, it gets done'. "It marks paradigm shift from the traditional practice of measuring physical and financial progress to a more rigorous system of evaluating the performance of government departments for their results/outcomes". While this effort was attempted by the Central government and some subnational governments in a war mode, it was abruptly withdrawn first by the Central government followed by the subnational governments in a quick succession.

It may be noted that in 2010–11, Karnataka government initiated steps to introduce PMES. The generic RFD framework and guidelines issued by Government of India were adopted by Government of Karnataka. All departments are expected to formulate at the beginning of the financial year. A rapid appraisal of RFD of select departments revealed that a number of issues with the RFD and did not aid much in ensuring a sound performance monitoring and evaluation. This is in view of the fact the country experiences from 1960s reveal that shifting from "input/outlays" focus on "results/outcome" is not a simple process. Its success involves not merely changing the manner in which information is presented but by bringing about effective changes for expenditure planning and management in its entirety covering the stages of programme planning, execution and evaluation. Its success depends to a large extent on effective change in the mindset of all stakeholders.

Among the many implementation challenges, the country has faced several challenges both in identification of performance indicators, generation of objectively verifiable and reliable performance data and usage in the expenditure decision-making process which is a very essential requirement to enhance allocative efficiency of public expenditure.

Some of the important problems identified by her in the implementation of the scheme are:

- Gaps are found between the guidelines and the information provided in the RFDs of the departments.
- Problem of identification of success indicators. Instead of identifying the success indicators that measures outcomes or impact indicators are identified for activities.
- Another problem is relating to the problem in which weights are distributed which results in less important activities getting larger weights and vice versa.

6 Conclusion

The FCs have suggested measures to improve transparency and accountability, better monitoring of expenditure and evaluation to improve the link between outputs and outcomes, working efficiency in public management fiscal effort and outcome. "There is a general consensus that India's main development challenge is to improve governance and effectiveness of public institutions" (Finance Ministry, GoI).

Managing the government expenditure is definitely a complex task, particularly in democratic countries, like India. There will be always pulls and pressures on the government. Also in a government set-up, expenditures are incurred at many different levels. This necessitates the need for taking decisions at every level of government, strictly as per rules and regulations and with full responsibility. In this context, it may also be noted that fiscal responsibility legislations will go a long way, in taking decisions and maintaining fiscal discipline. However, it is important to keep in mind that FRL's (Fiscal Responsibility Legislation), hold promise for strengthening fiscal management, but cannot by themselves, buy credibility or substitute for a commitment to prudent fiscal policy. (Promoting fiscal discipline-IMF) Bagchi 2005 says the only deterrent against fiscal profligacy in a democracy is a vigilant parliament and well-informed public.

References

Ahluwalia, M. S. (2000). State level performance under economic reforms in India. In *Center for research on economic development and policy. Reform conference on indian economic prospectives: Advancing policy reform.* Stanford University.

Akhtar Ali, S. (1997). *Pakistan & gulf economist*.

Ashford, D. E., & Kelley E. W. (Eds.). (1986). *Nationalizing social security in Europe and America* (Vol. 4). Jai Press.

Bagchi, A. (2005). *Readings in public finance*. New Delhi: Oxford University Press.

Gayithri, K. (2011). *Public Expenditure Review of Karnataka.* A report submitted to the Expenditure Reforms Commission, Government of Karnataka, Bangalore.

Gayithri, K., & Raju, K.V. (Ed.). (2014). Financing development: Financing India's development: Issues and challenges. New Delhi: Cambridge University Press.

GoI. (2005). *Reports of the finance commissions of India: First finance commission to the twelfth finance commission*. New Delhi: Academic Foundation.

GoI. (2009). *Economic Survey*. New Delhi: Ministry of Finance.

GoI. (2014). 14th finance commission report. New Delhi.

GoI. (2015). *Economic Survey*. New Delhi: Ministry of Finance.

GoI. (2017). *Economic Survey*. New Delhi: Ministry of Finance.

GoI Ministry of Finance, G. (n.d.). www.finance.nic.in.

Kapila, U. (Ed.). (1994). *Indian economy since independence* (Vol. 6). Academic Foundation.

Kapila, U. (1996). *India's economic reforms*.

Madheswaran, M. (2016). *Performance management: Current and best practices*.

Mohanty, R. K., & Bhanumurthy, N. R. (2018). *Assessing public expenditure efficiency at Indian states*. Working paper no 225, NIPFP, New Delhi.

Musgrave, R. A., Peggy, B., & Musgrave, R. (2004). *Public finance theory and practice*. New Delhi: Tata McGraw Hill publishing company Limited.

Panagariya, A., & Rao, M. G. (2014). *State level reforms, growth and development in Indian States*. New Delhi: Oxford University Press.

Panagariya, A., Chakraborty, P., & Rao, M. G. (2014). *State level reforms, growth, and development in Indian states* (Vol. 3). Studies in Indian Economic Policies.

Ramon, E., & Lopez, V. T. (2010). *The effect of fiscal policies on the quality of growth.* World Bank: Washington, D. C.

Rangarajan, C., & Subbarao, D. (2007). *The importance of being earnest about fiscal responsibility*. Madras School of Economics.

Samuelson, A. P. (1954). The theory of public expenditure. The Review of Economics and Statistics.

Samuelson, A. P. (2010). Economics. New Delhi: Tata Mac Graw Hill Education Private Limited.

Samuelson, P. A., & Nordhaus, W. D. (2010). *Economics*. New Delhi: Tata McGraw Hill Education Private Limited.

Tanzi, V.,& Ludger Schuknecht, L. (2000). *Public spending in the 20th century: A global perspective*. Cambridge University Press.

Virmani, A. (2006). *The sudoku of India's growth*. New Del: B S Books.

Chapter 6
Public Expenditure in India: Some Issues and Concerns

Gayithri Karnam

1 Introduction

Government activity measured in terms of the proportion of government expenditure in the gross domestic product (GDP) expanded considerably across the globe during the sixties (The World Bank 1997). This was a result of the immense faith countries had in the state-led growth strategy. Market failure accorded the governments a central role in making corrective interventions in the essential areas such as allocation, production, distribution and regulation. Governmental control prevailed in almost all sectors. The enormous growth in government expenditure that had occurred during the state-led regime has resulted in mounting fiscal deficits in the case of many countries.

There has been a sea change in the recent thinking on the role of government, which has led to the launching of the economic reform/structural adjustment programme process in many countries. The economic reform process emphasizes upon the need to reduce the fiscal deficit in bringing about higher growth. Thus, fiscal deficit reduction has been an important component of the stabilization measures initiated in many countries. While some countries have been able to successfully reduce their deficit levels, some countries are still struggling to find appropriate measures to bring down the same.

In Indian context, the size of government had grown enormously as a percentage to the gross domestic product. Government has assumed many responsibilities in the course of planned development, therefore has initiated a number of programmes resulting in a huge increase in government expenditure. The government over a period of time has not been able to meet the expenditure from its resources. The growing

G. Karnam (✉)
Centre for Economic Studies and Policy, Institute for Social and Economic Change, Bengaluru, Karnataka, India
e-mail: gayithri@isec.ac.in

G. Karnam (ed.), *Public Budgeting in India*, India Studies in Business and Economics, https://doi.org/10.1007/978-81-322-3917-8_6

imbalances between the resources and expenditure of government have resulted in a large-scale increase in the size of fiscal deficit.

The 1991 reforms aimed at containing the size of fiscal deficit through both tax and expenditure measures. Unfortunately, in Indian context the experience of expenditure reduction so far has not been very encouraging as the expenditure cuts both at the Central government and state government level are more revealing on the crucial sector like the infrastructure, social sector, capital expenditure.

Broad trends in the Central government expenditure and its composition especially during the economic reform phase are analysed in the present paper. An attempt is also made to address the hitherto neglected issues concerning expenditure impact, management and control of government expenditure.

2 Trends in Fiscal Deficit

India launched economic reforms in the year 1991 comprising of stabilization and structural adjustment measures in order to overcome the macro-economic crisis the country faced in the 1990s. Fiscal deficit reduction was an important element of the fiscal stabilization programme. This was very essential in view of the huge fiscal deficit that the governments both at the Centre and State levels had amassed over a period. It was as high as 10% of GDP and the rate of inflation, generally associated with high fiscal deficits, was 17% per annum. The gross fiscal deficit of the centre alone was as high as 7.8% of GDP (Table 1) in 1990–1991, which has been brought down to 4.1% in 2005–2006. However, there was a reversal in the falling trend after the global financial crisis in 2008. While the ruling government claimed that the rise in fiscal deficit was on account of the fiscal stimulus provided by the Central government to revive the economy from recessionary trends, studies argued that the reversal was more on account of structural factors than the stimulus. (Rao 2015) Increase in expenditure after 2007–2008 is argued to be on revenue account caused by election decisions to revise pay scales of government employees, farm loan waiver and expansion of rural employment guarantee programme from 200 districts to the entire country. The fiscal consolidation debate has two strong points of view, supporting enhanced fiscal deficit level in support of growth augmenting investments and another strong point of view desisting such increase owing to its potential adverse macro-economic impacts. The N.K Singh committee has laid down a road map for fiscal consolidation by 2022. There has been a slippage from the targets set for 2017–2018 and 2018–2019 caused by revenue shortfalls on account of Goods and Services Tax (GST). While the efforts to reduce the fiscal deficit are laudable and in line with the overall fiscal objectives of the Government of India, the share of revenue deficit has been on the increase from 41.59% in 1990–1991 to 73.77% in 2017–2018 (R.E.) (Table 2), implying that the corrective measures have been increasingly sacrificing the capital investments made by the government (Table 2, Fig. 1).

Table 1 Trends in Central government fiscal deficit

Years	Fiscal deficit (Rs. in crores)	Fiscal deficit as % of GDP
1990–1991	44,632	7.8
1995–1996	60,243	5.05
2000–2001	118,816	5.65
2005–2006	146,435	4.10
2010–2011	373,591	4.79
2015–2016	532,791	3.77
2016–2017	534,274	3.51
2017–2018 (RE)	594,849	3.54
2018–2019 (BE)	624,276	3.33

Table 2 Share of revenue deficit in fiscal deficit

Years	Revenue deficit (Rs. in crores)	Fiscal deficit (Rs. in crores)	Revenue deficit as per cent of fiscal deficit (%)
1990–1991	18,562	44,632	41.59
1995–1996	29,731	60,243	49.35
2000–2001	85,234	118,816	71.74
2005–2006	92,299	146,435	63.03
2010–2011	252,252	373,591	67.52
2015–2016	342,736	532,791	61.68
2016–2017	316,381	534,274	59.06
2017–2018(RE)	438,877	594,849	73.77
2018–2019(BE)	416,034	624,276	66.64

Source Indian public finance statistics 2015–16

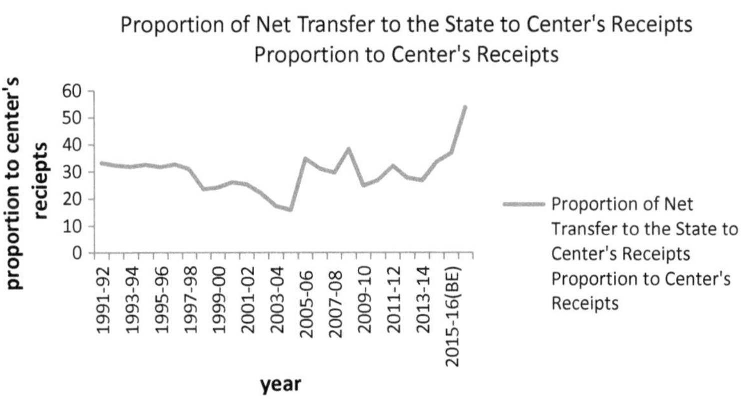

Fig. 1 Proportion of net transfer to the State to Centre's receipts

Table 3 Central government expenditure (Rs. in crores)

Year	Revenue expenditure	Revenue expenditure as % of GDP	Capital expenditure	Capital expenditure as % of GDP	Total expenditure	Total expenditure as % of GDP
1986–1987	40,860	13.13	22,056	7.09	62,916	20.22
1991–1992	82,292	12.60	29,122	4.46	111,414	17.06
1996–1997	153,933	11.25	42,074	3.08	201,007	14.69
2001–2002	301,468	13.27	60,842	2.68	362,310	15.95
2006–2007	514,609	12.47	68,778	1.66	583,387	15.64
2011–2012	1,145,955	12.71	141,042	1.60	1,286,997	14.28
2016–2017	1,734,560	11.40	279,847	1.80	2,014,407	13.26
2017–2018 (RE)	1,836,934	10.90	309,801	1.80	2,146,735	12.70
2018–2019 (BE)	2,141,772	10.20	300,441	1.60	2,442,213	13.04

Source Handbook of statistics of Indian economy and union budget of India: various years

3 Broad Trends and Composition of Central Government Expenditure

The out-pacing of the growth in government expenditure to that of government receipts has been causing considerable concern. This is more so on account of the fact that revenue expenditure has been growing faster than revenue receipts, thus causing revenue deficits. One cannot ascribe these developments entirely to the fiscal reform process in India. An analysis of growth of real public expenditure (Mundle and Govinda Rao 1997) revealed that from mid-70s to 1980, expenditure increased at a marginally higher rate than that of receipts and thus borrowings were modest. The second phase (1981–1986) caused a great damage to the fiscal situation due to excessive utilization of borrowed funds to meet the current expenditure. Some attempts were made to contain the expenditure during the third phase (1987–1990). These measures only resulted in compression of capital expenditure. By the end of this phase, revenue deficit had a sharp increase, which resulted in substantial diversion of borrowed funds to meet the current expenditure.

The trend analysis attempted in the present context for the period 1986–1987 to 2018–2019 (BE) reveals that the legacy of huge revenue deficits persisted and sharper decline is observed in the size of capital expenditure. While revenue expenditure has had a decreased share in GDP from 13.13% (Table 3) to 10.9% that of capital expenditure has recorded a shaper decrease from 7.09 to 1.6%.

The percentage composition of the total expenditure reveals that while the proportion of revenue expenditure has increased from 64.94% (1986–1987) to 77.23% (2004–2005) and further to 87.69% in 2018–2019 (BE), the share of capital expendi-

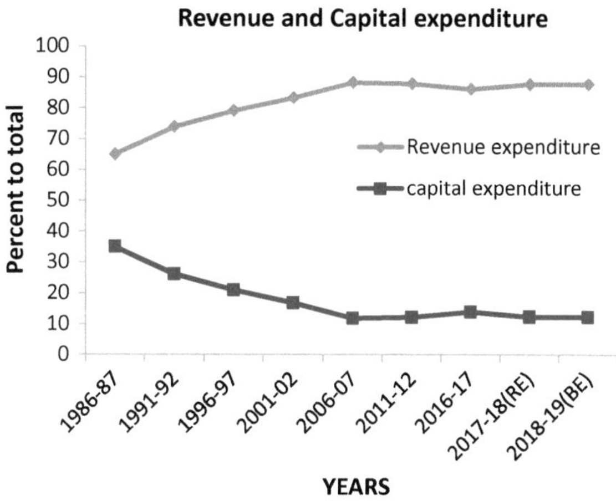

Fig. 2 Composition of government expenditure. *Source* Compiled by the author

ture has declined from 35.06 to 22.77% and 12.31%, respectively, during the above period (Fig. 2).

However, the purpose of stating these facts is not to subscribe to the view that the entire revenue expenditure is wasteful and all capital expenditure is productive. These trends are disturbing due to the increased diversion of capital receipts to meet the growing revenue expenditure needs. Greater fiscal instability emerges from this on account of the mounting debt servicing liabilities caused by diversion of capital investment funds. The governmental investment on infrastructure development is getting adversely affected due to paucity of funds. The deceleration in the infrastructure investment during the reform phase will have serious setback to investment prospects. The problem has been further compounded, as the much-awaited private investment in infrastructure development has not come forth in adequate quantity, despite many concessions. It is also disturbing to note that whatever private investment has taken place is more in the areas that have commercial viability which is quite obvious as private investments are guided by profit motive. A recent study (Anantharamu and Gayithri 2017) has revealed (Table 4) that while there is excess investment in certain sectors like telecom, road and power sector by the private sector, there is dearth of investment in rural infrastructure, sanitation and rural water supply. These are typically the areas that the government has to invest as the private sector shies away from such investments. Studies have also proved that public spending on social and physical infrastructures, besides being low are beset with poor productivity (Rao 2015). The declining capital investments by the government will have serious adverse implications for the development of sectors with infrastructure deficit.

Table 4 Sector-wise projections and actual infrastructure investments in the 11th plan period (INR billion, 2006–2007 prices)

Sector	11th plan	
	Projections	Investment (%)
Electricity (incl. NCE)	6665.25	6346.13 (95%)
Roads and bridges	3141.52	3618.22 (115%)
Telecommunications	2584.39	3359.32 (130%)
Railways (incl. MRTS)	2618.08	1954.22 (75%)
Irrigation (incl. watershed)	2533.01	1956.88 (77%)
Water supply and sanitation	1437.30	962.49 (67%)
Ports (incl. inland waterways)	879.95	347.73 (40%)
Airports	309.68	292.82 (95%)
Oil and gas pipelines	168.55	468.51 (278%)
Storage	223.78	142.03 (63%)
Total	20561.50	19447.96 (95%)

Source Anantharamu and Gayithri (2017)

4 Economic Categories of Expenditure

The composition of expenditure by economic categories reveals that government consumption expenditure (comprising of compensation to employees and net government maintenance) and current transfers have had a substantial increase from 54.42% in 1981–1982 to 78.76% in 2003–2004 and further to 83.1% in 2015–2016 (Table 5). While the gross capital formation has had a decline from 10.4% (1981–1982) to 6.34% (2105–2016) and capital transfers have had a marginal increase from 6 to 7. 78%, the share of financial investments and loans to rest of the economy had a sharp decline from 29.52 to 2.73%, respectively, during the above reference period. This growth in government expenditure which is turning out to be largely in the nature of transfer payments can have adverse macro-economic implications. Rao (2015, 65) states "…over the years, there has been significant increase in transfers such as for employment guarantee and food security, national housing scheme, apart from periodic loan waivers and recapitalization of banks to meet capital adequacy norms".

Tanzi and Shome (1993) rightly observe that "When on the one hand, a large part of the expenditures is explicitly or implicitly transfer payments to groups with high marginal propensity to consume and, on the other, infrastructural bottlenecks resulting from relative neglect by the government exist on the production side, low growth and inflation might be expected. If prices are attempted to be controlled either directly, or indirectly through administered prices, the inflationary tendencies crop up in the uncontrolled markets (e.g., rents, professional consultation fees etc.) or in the black economy (real estate prices, professional incomes, etc.), causing tax

Table 5 Economic classification of expenditure

		Final outlays	Transfer payments to the rest of the economy					
Year	Government consumption expenditure	Gross capital formation	Total	Current	Capital	Total	Financial investments and loans to rest of the economy	Total expenditure
1981–1982	6096	2551	8648	7728	1524	9253	7499	25,401
	24.00	**10.04**	**34.05**	**30.42**	**6.00**	**36.43**	**29.52**	
1985–1986	11,210	4557	15,768	18,347	3825	22,172	15,171	53,112
[a]	**21.11**	**8.58**	**29.69**	**34.54**	**7.20**	**41.75**	**28.56**	
1990–1991	22,359	8601	30,961	45,134	7117	52,251	21,760	104,972
[a]	**21.30**	**8.19**	**29.49**	**43.00**	**6.78**	**49.78**	**20.73**	
1995–1996	41,881	16,684	58,565	85,303	15,262	100,566	26,101	185,232
[a]	**22.61**	**9.01**	**31.62**	**46.05**	**8.24**	**54.29**	**14.09**	
1999–2000	68,831	26,074	94,906	161,548	20,481	182,030	30,572	307,509
[a]	**22.38**	**8.48**	**30.86**	**52.53**	**6.66**	**59.20**	**9.94**	
2005–2006	116,305	34,450	150,755	297,267	41,681	338,948	11,380	501,083
[a]	**23.21**	**6.87**	**30.08**	**59.32**	**8.3**	**67.64**	**2.27**	
2010–2011	230,262	65,059	295,321	656,300	150,312	806,612	62,795	1,164,728
	19.76	**5.58**	**25.35**	**56.34**	**12.90**	**69.25**	**5.39**	
2015–2016 (BE)	373,276	108,683	481,959	1,049,553	133,317	1,182,870	46,811	1,711,640
	21.80	**6.34**	**28.15**	**61.31**	**7.78**	**69.10**	**2.73**	

Note [a]Indicates percentages
Source Economic survey 2005–06, 2010–11 and 2016–17

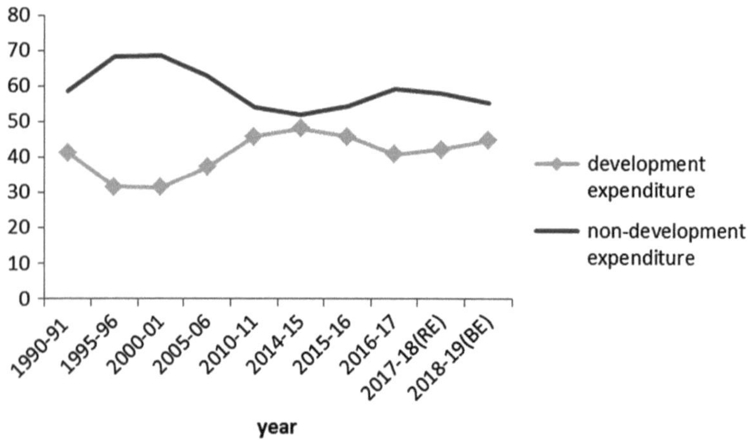

Fig. 3 Development and non-development expenditure

evasion and concomitant vicious circle of unfavourable effects" (as quoted in Shome et al. 1996).

These trends clearly account for the fact that expenditure compression measures have adversely affected the productive investment while the wages and salaries and current transfers have continued to increase unabated. The Fifth Pay Revision has enhanced the share of salaries and pensions from 17% of revenue receipts in 1995–1996 to 21% in 1997–1998. This is further followed by pay revisions effected by the Sixth Pay Commission. The substantial increase in subsidies and transfers is stated to be an important political economy development (Rao 2015). Composition of expenditure by the development and non-development expenditure categories plotted in Fig. 3 reveals that there has been a considerable increase in the share of non-development expenditure contrary to a decline in the share of the development expenditure.

5 Trends in Non-plan Expenditure

Composition of government expenditure by the plan and non-plan categories reveals that a major portion of the total expenditure is under non-plan category. Main items under them are interest payments, defence, subsidies, etc. (Table 6). It is generally argued that non-plan expenditure is sticky downwards and thus cannot be compressed, which means very little fiscal adjustment can be effected by way of expenditure reduction. The withdrawal of plan and non-plan distinction is a welcome change.

The broad trends (Table 6) reveal that the Central government expenditure during the last few years is characterized by larger increases in the expenditure under

Table 6 Trends and composition of non-plan expenditure (Rs. in crores)

Items	1990–1991	1995–1996	2000–2001	2004–2005	2005–2006	2010–2011	2015–2016
Interest payments	21,498	50,045	99,314	126,934	132,630	234,022	441,659
a	**27.94**	**37.94**	**40.88**	**34.74**	**36.29**	**28.59**	**34.56**
Defence expenditure	15,426	26,850	49,622	75,856	80,549	154,117	225,894
a	**20.05**	**20.36**	**20.43**	**20.76**	**22.04**	**19.00**	**17.00**
Subsidies	12,158	13,372	26,838	43,653	47,520	177,747	258,471
a	**15.80**	**10.14**	**11.05**	**11.95**	**13.00**	**22.00**	**20.00**
Grants to State and Uts	3982	5967	14,717	14,784	30,475	80,868	52,675
a	**5.18**	**4.52**	**6.06**	**4.05**	**8.34**	**9.88**	**3.99**
Loans and advances to States and Uts	7606	10,538	−140	612	89	971	3307
a	**9.89**	**7.99**	**−0.06**	**0.17**	**0.02**	**0.11**	**0.25**
Others	16,263	25,123	47,083	64,799	65,548	104,327	128,137
a	**21.14**	**19.05**	**19.38**	**17.73**	**17.93**	**12.74**	**9.70**
A. non-plan expenditure	76,933	131,901	242,923	365,406	365,485	818,263	1,319,700

Note [a]Denotes percentage to total non-plan expenditure
Source Data for 2015–2016 for grants and loans and advances to states and union territories are budget estimates

categories such as revenue head, non-plan, non-developmental and current transfer payments. Inadequate and low levels of spending on social services and physical infrastructure are key concerns. "The important point to be noted is that much remains to be done to achieve developmental objective through public expenditure policy. Both low allocations to social services and physical infrastructure and poor quality of spending have severely constrained the effectiveness of the instrument" (Rao 2015).

5.1 *Corrective Measures*

In the light of the ongoing reform process, there is a need to take a fresh look at the governmental role and responsibilities. Despite the fiscal reform process in India, the government has still not clearly defined its role, being fully aware of the fact that the past over-extension of government without an adequate backing of the resource growth has been mainly responsible for the present fiscal problems. The government has not effectively shed down some of its responsibilities that the private sector should be taking on. There is no justification whatsoever for direct participation of government in the areas like hotel business, fertilizers, air lines, textiles.

About the programmes under various departments, there is a need for a comprehensive review of the role of government in the changing context. As a first step, the government should redefine its role and confine itself to some core activities. This, however, is easier said than done. Deciding as to what the core activities are that help maximize the social welfare has to be based on a comprehensive review of the existing programmes and ensure adequate private sector participation in the gaps left by the government. Core functions of a government vary from one country to another and even from one state to another. Generally, governments can enhance the social welfare by participating in:

- An effective macro-economic management that would prevent serious fiscal imbalances.
- Provision of internal and external security.
- Regulation of private sector activity.
- Poverty alleviation and provision of basic minimum needs to the vulnerable sections of the society.
- Provision of basic social and economic infrastructure.

It is very important to decide on the appropriate size of public expenditure in the first instance. In India, it is generally assumed that compression of non-plan expenditure, which constitutes a very big share in the total expenditure, is difficult in view of its stickiness downwards. However, reforms in the budgeting practices from one of the current incremental budget to a suitable form of performance-based budgeting can certainly help in containing a routine increase in the size of public expenditure which can in the long run result in bloating of public expenditure.

6 Insights into Impact of Public Spending

There are two means of getting to know the impact of public spending, i.e. the Comptroller and Auditor General (CAG) reports and Performance Budget reports of development departments which have been in existence for long, with a recent initiative introduced in 2005–2006 are in the form of "outcome" budgeting and a failed Results Framework effort attempted between 2009 and 2015–2016.

6.1 CAG Source

CAG carries out two types of auditing: procedural/regularity auditing and performance auditing. Procedural/regularity audit is undertaken largely to verify whether the expenditure has been authorized, disbursements sanctioned and whether rules and regulations have been followed. The issue of whether value for money is ensured and whether the results are in consonance with the objectives of the government are not addressed in the procedural audit. On the contrary, efficiency-cum-performance audit seeks to evaluate whether the objectives of the expenditure have been met at the lowest cost, and whether the expenditure made has been able to deliver what was expected. However, the performance audit is taken up only for select schemes and thus its coverage is very limited. This acts as a major limitation on the checks and balances that we have on the performance/results of the financial operations of the government.

An important issue that largely escapes the attention is with reference to the wastage and improper use of public funds caused by multiplicity/duplication of government schemes in achieving the certain objectives of the government. Instances are evident from many sectors like education, housing, rural development, even while there are schemes existing to fulfil a particular objective, there are more introduced, without having a clear understanding of the need for such new additions amounting to improper use of public funds. Instances of this kind are evident even at the sub-national level, even in a fiscally progressive state like Karnataka that has introduced a number of fiscal reforms. Housing subsidy is one such scheme on account of which there has been a substantial increase in the expenditure by the government. It has been observed that (Gayithri 2003a) in view of the multiplicity of schemes and the involvement/participation of many departments in providing the service, problems like keeping track of total investments made for the purpose and the total impact of such financial operations by the government crop up. To the best knowledge of the author, none of the agencies are addressing these kinds of issues. However, some such evidences may come to limelight based on some evaluation studies carried out by independent agencies, these obviously will be only stray cases that are taken up for study even, while a large number of other programmes may not be evaluated at all for their usefulness to the citizens that the programmes are serving. Similarly, there are some agencies/autonomous institutions, such as Public Affairs Centre, Bangalore, that use Citizen Report Cards to assess the quality of public services provided by the government; these again will be focusing on limited number of themes, and thus, a major component of expenditure falls outside the scrutiny of public usefulness.

Agencies that have some constitutional backing and cover a wide gamut of control on public finances, such as CAG, would be the appropriate agency to address such issues.

6.2 Performance Budget Source

Performance budgeting is a system introduced based on the Administrative Service Commission recommendation in 1969, as per its directives Departments have to report performance of their plan programmes on an annual basis to the legislature. These are often taken up for discussion by the Subject Committees, which have the powers to seek explanation for non/poor performance. This is yet another good practice that has been in existence for over four decades.

However, there are many weaknesses associated with this system. The current performance budgeting largely presents financial targets vis-à-vis achievements and physical targets vis-à-vis achievement. While it is important to know whether money allocated is spent or not, outlays cannot be treated as outcomes. It is important to know the impacts of government expenditure rather than know about the quantum of expenditure itself. While these issues are addressed to some extent under the physical targets and achievements, these are largely with reference to the outputs rather than the outcomes. Outputs basically indicate the work carried out by the departments in the process of delivering some final product to the public. In essence what is highlighted is the activity that has been undertaken and not the impact. Yet another weakness of the system is that performance reporting is largely limited to the plan programmes and centrally funded schemes (at the state government level), and the huge non-plan expenditures is left outside the purview. Non-plan expenditure constitutes a very large share in the total expenditure as observed earlier.

Citizens will not be interested in knowing how many pulse polio camps have been conducted or how much has been spent on procuring polio vaccine; they will be interested in knowing about how safe their own wards are from the polio menace. Similarly, the interest is not in knowing about what the government has been spending on law and order situation, rather they would be concerned about the safety to their own lives and property which is largely dependent on the crime rate in the society. Governments are accountable to the public in the delivery of services and the effectiveness with which they are delivered. There is currently a big information gap with reference to the impacts of government programmes on the citizens. While the CAG does attempt an evaluation of this nature in its performance audit, the coverage is very small and there is an urgent need to address this issue.

'Outcome budgeting' is yet another initiative implemented by the Government of India, and the design and its utility in tracking the results in a meaningful manner has been a major issue in the context of framing informed budgetary decisions to eliminate redundant schemes that have outlived their utility.

7 Management and Control of Government Expenditure

Issues pertaining to management and control of public expenditure are two essential aspects that need considerable attention. This gain added importance during the reform process. Unfortunately, "the increased size and complexity of the public sector had clearly over-stretched the management capabilities of many governments even before the crisis of the 1980s" (The World Bank 1998). Control of public expenditure in India has to be ensured by the office of the Comptroller and Auditor General, legislature and the legislative committees and the judiciary.

One of the important indications of the presence of a sound public financial accountability in a country is when its legislative committees and audit committees provide for its citizens crucial oversight of the country's public finances. A country may be publicly accountable financially if it maintains internal control and performance reporting systems that make the results of public operations transparent to the citizens and corrective actions initiated wherever public funds are not efficiently used. In Indian context, checks and balances are imbibed on the government financial operations in the form of internal controls, external auditing and legislature reviews of the government financial operations, which have become a part of the system attempting to ensure accountability on a regular basis.

7.1 *External Control*

External control mechanisms on public spending have been laid out in the Indian Constitution. The office of the Comptroller and Auditor General (CAG) of India is the agency, which oversees the compliance of the laws by the executive. The office of the CAG is an independent constitutional agency and derives its authority from article 148–152 of the Constitution. Further legal basis for powers and duties of the CAG is provided in the Comptroller and Auditor General's Act of 1971.

External control on public financial operations is in the form of auditing by the Comptroller and Auditor General (CAG) of all receipts and expenditure of the government, which is conducted throughout the year based on which audit reports are prepared. These reports highlight many important observations regarding government financial operations, which get tabled in the parliament/legislatures. The legislative bodies such as Public Accounts Committee (PAC) and Committee on Public Sector Undertakings (COPU) examine these reports and question the Departments concerned. Reports of the PAC and COPU in turn are submitted to the parliament/legislature. These procedures are very well streamlined over the years, and auditing goes on a regular basis and can be broadly termed as procedural/regularity audit.

An important question that needs to be addressed in the context of prevailing mechanisms to imbibe public financial accountability is whether these have ensured effective control on the use of public funds and public financial accountability. There are three aspects that throw some light on the above question: first, whether the current control mechanism captures entire public spending, secondly, adequacy of the control mechanism in terms of providing insights on the results of public expenditure, thirdly response to the CAG audit findings.

7.2 *Partial Coverage*

CAG has powers under its Act 1971 (C&AG Act 1971) sections 13, 16 and 17 to audit all expenditure from and receipt into the Consolidated Fund of India and the state. CAG has the authorization under sections 14, 15 and 20 to audit receipts and expenditure of bodies or authorities substantially financed by loans or grants from Union or State or Union Territory (National Commission to Review the Constitution, 2001).

There are certain items of expenditure incurred by the governments at the Central as well as at the State level revenues that do not form a part of audit by the CAG. These include grants that are made to autonomous bodies and institutions, when not very substantial, non-government organizations (NGO). Utilization certificates are, however, produced; the results of such grants (as very often they are meant to provide the services that the government should have provided otherwise) are not known to the government let alone the public. It is worthwhile an exercise to examine the quantum of such expenditure in the form of grants to such agencies on a year-to-year basis. Even in the cases, which receive substantial grants that fall within the jurisdiction of CAG audit, are not submitting their annual accounts for audit in time and there is a time gap of two to three years. Hence, all such expenditure incurred by the government is escaping even procedural audit let alone performance audit.

With the 73rd and 74th amendment of the Constitution, the local bodies have been playing a greater role in the provision of services, for which substantial transfers take place from the Central and State governments. Very often these are direct transfers, from the Central government, the magnitude of which has substantially increased in the recent years. There is a need to develop satisfactory audit systems of these local bodies (some states like Karnataka have developed these already).

7.3 *Tax Expenditures*

State governments in India have until the recent past indulged in fierce competition with one another in attracting industry to their respective states by resorting to fiscal tools. While the financial implications of direct subsidy are available in black and white in the budget documents, the tax incentives doled out by the governments which result in loss of revenue to the government, popularly known as "Tax Expenditures" is a grey area. Strictly speaking these incentives are offered to fulfil certain specific objectives, and there is every need to assess the results of such tax expenditures.

While the CAG audit does look into any improprieties associated with such incentive schemes, it is very important to know the impact of such schemes vis-à-vis the objectives with which such incentives are provided. A study carried out at the Institute for Social and Economic Change (Gayithri 2004) reveals that while the revenue loss on account of sales tax concessions to the mega industries alone in Karnataka has increased in a very substantial way from Rs. 7.38 crore in 1994–1995 to Rs. 514.51 crore in 2002–2003, total amount of revenue loss during the above period being Rs. 1946.52 crore, the results are not very satisfactory. In addition, medium, small and tiny units had also availed such concessions. In many a states' cases, these do not even get estimated, however, in Karnataka tax expenditures are reported in the Overview to the Budget on an annual basis. There are many other concessions of this nature provided through the other departments; the fiscal implications and the results of such fiscal operations are not known. Similarly, studies reveal that (Gayithri 2003b) the programmes like capital investment subsidy have not really aided much in the dispersal of industry to the backward areas, the objective with which the scheme was originally conceived. On the contrary, it has inadvertently helped the industries in the industrially developed regions.

Hence, public financial accountability does not make sense if the results of complete fiscal operations of the government are not captured. There is a need to subject all government spending to external scrutiny to ensure efficiency and effectiveness in spending.

Unfortunately, in Indian context, "this elaborate system tends to control expenditure in a mechanical or legal way: checks are made for the necessary approvals and completed forms: the contents of various expenditure proposals and their worth rarely gets a scrutiny once past the formulation stage. The system is not very successful in controlling leakage either: it has been stated that a non-negligible part of public expenditure ends up in the underground economy" (Shome et al. 1996).

In Indian context, an important issue that needs to be addressed pertains to the control of committed expenditure. Shome (1998) make an interesting suggestion in this context. The expenditure could be bifurcated into committed and discretionary components, while discretionary expenditure has to be strictly controlled to their ceiling levels; adequate guidance should be given for the committed expenditures.

Reduction in sectoral allocations while getting the budget cleared by the parliament does not carry any significance if the reductions are more than made good in the form of supplementary grants. Inadequate control and monitoring of the government expenditure have resulted in practices like bunching of expenditure towards the last quarter of the financial year. While only about 30% of the expenditure is incurred in the first two quarters major chunk of the expenditure is incurred in the last two quarters. Statistics presented for the financial year 2015–2016 (Fig. 4) clearly account for these. In order to ensure proper returns from government expenditure, there is need for proper monitoring of its growth. Quarterly monitoring of the departmental expense will put a stop to the present practices of rushing through the spending in the last quarter of the year. These practices exist in countries like UK, (cash limits), Canada (envelope system), Japan (Scrap and burn), New Zealand (Tit for Tat) which are aimed at apportioning spending every quarter. (Premchand 1983, 281).

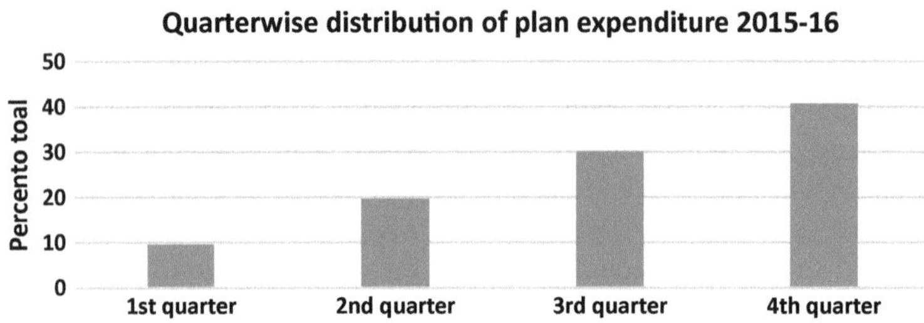

Fig. 4 Quarterly growth in Central government expenditure 2015–2016. *Source* Plotted using data from Controller General of Accounts

7.4 Quality of Public Expenditure

Quality of public spending is one aspect that has not drawn any serious attention of the policy makers until now. Although there are couple of promises made in certain budget speeches and announcement of formulation of committees to look into the quality of government spending, none of these have been given a concrete shape.

Notwithstanding the recommendations of various committees to undertake a careful review of public spending in containing the sharp growth, the progress has been far from satisfactory. The government even today continues to have multiple schemes that are duplicative in nature. As a result, the resources are thinly spread on multiple schemes which are not adequate at all for any of these programmes. There is also improper targeting under many programmes. A proper control of expenditure by examining each item of expenditure is needed as opposed to the present practice of automatic approvals. There is an urgent need to review the government expenditure by programmes rather than plan and non-plan categories, which thankfully the government has given up. Based on a review of programmes, there is a need to drop the programmes that have outgrown their utility and become redundant. This, however, cannot be achieved overnight. The process has to begin without further wasting any more time and resources.

References

Anantharamu, M. R., & Gayithri, K. (2017). Fiscal consolidation versus infrastructural obligations: Evidence from India. *Journal of infrastructure development, 9*(1), 1–19

Gayithri, K. (2003a). Housing subsidies in Karnataka. In G. Rao (Ed.), *Volume and composition of budgetary subsidies in Karnataka*, Monograph 1. Bangalore: ISEC.

Gayithri. (2003b). *Who benefits from industrial incentives: A study of capital investment subsidy in Karnataka*. Working paper, ISEC (No 124).

Gayithri, K. (2004). *Spin off effects of industrial incentives in Karnataka, a study of mega industrial units*, Mimeograph. Bangalore: ISEC.

International Monetary Fund. (1991). *Public expenditure hand book: A guide to public policy issues in developing countries*. Washington, DC.

Mundle, S. & Govinda Rao, M. (Eds.) (1997). *Public Finance: Policy issues for India*. New Delhi: Oxford University Press.
Premchand, A. (1983). *Government budgeting and expenditure controls: Theory and practice*. Washington, D.C.: International Monetary Fund.
Rao, M. G. (2015). Political economy of government finance in India. *India Review, 14*(1), 58–72.
Shome, P. (1998). A critical assessment of the public finances and a future agenda for reform. In A. V. Desai (Ed.), *Economic reforms, the next step*. New Delhi: Frank Bros and Co.
Shome, P., Sen, T. K., & Gopalakrishnan, S. (1996). *Public expenditure policy and management in India: A consideration of the issues*. Paper presented at Department of Expenditure, Ministry of Finance, Government of India, Vigyan Bhavan, New Delhi.
Tanzi, V., & Shome, P. (1993). *A Primer on tax evasion*. IMF Staff Papers, International Monetary Fund, Washington, D.C.
The World Bank. (1998). *Managing public expenditure: An evolving world bank perspective*. Washington DC: The World Bank.
The World Bank. (1997). *World development report*. Washington, D.C.

Chapter 7
Budgeting Techniques of Rural Local Bodies in Karnataka

M. R. Anantha Ramu

Background

The State of Karnataka is a forerunner in decentralization reforms in India. One of the most important initiatives toward decentralization in Karnataka was taken place in 1983 with the enactment of Karnataka Zilla Parishads, Taluk Panchayat Samitis, Mandal Panchayats, and Nyaya Panchayats Act, 1983, and it got implemented in 1987. The 1983 Panchayat Act passed by Government of Karnataka was a landmark legislation in India and it provided a model of decentralization envisioned in the country subsequent to the 73rd Constitutional Amendment (Rao et al. 2003).

The 73rd Amendment to the Indian Constitution has brought the standardized system of decentralization in the country. This amendment was made to enable the Panchayats to work as institutions of self-government by providing required powers and authority. The law also contains provision for power devolution along with responsibility at different levels of the Panchayat system (IPAI 2016). Consequent to the amendment, Karnataka Panchayat Raj (KPR) Act was enacted in 1993 and the Act specifies three-tier structure of rural local governments namely at district level, taluk level, and village level.

With the Constitutional Amendment, Panchayats can act as an independent body and make plans for social and economic development. It has provided sufficient representation for marginalized section of the society. Having adequate transfer of powers and financial resources, it requires the Panchayats to properly formulate and implement the budget to achieve overall social and economic development of the people under its limit.

This paper concentrates on the budgeting practices of panchayats in Karnataka and also draws the lessons to be learned from the best practices across the world. The paper is structured as follows. First section explains the structure of rural local bodies (RLBs) in Karnataka. Section 2 elaborates the sources of revenue to the Panchayats

M. R. Anantha Ramu (✉)
Fiscal Policy Institute, Bengaluru, India
e-mail: anantharamu.m.r@gmail.com

G. Karnam (ed.), *Public Budgeting in India*, India Studies in Business and Economics, https://doi.org/10.1007/978-81-322-3917-8_7

and also the major expenditure items. Third section discusses the budgeting practices to be followed by RLBs in Karnataka as per Karnataka Panchayat Raj Act, 1993, and also draws several important lessons to be learned from the international best practices with regard to local budgeting. Final section concludes paper.

1 Structure of PRIs

Karnataka follows three-tier structure of Panchayat Raj system, namely Zilla Panchayats, Taluk Panchayats, and Gram Panchayats. There shall be a Zilla Panchayat for each district having dominion over entire district. However, it is exclusive of municipal areas. Each taluk will have a Taluk Panchayat and it has jurisdiction over entire taluk excluding municipal area. The Gram Panchayats are constituted for a village or a part of a village or cluster of villages having population of not less than 5000 and not more than 7500. There are 6022 Gram Panchayats exists in Karnataka along with 176 Taluk Panchayats and 30 Zilla Panchayats as on May end 2017 (GoK 2017). All the three tier of decentralized government in Karnataka is bestowed with the executive power and are expected to be independent of each other. However, Rao et al. (2003) argue that in actual practice administrative guidelines, supervision and reporting necessities and capacity differences have resulted in a hierarchical structure. Taluk Panchayats supervise Gram Panchayats and Zilla Panchayat supervises other two tiers of the Panchayat Raj system in Karnataka.

Grama Sabha is one of the important components under the Panchayat Raj system in Karnataka. Grama Sabha is a body consisting of persons recorded in the voters' list of each Gram Panchayat constituency. The Grama Sabha shall approve plans, programs, and budget prepared by the Gram Panchayat.

Article 243G of Indian Constitution provisions that State Legislature may, by law, award powers and authority which is required for Panchayat Raj Institutions to function as institutions of self-government. Accordingly, law also mandates the devolution of powers and to panchayats (GoI 2011). This provision enables the Gram Panchayats to preparation of plan and implementation of schemes for economic development and social justice.

2 Receipts and Expenditure of RLBs in Karnataka

2.1 Receipts of RLBs

As per the provisions under Article 243H of Indian Constitution, State Legislature may assign certain taxes, tolls, duties, etc., collected by the State Government to Panchayats, providing grants-in-aid to Panchayats from Consolidated fund of the State and also authorize Panchayats to levy and collect taxes. Tax receipts of Gram

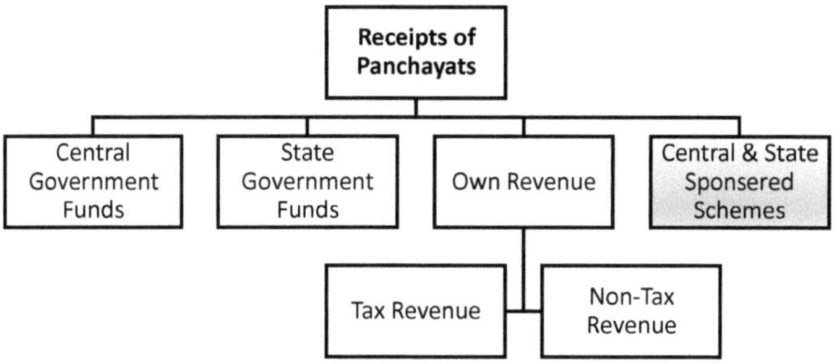

Fig. 1 Structure of receipts of Panchayats

Panchayats include income from property tax, collection of fess and cess, water rate, street light cess, license fee, entry fee for shopkeepers in fairs other than cattle fairs, katha transfer fee, shop and establishment license fee and others. Non-tax receipts of Gram Panchayats mainly consist of share of land revenue, income from movable and immovable properties, sale of movable and immovable properties, income from endowments or trusts, interest receipts on loans advanced, interest on deposits, donations and contributions, etc.

Secretary/PDO of the Gram Panchayat shall collect revenue unless Gram Panchayat authorizes a person like bill collectors to collect revenue. Gram Panchayat should maintain a receipt book and a day book and all particulars of amount received should be entered into it. The collected amount has to be remitted to Gram Panchayat fund. Gram Panchayats should maintain a demand and collection register of taxes. Each major taxes of Gram Panchayat like taxes on land and buildings, taxes on advertisement, water rates, license issued, taxes on entertainment, etc., has to be entered in separate registers.

Central Finance Commission is mandated in the terms of reference to recommend the measures required to enhance the consolidated fund of a State to supplement the resources of the local bodies in the State (GoI 2015). The recommendations of Central Finance Commission are based on the report submitted by respective State Finance Commissions. Central Government as per the recommendations of Central Finance Commission transfers the funds to State Governments to strengthen the local bodies. After receiving funds from the Central Government, Finance Department of Karnataka transfers the fund directly to the accounts of concerned local bodies. State Government based on recommendation of State Finance Commission transfers the State grants to local bodies through treasury. Zilla Panchayats draw funds from the treasury and transfer it to the bank account of Gram Panchayats. The Central and State sponsored schemes' funds will be transferred to a separate bank account maintained by Gram Panchayats for specific schemes (Fig. 1).

The Gram Panchayat funds include all grants from Central and State government, all taxes, duties, cesses, fines and fees imposed, donations, loans received, income from lease or sale of land or property. The Panchayat Development Officer (PDO) or President of Gram Panchayat can operate the Panchayat fund. The Gram Panchayat fund has to be deposited in a bank to which Government Treasury business is assigned including a scheduled bank or cooperative bank situated in the jurisdiction of Gram Panchayat or in the neighboring Panchayat area.

2.2 *Expenditure of RLBS*

Expenditure of RLBS mainly constitutes spending on administration, maintenance, and pay allowances. Community welfare, education and health, sanitation works, etc., are the other key areas of RLBs spending. Sectors like education, rural employment, welfare of women and children, welfare of scheduled caste and scheduled tribes and rural housing have been the priority sectors of the Panchayats in Karnataka (GoK 2017). For instance, in 2016–17, out of total allocation toward District Sector Plan Funds, education sectors received 29.3%, rural housing received 9.16%, and rural employment sector received 12%.

3 Budgeting Practices

Budget is a means to implement the development plans and should enable all-round development of people in a society. There are various types of budgets namely zero-based budgeting, performance budgeting, participatory budgeting. The zero-based budgeting requires every department or decision-making body to make all its budgetary decisions as if they were totally new decisions and it adopts zero base at the commencement of each budget schedule. Performance budgeting, in simple terms, refers to linking of expected result to the budget. It stresses on targeting and assessing outputs and performance with data analyzed against given aims and standards (Folsher 2007). Participatory budgeting can be viewed as the process of directly involving local people in decision making by the way of sorting out of the priority area and spending for given amount of public budget (World Bank 2017).

Generally, budgeting is carried out in four different levels starting with preparation, followed by approval, implementation, monitoring and evaluation.

Budgeting Procedure as Per KPR Rules, 2006

The Karnataka Panchayat Raj (Gram Panchayats' Budgeting and Accounting) Rules, 2006, specifies procedure for preparing and presenting budget at Gram Panchayat level. Section 241 of the Karnataka Panchayat Raj Act, 1993, specifies that the Secretary of the Gram Panchayat shall prepare a budget and place it before the Gram Panchayat at a meeting which is mandated to be held between 1st February and 10th March (Puliani 2014). Gram Panchayat secretary is mandated to prepare statement of expected receipt and projected expenditure. The State or Central government or the Zilla Panchayat or the Taluk Panchayat, as entrusted, before the end of each year are to intimate Gram Panchayats the amounts of contribution, grants, and loans, if granted any, to prepare estimates of revenue and expenditure for the ensuing year (IPAI 2016). Expenditure should be estimated based on administrative expenditures like salaries and wages, office expenses, office equipment, electricity charges, etc., incurred during previous year with the addition of expected increment due to inflation, dearness allowance, and annual increment. Estimates of expenditure on civil works have to be drawn with the help of engineering department or by indicating an approximate figure on the basis of existing prescribed rates. The budget estimates shall consist of three statements and they are as follows:

1. Statement 1: Budget Abstract
2. Statement 2: Detailed estimate of receipts anticipated
3. Statement 3: Detailed estimate of expenditure proposed

The budget estimate has to be supported by subsidiary statements like

1. Estimate of demand, collection, and balance under Gram Panchayat rates and taxes;
2. Estimate of expected revenue, collection, and balance of income from Gram Panchayat property;
3. Estimate of expected receipts, collection, and balance of the revenue from constitutional powers of Gram Panchayat;
4. Statement of salary establishment;
5. Statement of loans availed and anticipated grants, etc.

Gram Panchayats should follow accrual accounting method. It means the system of recording transactions of revenue when it is received and outlay when it is incurred, regardless of cash under normal double-entry accounting system. Gram Panchayat Secretary/PDO should follow following guidelines while preparing the budget:

1. Budget estimate shall be for expected receipts and payments during the year and not for demands or liabilities likely to fall due within the year.
2. The liabilities which cannot be discharged before the beginning of the financial year shall be ascertained and provided for.
3. Panchayats have to allow a balance at the end of each year as fixed by the Government periodically.

Expenditure should not cross the amount as provisioned in the budget. However, with the revision of allocations in the budget excess expenditure can be accommodated. If the Gram Panchayat considers to revise the budget during course of financial year, it should obtain approval from the Chief Executive Officer of concerned Zilla Panchayat. It is also mandated that there shall not be any reduction of over ten percent in the grants approved for developmental functions (Puliani 2014).

Best Practices: Indian and International Experience

Participatory budgeting has gained momentum in many places of the world in the last two and half decades. The participatory budgeting evolved in Brazil in the late 1980s. The 1988 Brazilian Constitution provides several mechanisms which permit grassroots' movements to take part in decision making and also to supervise public matters at local level (Souza 2001). Participatory budgeting is a method in which people place their demands and priorities for public improvement. Through debates and discussions, citizens influence the allocation of funds in the budget participatory budgeting began in Brazilian city, Porto Alegre where one-third of city's population survived in remote slums and lacked access to basic requirements like water, sanitation, schools, and medical facilities in the late 1980s. To overcome this situation, several innovative reform programs were initiated in 1989 and participatory budgeting emerged as the flagship of these programs. Representatives generally from low-income districts decided upon the allocation of resources through participatory budgeting (Bhatnagar et al. 2003). These representatives determine the investment priorities together and priority is given to progressive distribution of the resources, irrespective of demands by individual representatives, so that backward areas receive more funding. Bhatnagar et al. (2003) also listed out the key elements of empowerment in Brazil and they are as follows:

1. Information disclosure.
2. Participation of low-income sections of population in the decision-making process.
3. Transparency remains the core of participatory budgeting. The administration has to disclose its economic and financial position.
4. Local community groups were formed to place the demand and influence the budget decisions.

The positive impact of participatory budgeting was noticed in terms of improvement in accessibility and quality of various public welfare facilities in the municipalities where it was being adopted. Active involvement and influence of people belonging to low-income groups in the budgetary allocation process are a proof of their empowerment. As mentioned earlier, participatory budgeting began in Brazil in 1989 and by 2013, this kind of budgeting method was found in more than 2500 municipalities worldwide (Gilman 2016).

The role and commitment of elected leaders become crucial for success of participatory budgeting. In Kenya, with the support of Kenya Participatory Budgeting Initiative and commitment from West Pokot and Makneni county leaders, participatory budgeting is being tested as a means to achieve more inclusive and effective people participation (World Bank 2017). Kenya's Constitution emphasizes that people participation, transparency, and accountability are the means to improve efficiency, equity, and inclusiveness of government service delivery. The framework is strong as it is backed by Constitution of Kenya with supportive legal framework (World Bank 2017). Participatory budgeting in many counties of Kenya has increased occasions for women and remote population to take part in prioritization of the expenditure and the budget allocation was aligned with citizens' priorities. This framework has also made the elected members to compulsorily participate in the discussions so that it will allow swifter approval of budgets and reduces the changes in proposed budget. As shown in Fig. 2, participatory budgeting should consist of government officials, elected people representatives/politicians, and public.

Fig. 2 Participatory budgeting: stakeholders

Participatory budgeting is taking root in USA in the present decade. It was found that number of participants in participatory budgeting and dollar allocated has roughly doubled each year between 2011 and 2015 (Gilman 2016). In USA, Department of Housing and Urban Development funds the participatory budgeting programs.

The World Bank has concluded that participatory budgeting, especially in developing democracies, has the potential to limit government inefficiency and restrict clientelism, corruption, and patronage (Shah 2007). In India, 73rd and 74th amendment to the Constitution provided autonomy at grassroots level. These amendments devoted greater responsibilities and role to local governments. Experiences around the world suggest that constitutional provision for decentralization and people participation are required to create an enabling environment for these institutions (Folsher 2007). Citizen participation in deciding allocation and usage of funds is very important to achieve development goals. Folsher (2007) lists out several reasons in this regard.

1. People have the best knowledge of their requirements and local conditions.
2. Citizens' participation in decision-making process helps in allocating available funds to catering most needed goods and services.
3. People participation enables policy decision and implementation efficient.
4. It improves government effectiveness.
5. It helps in making officials more accountable and efficient.
6. It builds social unity, which can lead to concrete benefit of increased tax collection.

The participatory budgeting has the greater potential to strengthen the democratic quality and values. Participation in public decision making is a method of direct democracy that accommodate more meaningful democratic relationship between citizens and government than that provided by representative democracy (Folsher 2007).

Ministry of Panchayat Raj, Government of India has initiated a Central Sector Plan Scheme called Panchayat Empowerment and Accountability Initiative Scheme (PEAIS) in 2005–06 by aiming at:

1. Incentivizing States to empower Panchayats through devolution of functions, funds, and functionaries in accord with Article 243G of Indian Constitution.
2. Incentivize local bodies to put in place accountability systems to make their functioning transparent and efficient.

Under this scheme, States are ranked based on devolution index which measures the extent of devolution of functions, funds, and functionaries from State to Panchayats. Since 2011–12, best performing Panchayats are also being incentivized (PIB 2017). Some of the major indicators to assess the schemes are as follows:

1. Panchayat functioning: regular conduct of Panchayat meetings, Grama Sabhas, and formation of standing committees;
2. Management of employees and capacity building;
3. Planning and budget preparation;
4. Revenue mobilization: collection of taxes, dues, etc.;
5. Performance: physical achievement;
6. Accountability and transparency: maintenance of accounts and audit.

A Gram Panchayat, namely Bearhatty Gram Panchayat in Nilgiris district of Tamil Nadu, has performed well in all the above indicators. It also received number of awards like 'Nirmal Gram Puraskar', 'Panchayat Sashaktikaran Puraskar' from the Indian Government. Concerning the planning and budget formulation, which is the thrust of this study, Bearhatty Panchayat has prepared annual plan in advance and it was discussed in Grama Sabha and with various stakeholders. More importantly, the suggestions received in the Grama Sabha were incorporated. Budget was prepared as per the norms. And the Gram Panchayat has also prepared Gender Budget. Accounts were maintained under given format, updated, and validated and have been placed before Grama Sabha (GoI 2015). The Grama Sabhas were conducted regularly and frequently. One more noticeable fact is that, the Grama Sabhas were conducted in different hamlets to ensure that all the people get an opportunity to participate. This has resulted in improving presence as well as consciousness among the community about Panchayat activities.

Dakshina Kannada Zilla Panchayat in Karnataka conducts regular meetings once in two months. It publishes annual administrative report every year. It includes details on total funds received, expenditure, grievances addressed, etc. Active participation of Panchayat office holders and public is very important to achieve any of the set goals. In 2005, Dakshina Kannada Zilla Panchayat conducted a survey to measure the sanitation status in the district. The finding revealed that nearly 61% of the families had no toilets including many above poverty line families. Minimum cost of building a toilet was around INR 4000 (in the year 2003), whereas the Government provided only INR 1200. In these circumstances, Ira Gram Panchayat in Dakshina Kannada district came up with the idea of 'Shramadan' where many people including the Panchayat officials took personal interest to dig pits for toilets (GoI 2015).

This motivated other Gram Panchayats. Through 'Shramadan' 110 toilets built in a single day in GolthaMajal Gram Panchayat of Dakshina Kannada district. With many innovative ideas and efforts, Dakshina Kannada Zilla Panchayat awarded with 'Nirmal Gram Puraskar' from the Indian Government.

Another example of active people participation in Panchayat activities is Ghatboral Gram Panchayat of Bidar district in Karnataka. The Gram Panchayat members meet regularly and conduct meetings at least once in a month to discuss status of developmental activities in the Panchayat area (GoI 2015). It was noted that overall attendance has been above 90%. The Ghatboral Gram Panchayat has the practice of conducting compulsory number of Grama Sabhas. One of the best practices of the Panchayat is that the elected representatives of the Panchayat address the issues as a group rather than individually.

Transparency in planning and budgeting process and active participation and representation of people, especially youth is very essential for successful implementation of any programs. Gerethang-Labing Gram Panchayat in Sikkim follows participatory planning process and has formulated Gram Planning Forum (GPF). They have adopted a bottom-up method for planning, and in the first stage, planning is prepared by a committee at the ward level and then compiled at Gram Panchayat level and finally passed and approved by GPF (GoI 2015). This Gram Panchayat has 12 standing committees. Along with elected representatives of Panchayat, villagers are also being included in the standing committees. The committees are very active and members regularly meet to take necessary decisions. Gerethang-Labing Gram Panchayat has also given high importance to revenue generation. It has identified number of sources to raise revenue like building permanent shops, charging animal transactions, etc., and also mobilized people to pay tax. Functioning of Gram Panchayat is very transparent and it declares amount of revenue generated and expenditure incurred in the Grama Sabha. This transparency has helped the Gram Panchayat to raise more revenue. The villagers keenly pay taxes and fees and even they come to Gram Panchayat in person to take information on the pending amount to be paid (GoI 2015). Gram Panchayat also gives much importance to Grama Sabha and has put in effort to strengthen it. Gram Panchayat issues prior notice to all Grama Sabha members to attend the meeting. In case of absence, the members need to inform the Gram Panchayat stating the reason for absence in writing. Gram Panchayat has constructed separate hall to conduct Grama Sabha proceedings and even people have contributed around INR 2 lakh for construction of the hall. Attendance in Grama Sabha was almost 80%. Youth in the villages participates very actively and GPF does encourage their by recognizing and awarding them with 'Best Youth Award'.

4 Conclusion and Way Forward

International and few Indian experiences reveal that participatory budgeting is necessary and needed to ensure that the demands by people are fulfilled. Participatory budgeting provides a platform for the people to express their needs and also to cross-check status of work as budgeted earlier. Grama Sabha, which has a special place as per KPR Rules, 2006, should further strengthened by mandating an exclusive Grama Sabha meeting to discuss the budget of the Panchayat. The Grama Sabha should provide equal representation to all and particularly to women and deprived section of the society. Youth should be encouraged to participate in the meetings. Gram Panchayats should conduct their Grama Sabha meetings in different locations (wards) within the Panchayat jurisdiction on rotation basis so that it gives an opportunity for all to participate in the discussions.

Providing incentives in the form of 'citations' or 'awards', etc., would encourage younger generation to participate in the discussions. In the Grama Sabha meeting, Panchayat officers should give details of works which have been completed and also to be undertaken. Grama Sabha members should give suggestions on the kind works to undertaken. Based on availability of funds, Panchayat officers need to estimate likely expenditure and prioritize the works suggested by the members of Grama Sabha. Along with spending activities, ways to raise revenue should also be discussed in the meeting. Eventually, a budget should reflect the wish of the people.

References

Bhatnagar, D., Rathore, A., Torres, M. M., & Kanungo, P. (2003). *Empowerment case studies: Participatory budgeting in Brazil.* Washington, DC: The World Bank. Retrieved June 2, 2017, from http://poverty.worldbank.org/files/14657_Partic-Budg-Brazil-web.pdf.

Folscher, A. (2007). Participatory budgeting in Asia. In A. Shah (Ed.), *Participatory budgeting* (pp. 157–190). Washington, DC: The World Bank.

Gilman, H. R. (2016). Engaging citizens: Participatory budgeting and the inclusive governance movement within the US. *Ash Centre Occassional Paper* 1–32.

GoI. (2011). *The constitution of India.* New Delhi: Ministry of Law and Justice, Government of India. Retrieved from http://lawmin.nic.in/olwing/coi/coi-english/Const.Pock%202Pg.Rom8Fss s(13).pdf.

GoI. (2015). *Best practices in Panchayats management and services delivery.* New Delhi: Ministry of Panchayat Raj, Government of India.

GoK. (2017). *Economic survey of Karnataka, 2016–17.* Bangalore: Planning Program Monitoring and Statistics Department, Government of Karnataka.

IPAI. (2016). *Budget and accounts Manual of Panchayat Raj institutions in Karnataka.* New Delhi: Institiue of Public Auditors of India.

PIB. (2017). *Press information Bureau.* Retrieved from: http://pib.nic.in/newsite/PrintRelease.asp x?relid=93829.

Puliani, S. (2014). *The Karnataka Panchayat Raj Manual.* Bangalore: Karnataka Law Journal Publications.

Rao, M. G., Amarnath, H. K., & Vani, B. P. (2003). Fiscal decentralization in Karnataka. In G. Sethi (Ed.), *Fiscal decentralizatio to rural governments in India* (pp. 43–106). Washington, DC: The World Bank.

Shah, A. (2007). *Participatory budgeting.* Washington, DC: The World Bank.

Souza, C. (2001). Participatory budgeting in Brazilian cities: Limits and possibilities in building democratic institutions. *Environment and Urbanization, 13*(1), 159–184.

WorldBank. (2017). *Inclusive and effective citizen management-participatory budgeting.* Washington, DC: the World Bank.

Chapter 8
Program Performance Budgeting Approach to Enhance Quality of Public Expenditure: Approach and Challenges in Karnataka

Gayithri Karnam

1 Background[1]

State finances in India reeled under severe fiscal stress in the decade of nineties featuring growing fiscal and revenue deficits. Karnataka state was no exception to the general trend as it experienced severe fiscal stress in the decade of nineties, with the exception of a few years during mid-nineties. This period was marked by rising fiscal and revenue deficits owing to poor tax buoyancy and a fall in the non-tax revenue resources of the state government coupled with unbridled growth in revenue expenditure. However, even during such distress phase, Karnataka's fiscal position compared well with other states, the growing distress in the state was a cause for serious concern. The state government prepared a white paper on state finances in 2000. Closely following suit was a slew of legislations such as Karnataka Transparency in Public Procurement (KTPP), Ceiling on Government Guarantee, both of which were framed in 1999. An important legislation 'Karnataka Fiscal Responsibility Act' was passed in 2002, the state being the first in the country to frame such a legislation. The fiscal reform initiatives introduced by the Government

[1] This section draws from the author's contribution to the preparation of Program Performance budget case study to the USAID REFORM project. See USAID-REFORM (2008a, b).

The author had provided extensive training sessions at the instance of the Planning Commission and UNDP on Program Performance Budget (PPB) approach in Karnataka which is included in their trainers training manual. Excerpts from the manual can be found across this chapter. Some technical features of PPB are discussed by the author in Institute for Social and Economic Change (ISEC) Working paper 334 entitled 'Performance-Based Budgeting: Subnational Initiatives in India and China' (see Gayithri 2015).

G. Karnam (✉)
Centre for Economic Studies and Policy, Institute for Social and Economic Change, Bengaluru, Karnataka, India
e-mail: gayithri@isec.ac.in

G. Karnam (ed.), *Public Budgeting in India*, India Studies in Business and Economics, https://doi.org/10.1007/978-81-322-3917-8_8

of Karnataka have reversed the trend and today, the state's macro-fiscal indicators seem very sound, marked by revenue surpluses and a fiscal deficit level which is well within the targets of the Fiscal Responsibility Act passed in 2002 by the Government of Karnataka. Adherence to the fiscal targets even during the global recession phase that started in 2007 is a remarkable feature. However, a key challenge is to sustain the sound fiscal health in the long run given the fact that the recovery is largely revenue led caused by the revenue reform initiatives and in the event, there is lack of prudent and effective spending, and there is every possibility of a relapse of fiscal stress. Sustaining a sound revenue growth is also subject to the overall economic growth of the state.

On the growth front, the state's performance is good especially on account of the growth in service sector. The state is also attracting considerable amount of investment, both from domestic and foreign sources. In terms of public spending, the state has had the distinction of having the highest per capita plan and development spending for a number of years among the Indian states. The state's per capita spending on the social sectors and capital investments have considerably increased after the framing of the KFRA, and sectors such as 'Education' 'Health', etc. have been given thrust status. However, the state's poor achievement levels in the social and economic infrastructure have remained a cause for concern, which pose serious threat to the sustenance of the recent growth experience (Gayithri 2017b). In this context, it becomes important to address issues as to how well/ill-informed are and whether the inter-/intra-sectoral allocations to reflect the needs of the sections of the people concerned. The situation in the state thus has on the one hand a very sound fiscal situation largely led by good and increasing revenue yield due to various reform initiatives, on the other hand on its expenditure front has weaknesses revealed in the form of allocative and technical inefficiencies. The state may experience overall fiscal improvements for a few more years owing to the initiatives on the revenue front, ensuring everlasting results sans expenditure reforms and toning up of technical and allocative efficiency of public spending. The current weaknesses in allocative and technical inefficiencies in the expenditure referred to earlier can largely be attributed to lack of comprehensive and meaningful expenditure reform initiatives until the recent past.

It is in this backdrop that the present paper addresses the weaknesses in the areas of expenditure planning and management and presents the broad features of the reform initiatives experimented with by a forward-looking state like Karnataka in the form of Program Performance Budgeting (PPB) for a few years. It is important to examine if the features of such experiments need to be incorporated into the budgetary systems in the state to achieve sustained improvements. First, a brief outline of the Karnataka state's fiscal scenario is presented.

2 Karnataka State's Fiscal Scenario[2]

2.1 Karnataka State's Macro-Fiscal Indicators

Karnataka's fiscal scenario as assessed by the trend behavior of the fiscal indicators reveals that the state that had experienced severe fiscal stress during the decade of nineties, recovered ever since the launch of Fiscal Responsibility Act (FRA) in 2002. Since then, the state government's fiscal and revenue deficits have been well within the targeted levels and the state-attained revenue surplus to enable much sought after capital and social sector investments. The fiscal and revenue deficit trends are depicted in Fig. 1. Fiscal recovery was largely revenue led contributed by the reforms introduced by the state.

2.2 State's Revenue Position

The state's revenue resources comprise of state's own revenue in the form of tax and non-tax revenue and that of transfer of resources from the Central government by way of tax and grants. Karnataka's own tax performance has played a key role in reviving the state's finances from severe stress experienced in the decade of nineties. The state's initiative to appoint the Tax Reforms Committee and the subsequent implementation of several of its recommendations has brought about a sea change in the revenue performance (Table 1).

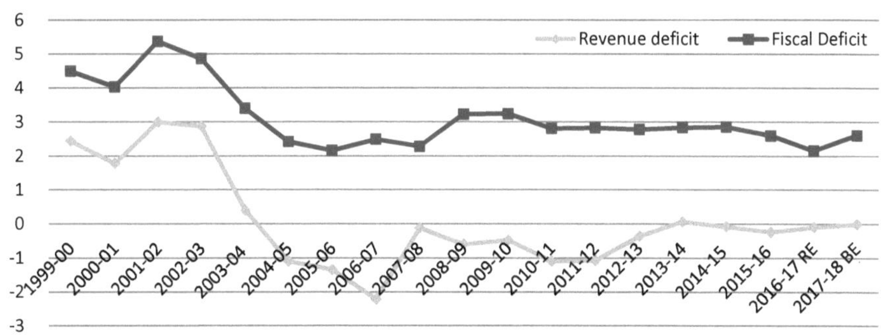

Fig. 1 Trends in fiscal and revenue deficits in Karnataka. *Source* Gayithri (2017b)

[2]This section has excerpts from author's unpublished reports on "Evaluation of State Finances of Karnataka" submitted to the Fourteenth Finance Commission, Government of India, see Gayithri (2014) and "Karnataka State Fiscal transfers to local bodies: The current status and the state's fiscal Capacity", 2017, submitted to the Fourth State Finance Commission, Government of Karnataka.

Table 1 Major fiscal indicators of Karnataka

Fiscal indicators	2008–09 (Accounts)		2009–10 (Accounts)		2010–11 (Accounts)		2011–12 (Accounts)		2012–13 (Accounts)		2013–14 (Accounts)		2014–15 (RE)		2015–16 (BE)	
	KAR	All states	KAR	All states	KAR	All states	KAR	All states	KAR	All states	KAR	All states	KAR	All states	KAR	All states
RD/GFD	−18.7	−9.4	−14.9	16.4	−39	−1.9	−38.13	−14.23	12.98	10.4	−2.04	4.26	−0.84	5.01	−4.5	−16.1
Capital out-lay/GFD	113	106	111.6	79	125	94.1	126.1	101.72	106.69	98.83	99.18	88.98	99.21	90.84	101.68	110.37
NDE/AD	23.6	28.9	21.1	30.3	20.2	30.8	20	29.7	21.5	28.8	23	29.6	21.4	26.6	22.8	28.2
STR/RE	66.4	47.2	64.3	45.4	71.2	49.4	71.4	75.66	87.03	76.81	74.1	61.2	67.1	53.6	70.7	57.1

Source Gayithri (2017b)
RD Revenue deficit; *GFD* Gross fiscal deficit; *STR* State tax; *NDE* Non-development; *RE* Revenue expenditure; *AD* Aggregate disbursement

2.3 Revenue Receipts in Karnataka

Karnataka state's revenue resources have had an absolute increase from Rs. 4775 crore in 1991–92 to Rs. 144,892 in 2017–18 BE revealing a 30 to 34 times increase. State tax revenue being the largest component of revenue resources of the state has had 31 times increase growing from Rs. 2900 to Rs. 89,957 crore (Table 2). Non-tax revenue has had a very small increase of 11 times. The share of revenue receipts as percent of GSDP is presented in Table 3, revealing that the share has increased from 15.87 in 1991–92 to 16.14% in 2015–16 reaching its peak of almost 20% level in 2006–07. State's tax revenue has had a share of 9.64% and increased to 10.27% during the reference period, while that of non-tax revenue declined from 2.06 to 0.73% during the above reference period.

Distribution of revenue receipts by its major components reveals that state's own tax revenue has constituted the largest share with a large part of the time period having over 60% of the total and almost reaching 70% in 2013–14. The share of state's non-tax revenue has come down from 13% in 1991–92 to 4.79% in 2017–18 BE. Share in central taxes has had a marginal decline from 16.38 to 14.07% in 2014–15, however, owing to the Fourteenth Finance Commission recommendation which increased the states 'share to 42% has enhanced the Centre's share to 22% in 2017–18 BE (Table 4; Fig. 2). The sound performance of state's own tax revenue inclusive of some of major components, especially after the promulgation of Fiscal Responsibility Act is also borne out by the rates of growth (Table 5). Details presented in Table 6 reveal the poor performance of non-tax revenue.

Table 2 Karnataka state's resource position

Year	STR	SNTR	Grants	SCT	RR
1991–92	2900	621	472	782	4775
1994–95	4289	848	695	1136	6968
1997–98	6412	1264	767	2176	10,613
2000–01	9043	1660	1546	2574	14,823
2004–05	16,072	4472	2147	3878	26,570
2007–08	25,987	3358	5027	6779	41,151
2010–11	38,473	3358	6869	9506	58,206
2015–16	75,550	5355	13,929	23,983	118,817
2016–17 RE	82,211	7099	14,798	28,760	132,867
2017–18 BE	89,957	6945	16,082	31,908	144,892
Percent increase	3101.75	1117.85	3407.85	4079.89	3034.09

Source Gayithri (2017b)

Note: *STR* State tax revenue; *SNTR* State non-tax revenue; *SCT* Share in central taxes; *RR* Revenue receipts. Please refer A-3.3 for detailed information

Table 3 Resources as percent of GSDP

Year	STR	SNTR	Grants	SCT	RR
1991–92	9.64	2.06	1.57	2.60	15.87
1994–95	8.95	1.77	1.45	2.37	14.54
1997–98	8.94	1.76	1.07	3.03	14.80
2000–01	8.26	1.52	1.41	2.35	13.55
2004–05	10.82	3.01	1.45	2.61	17.89
2007–08	11.11	1.44	2.15	2.90	17.60
2010–11	10.10	0.88	1.80	2.50	15.28
2015–16	10.27	0.73	1.89	3.26	16.14
2016–17 RE	9.16	0.79	1.65	3.20	14.81
2017–18 BE	8.75	0.67	1.56	3.10	14.09

Source Gayithri (2017b)

Table 4 Composition of revenue receipts (percentage to total revenue receipts)

Year	STR	SNTR	Grants	SCT
1991–92	60.73	13.01	9.88	16.38
1994–95	61.55	12.17	9.97	16.30
1997–98	60.42	11.91	7.23	20.50
2000–01	61.01	11.20	10.43	17.36
2004–05	60.49	16.83	8.08	14.60
2007–08	63.15	8.16	12.22	16.47
2010–11	66.10	5.77	11.80	16.33
2015–16	63.59	4.51	11.72	20.18
2016–17 RE	61.87	5.34	11.14	21.65
2017–18 BE	62.09	4.79	11.10	22.02

Source Gayithri (2017b)

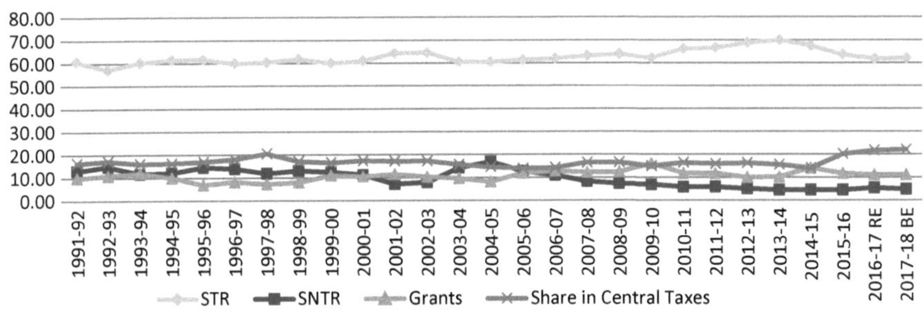

Fig. 2 Composition of revenue receipts. *Source* Gayithri (2017b)

2.4 Revenue Receipts and Revenue Expenditure

The sharper rate of growth of the revenue receipts over that of revenue expenditure from 2003–04 onwards (Table 5) has enabled the state to generate more revenue resources than its revenue spending. These trends not only expedited the fiscal correction process by way of attaining the fiscal and revenue deficit targets ahead of the prescribed timelines but also helped to generate savings on revenue account that could be used for capital investments. However, ever since the global meltdown, the rate of growth of revenue expenditure has been largely on the higher side resulting in reduction in the revenue surplus achieved by the state earlier on (Fig. 3).

Table 5 Revenue receipts and revenue expenditure: trends and growth

Year	Revenue receipts	Revenue expend	Growth rate of revenue receipts	Growth rate of revenue expenditure
1991–92	4775	4954		
1994–95	6968	7265	10.18	17.01
1997–98	10,613	10,890	10.30	6.76
2000–01	14,823	16,685	14.85	9.54
2004–05	26,570	24,932	27.99	17.14
2007–08	41,151	37,375	9.48	11.78
2010–11	58,206	54,034	18.41	13.67
2011–12	69,806	65,115	19.93	20.51
2015–16	118,817	117,029	14.09	12.95
2016–17 RE	132,867	131,805	11.82	12.63
2017–18 BE	144,892	144,755	9.05	9.83

Source Gayithri (2017b)

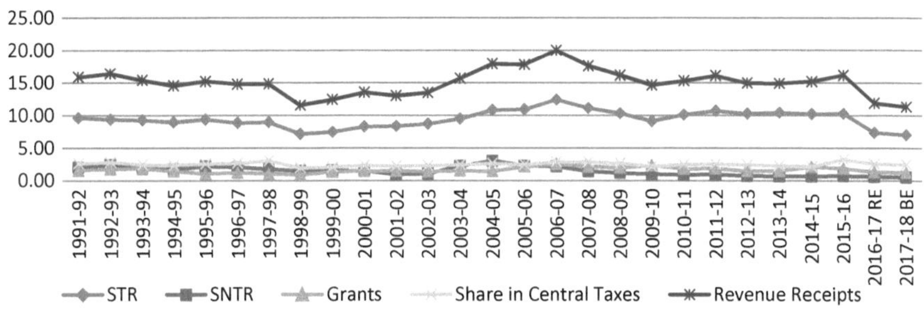

Fig. 3 Sources of financing revenue expenditure as a percentage of GSDP. *Source* Gayithri (2017b)

Table 6 Non-tax revenue as (% of expenditure of functional categories)

Year	General services	Social services	Economic services
1991–92	5.68	1.62	12.21
1994–95	4.19	1.90	9.25
1997–98	3.93	3.75	10.01
2000–01	3.34	1.90	10.42
2001–02	2.66	2.16	8.79
2004–05	20.90	1.79	19.56
2007–08	6.06	1.19	11.91
2010–11	0.67	1.34	9.19
2013–14	2.40	1.38	5.45
2015–16	2.66	1.06	5.35
2016–17 RE	2.68	1.35	7.18
2017–18 BE	2.51	1.37	5.58

Source Gayithri (2017b)

2.5 Non-tax Revenue in Karnataka

Karnataka's non-tax performance has not been satisfactory; it has not only deteriorated over time but also has trailed behind that of all states.

Non-tax revenue as percent of respective functional heads of expenditure reveals (Table 6) that there has been a decline during the reference period. The share of social services has dwindled to less than half from 1.62% in 1991–92 to 1.37% in 2017–18 BE and that of economic services has declined from 12.21 to 5.58% during the reference period. This is despite a sharp increase in the functional categories of expenditure. While one of the reasons is the retention of user charges by departments concerned, the cost recovery has been abysmally low and does not even cover the operation and maintenance charges incurred by the government in the provision of these services. Despite this, government has not put in a clear policy. ERC has recommended that government should articulate a policy on user charges so that it is firmly on the agenda of every department (GoK, ERC, 2011, 41).

2.6 Growth in Public Expenditure: Revenue and Capital Categories

Growth and composition of total Karnataka government expenditure by revenue and capital heads—the former denoting recurring and maintenance expenditure, and the latter capital investments incurred by the government is discussed in the following. It is important to note that while the revenue expenditure is largely in the nature of committed expenditure inclusive of salaries, pensions, interest payments and other

Table 7 Trends in revenue and capital expenditure

Year	Revenue expenditure (in crores)	Revenue exp as a % to total ex	Revenue exp as a % to GSDP	Capital expenditure (in crores)	Capital exp as a % to total ex	Capital exp as a % to GSDP
1991–92	4954	86.31	16.46	786	13.69	2.61
1994–95	7265	86.47	15.16	1137	13.53	2.37
1997–98	10,890	90.00	15.19	1210	10.00	1.69
2000–01	16,685	89.55	15.25	1947	10.45	1.78
2004–05	24,932	84.21	16.79	4674	15.79	3.15
2005–06	28,041	82.81	16.42	5822	17.19	3.41
2010–11	54,034	80.18	14.19	13,355	19.82	3.51
2015–16	117,029	85.28	15.90	20,198	14.72	2.74
2016–17 RE	131,805	86.05	11.80	21,369	13.95	1.91
2017–18 BE	144,755	84.60	11.30	26,341	15.40	2.06

Source Gayithri (2017b)

maintenance related expenditure and is difficult to be reduced unless the commitment itself is reduced. On the contrary, capital expenditure is highly susceptible to fiscal uncertainties.

2.7 *Trends in Revenue and Capital Heads of Expenditure*

An analysis of the broad trends by the revenue and capital expenditure in Karnataka reveals that revenue expenditure has increased sharply from INR 4954 crore in 1991–92 to INR 144,755 crore in 2017–18 (BE). On the other hand, capital expenditure has increased from INR 785.84 crore to INR 26,341 crore during the above reference period (Table 7). In terms of annual compound rate of growth capital expenditure reveals a higher rate at 13.89% per annum as compared to that of revenue expenditure at 13.31% during 1991–92 to 2017–18 (BE). This sharper growth in capital account has largely occurred during the current decade (after 2002–03) caused by the recovery experienced by the state government finances following pronouncement of FRA and sound revenue position. Rate of growth of capital expenditure during the period 2002–03 to 2017–18 (BE) was 17.41% as opposed to 9.37% for the previous period (1991–92–2001–02). These are positive trends given the capital investment inadequacy in the past; however, on an average, revenue expenditure constitutes a very large share in the total with 85.15% share whereas that of capital heads constitutes 14.81% share in total expenditure; 15.15 and 2.66% share in GSDP during the reference time period. Details are provided in Fig. 4. These trends clearly account for a large revenue expenditure commitment on the state government).

The current fiscal scenario discussed above clearly accounts for a revenue-led fiscal recovery in the state and the issues and concerns relating to the public expen-

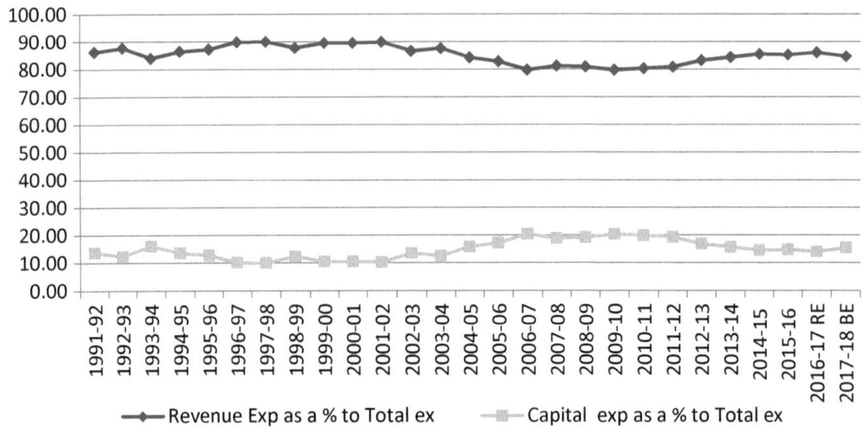

Fig. 4 Revenue and capital expenditure as a percentage of total expenditure. *Source* Gayithri (2017b)

diture. There are also concerns expressed regarding the poor translation of outlays into outcomes. In the context of human development, it is stated 'Karnataka's fiscal capability and the priority assigned to the social sector reveals that the state's performance with reference to financing of human development is comparable over time and with other states, However, this should not lead to complacency, as the state's performance on human development front has not been commensurate with the resources flowing into the sector. This is amply clear from the fact that the states with similar per capita spending like Tamil Nadu have achieved much better levels of human development as compared to Karnataka. Analyzing the relative performance of Indian states in various dimensions of human development, Ghosh (2006) observes that Madhya Pradesh, Rajasthan, and Tamil Nadu managed to improve their HDI position over time, Karnataka along with Andhra Pradesh, Gujarat and Maharashtra experienced deterioration in their relative position. Despite the overall improvement in the HDI-level overtime, the relative performance of the state has been a cause for concern'(Gayithri 2017a).

These instances clearly account for the need to carefully examine the issues in expenditure planning and management and the current lacunae in tracking the effectiveness of public spending.

3 Strengths and Weaknesses of the Current Expenditure Planning and Management Practice

3.1 *Line-Item Incremental Budgeting*

Line-item incremental budgeting is a budgetary practice wherein budget is prepared using the previous year's budget as a basis with incremental amounts added for the new fiscal year. The current incremental budgeting practices have many inherent strengths and weaknesses.

3.2 *Strengths*

A key advantage of the line-item incremental budgeting practice is that it is relatively simple and easy to operate. Expenditure prediction is straightforward and hassle free as the priorities are assumed to remain the same but with gradual increased allocation to account for the price and population factors. The line-item appropriations also render great ease in infusing control on expenditure and oversee the use of use of appropriations for the assigned purpose. Line-item budgeting itself happened to be a reform initiative that stood the test of time over a century.

Shah and Shen (2007, 139) state, 'A prominent feature of a line-item budget system is to specify the line-item ceiling in the budget allocation process and to ensure that agencies do not spend in excess of their caps. Hence the budget facilitates tight fiscal grip over government operations. The strengths of such a system rest on its relative simplicity and potential control of public spending through the detailed specification of inputs. Throughout much of the twentieth century, central budget offices and finance ministries have been aggressive proponents of control of public resources, which explains why line-item budgeting has been so enduring in spite of relentless efforts in budgeting reforms.'

3.3 *Weaknesses*

3.3.1 Input Focus

Governments in India and many nations across the globe have practiced for long incremental budgeting, wherein the expenditure proposals are largely based on the monies expended in the last year with some markup. While this practice makes the job of expenditure decision making very simple and easy, a major drawback lies in its underlying implicit assumption that sectoral priorities remain the same and they would not undergo any change over time, which is highly misleading. Thus, the incremental budgeting practices often result in bloating of public expenditure leading to large fiscal deficits with a very poor focus on the societal needs.

3.3.2 Lack of Incentives to Restrain Costs

Expenditure estimates may have often been overestimated at the time of scheme/program inception and would never get re-examined given the practice of incremental budgeting, thus giving rise to technical inefficiency in governmental operations. There is also a tendency to spend up to the budget and thus lead to cost escalation in the service provision.

3.3.3 Does not Facilitate Informed Expenditure Decision Making

Since the focus is on the inputs/money spent, it offers very little scope to take into consideration what services have been delivered with the resources used up in providing a particular service? Did such spending align with the government's proposed objectives? What is the current attainment level and what is the required level of intervention to achieve the originally stated goal? In other words, while the focus is largely on the effort in providing a particular service in the form of 'inputs' the results of the expenditure interventions by the government are not being taken into consideration while framing the expenditure plans, thus leading to framing of ill-informed expenditure decisions.

The results/impacts/outcomes of large and increasing government expenditure on account of the growing number of government schemes and programs are not currently being tracked, let alone being tracked; there are no appropriate indicators of outcomes developed by a number of departments barring a few departments and centrally sponsored schemes. Effectiveness of government schemes and programs in delivering the expected results has not been adequately assessed. Hitherto governments have been reporting scheme performance in the 'Performance Budgets' prepared by development departments; albeit, the focus in these reports is limited to 'outputs' and relating only to the 'plan schemes' of the respective departments. It is very rare that program 'outcomes' are tracked and reported in any of the reports. It is stated 'While it is very important to have information relating to 'outputs' which by and large amounts to listing out of goods and services provided by the government agencies, they are not tantamount to the final impact or the end result expected of a program. On the other hand, 'outcomes' indicate the final impact or the end results' (Gayithri 2015, 9). Major weaknesses in resource allocation and use are highlighted by the World Bank, 1998 in the following text box.

Weaknesses in Resource Allocation and Use
Weaknesses that undermine public sector performance include:
• Poor planning; • No links between policy making, planning, and budgeting; • Poor expenditure control; • Inadequate funding of operations and maintenance; • Little relationship between budget as formulated and budget as executed; • Inadequate accounting systems; • Unreliability in the flow of budgeted funds to agencies and to lower levels of government; • Poor management of external aid; • Poor cash management; • Inadequate reporting of financial performance; and • Poorly motivated staff

Source The World Bank (1998)

4 Budget Reform Initiatives

Current global thinking has been to move away from 'outlays' to 'outcomes' in attaining allocative efficiency. There have been variant forms of such reform initiatives attempted from time to time. These include[3]:

- Line item budgeting
- Performance budgeting
- Program budgeting
- Zero-based budgeting

4.1 Reform Initiatives in Karnataka

The state of Karnataka has been experimenting with some reform initiatives in the past couple of decades and these include:

4.2 Performance Budgets

'Performance Budget' reporting formats came into existence based on the recommendations of the Administrative Reforms Commission in 1969, and many state governments in India are preparing these reports also in addition to the line-item budgets. These reports are being annually prepared by the departments involved in the development works on a regular basis in the state of Karnataka. The reports pro-

[3]Discussion on Budget reform initiatives in Karnataka is sourced from Gayithri (2015).

vide a narrative description of the plan schemes and detail both financial and physical targets and achievements relating to such schemes. These reports are also serving well as the basis for a review of the departmental schemes and their implementation by the legislature committees. Their utility is however limited only to the plan schemes implemented by the respective departments and the huge non-plan expenditure, which typically constitutes 75–80% of the total expenditure, escapes a critical review. In addition, the targets and achievements provided in the report largely relate to the inputs and outputs, with very little coverage of outcome information.

4.3 Departmental Medium-Term Fiscal Plan

Yet another important reform initiative introduced by the Government of Karnataka in 2003 as a logical continuation of the provisions of the Fiscal Responsibility legislation relates to the preparation of Departmental Medium-Term Fiscal Plan (DMTFP) by some departments.

DMTFP encompasses reform features such as a medium-term program approach, strategies for achieving the goals and objectives of the programs, 'outcomes' and information related to them. These reports however are currently not prepared by all the departments; in addition, the programs are largely at the department level thus, they tend to become very aggregative. Programs are also not connected to their budget summary.

5 Program Performance Budgeting in Karnataka

In light of the weaknesses referred to above, the state government in collaboration with the USAID-REFORM (2008a, b) and on its own had experimented with some reform initiatives in the area of government expenditure; one of such initiative was in the form of 'Program Performance Budget'.

5.1 Programs Approach to Budgeting

The line-item description practice that normally depicts the expenditure breakup by each line item was brought under reform fold. A number of OECD countries have attempted programmatic reclassification of their Central government budget line items. Australia, France, Netherlands, Sweden, and the UK offer good examples of reclassified budgets based on program criteria (Kraan 2007). These reform initiatives shifted the focus from single line items which have for long served as the focal points of expenditure control to grouping of certain related line items that contribute to specified outputs and outcomes. The broad objective of a program focus is to enable result-oriented public expenditure decision making. In Australia, under Program Management and Budgeting (PMB), expenditures were classified on the basis of a hierarchy of programs, subprograms and activities, each related to purposes and objectives (as opposed to the line-item budgeting system previously in use). This exercise involves a careful reclassification of the line items into groups that collectively result in certain outputs and outcomes.

The usefulness of grouping related line items into programs and sub-programs lies in the fact that very often an individual activity or a single item of expenditure does not by itself contribute to the achievement of the end results expected of expenditure. It is generally a group of related activities a group of activities that collectively ensure the achievement of expected results. For instance, education outcomes get guided by spending on a number of line items such as construction of school buildings, procurement of infrastructure, recruitment of teachers and their training, etc. Hence, it becomes imperative that expenditure decisions are made for such group of activities that collectively influence the results, rather than framing the expenditure decisions at individual scheme level. In the PPB methodology, related individual schemes are grouped together to constitute a program, with clearly delineated objectives to be achieved within a time frame, and this in turn forms the basis for formulating expenditure decisions and providing actual allocations.

Thus, in the preparation of PPB, the first and the foremost task is one of defining the broad programs and subprograms of the department. A department is responsible for providing many services (resulting in outputs and outcomes) to the citizens, and toward this end, one or more activities are generally initiated. While framing departmental programs and subprograms, a complete list of the departmental schemes, both plan and non-plan, and under revenue and capital heads of expenditure have to be first prepared, and then, all the inter-related activities that aid in the provision of a particular service/group of related services grouped into programs and subprograms. The programs should be defined in such a manner that specific results/outcomes linked with the overall goals of the department could as far as possible be attributable to an individual program. A program could be subdivided into subprograms with identifiable contributions to the outcome of a program. Functionality charts mapping individual schemes to a subprogram and subprograms on to program to ensure that no schemes are lost sight of while narrating the program/subprogram details would be of great help in completing the PPB exercise. However, it is important to realize that these programs and subprograms can and should be reviewed from time to time in view of the addition/deletion of new/old schemes and the changing role of government from time to time.

5.2 *Program Performance*

5.2.1 Linking Policy, Expenditure and Outcomes

The PPB framework enables integration of policy, expenditure, and outcomes/results of all the government activities and provides the necessary inputs required for framing informed expenditure decisions. This is an improved form of budgeting over the traditional budgeting in the sense the latter provides merely a detailed statement of the line items of expenditure and very often the current year's expenditure serves as the basis for framing estimates for the next fiscal year. Very often governments base their year-to-year expenditure decisions on the line items by providing for an increase over the current year, popularly known as incremental budgeting. Many governments across the globe have for long resorted to incremental line-item budgeting and many of them still continue to do so. While the line-item budgeting is certainly very helpful in keeping proper checks and balances on the monies spent by the government departments on their schemes and programs, this form of budgeting does not provide information as to what the scheme is all about, how the schemes contribute to the achievement of broader goals and objectives of the government and also does not indicate the results of the spending activities on such schemes. 'Integrating policy, planning and budgeting is fundamentally about having expenditure programs that are driven by policy priorities and disciplined by budget realities' (The World Bank 1998, 32). Cycle depicting the links is presented in the following chart.

Linking policy, Planning and Budgeting in the planning and Resource Management Cycle.

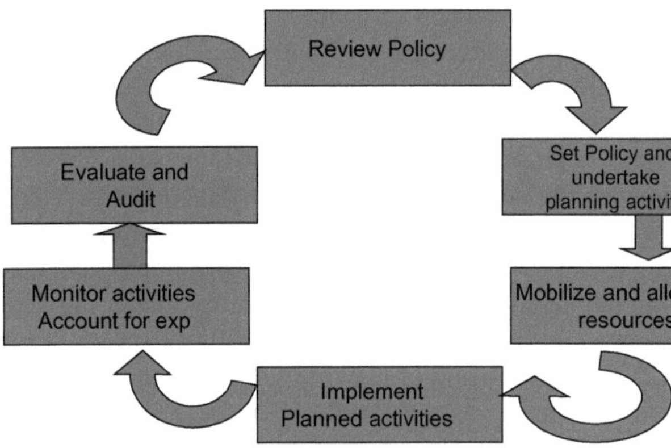

Source The World Bank (1998)

The PPB framework used in Karnataka was developed based on a careful study of international best practices and suitably amended to fit the Karnataka budget requirements.

5.2.2 PPB: The Structure

The PPB structure as adopted in Karnataka essentially comprises of three important components, these definitely are not sacrosanct, and additions/deletions are possible. The PPB structure provides scope to present both narrative descriptions of their operations:

Descriptive element of PPB	Statistical information
Departmental mission statement, goals, and objectives Key achievements and emerging concerns	Department level Summary of budget operations Presented in a medium-term time frame
Program descriptions to comprise of functions, performance Key community targets, special impacts on weaker sections	Budget summary of each program depicted by economic categories such as 'employee related' 'administrative costs', transfer payments by way of subsidies, local bodies, etc., presented in a medium-term time frame
Performance Indicators/Family of performance measures	Performance information to depict 'inputs' 'outputs', 'outcomes' and 'efficiency' to be projected in a medium-term time frame

5.2.3 Department Summary

The PPB framework adopted in Karnataka required that each department clearly identifies the major goals and objectives of each of the programs and subprograms, such an exercise is important as they guide the outcomes expected of the expenditure program. The departments were expected to prepare a summary of the department providing information on departmental activities, legal authority, goals, objectives, important achievements, emerging issues, and concerns. The departments can also present an organization chart on program lines summarize the departmental expenditure.

5.2.4 Program Narrative Description and Community Targets

The program budget format comprises of a narrative description of the program pages of each program and subprogram. The narrative provides a brief understanding of the program/subprogram and outlines the key achievements of program intervention and the important developments in the department. These are logically followed up by slating of future targets that invariably get guided by their past performance levels. A special focus is provided to describe the special impacts the departmental program is having on the downtrodden and weaker sections of the society.

The framework also recognizes the policy importance attached to inclusive development in Indian context and accordingly provides for tracking the special impacts that the programs and subprograms have on these sections of the society. Accordingly, an exclusive column is provided to capture the special impacts on Scheduled Castes and Scheduled Tribes and Women.

5.2.5 Departmental Constraints

An important component of the narrative description of the program pertains to the fact that not all achievements slated to be achieved at the beginning of the plan period can be achieved due to both foreseen and unforeseen hurdles to program delivery. While the risk element for the foreseen adversities can be factored in, that of unforeseen hurdles cannot be factored in, these aspects can be detailed by including a short note on the constraints faced by the departments in the implementation of a program. The department can highlight the constraints faced by the concerned in the provision of services under the program/subprogram. Correct identification of such constraints can guide in framing of strategies that aid in overcoming the same.

5.2.6 Budget Summary Page

Budget summary page provides information for each of the programs pertaining to expenditure, staff and performance results. USAID (2008a, b) outlines the detailed framework to present the budget summary and the expenditure classification included therein[4]:

5.2.7 Expenditure Statement

PPB provides a more meaningful depiction of economic significance of expenditure statement, wherein the object heads of expenditure pertaining to each of the programs are grouped into meaningful categories like:

- Employee related
- Administrative cost
- Operations and maintenance
- Capital works
- Capital investments and loans
- Transfers to local bodies
- Transfers to others
- Debt service

[4]USAID (2008a, b).

This grouping enables a clear understanding of the economic nature of the expenditure incurred and provides insights into areas of expenditure shortfall, such that much-focused intervention can be made in setting right the problem.

It has to be noted that care is exerted while preparing the budget summary that no item of the budget head is left out in one or the other program/subprogram and that all the object heads form a part of one or the other expenditure categories included in the budget summary. Thus, the expenditure statement is complete and inclusive of all kinds of expenditure incurred for the purpose, such as revenue and capital and plan and non-plan and thus provides a holistic idea of what is the total expenditure incurred on the program in one place unlike the line-item budget where each one of the above is listed separately. Such a complete tracking of total expenditure facilitates technical efficiency analysis of program spending.

A medium-term (three year) projection of expenditure for the program concerned is provided. PPB Budget Summary also provides the staff details pertaining to each program under two categories-Employees and staff and by gender. It has to be noted that this format is not sacrosanct and certainly its variants also designed so as to suit the requirements

5.2.8 Performance Results

Performance results indicate the results of the programs. Performance measures include variables such as 'inputs' 'outputs' 'efficiency,' and 'outcomes.'

Outcome: Effects/impact of the activities taken up by the government under the subprogram on the community/citizens under focus
Output: Work done by the department in delivering the proposed services to the community
Efficiency: Cost per unit of output/outcome.[5]
Input: Resources used, referring to the manpower/material/cost incurred in the supply of the services

In some countries, these are used as family of measures and all of them are used in assessing the effectiveness of programs.

Examples of 'outputs' and 'outcomes'

In view of the considerable merits that a framework like PPB offers in the toning up of effectiveness of public expenditure, it would be advantageous for a government-

[5]Calculation of cost efficiency is very important in order to assess the cost of providing services by the government. There are currently estimation problems faced on account of limited availability of required data and the indivisibility that exists among certain costs-such as the employees services which stretch to more than a single program, the administrative expenses common to more than a single program etc., There are also difficulties in the case of certain departments which produce multiple services such as 'Irrigation Projects' to estimate the unit costs of each service. While there are methodologies available in the context of other countries such as 'Activity based costing', such costing methods are yet to be adopted in the government sector in the country, and it is hoped that such methodologies are used in due course such that cost efficiency of services is measured by the government on a routine basis.

Outputs	Outcomes
Number of children distributed uniforms, textbooks	Survival rate of class 1 children reaching class 8
Number of teachers trained	Percent of children attaining desired levels of learning
Number of new tuberculosis cases detected or sputum examined	Rate of tuberculosis per lakh population
Number of children administered polio vaccine	Percent of children in the 2–5 age-group that contract polio

wide adoption. However, the following challenges can be addressed to make the system foolproof.

6 Key Challenges

The preparation of line-item incremental budgeting has been in vogue for long and has been carried out year on year with considerable amount of ease. Changing the mindset to switch over to a new system involving collating considerable amount of additional information is a formidable task.

Clear divisibility of activities and outcomes by programs and departments is difficult to be achieved as very often outcomes emerge due to the combined activities undertaken by different departments and programs. In addition, some results may occur after a considerable time lag in which case the progress in the intermediate outcomes may serve well as guiding force for expenditure decision making. There are also extraneous forces at play impacting on the final outcomes, such as the participation by the private sector.

There is a need to take stock of the current constraints and challenges faced in the preparation of PPB and initiate some measures to make an effective PPB to take roots in the GOK expenditure operations.

6.1 Identification of Subprograms: Practical Difficulties

Ideally in the context of outcome-based budgeting, the programs and subprograms need to completely synchronize with their goals and objectives. It is very essential that in framing of subprograms under each of the programs there is need to have a complete understanding of the departmental activities—their goals and objectives. The department officers executing these schemes and having good experience in the administration of various schemes of the department alone can undertake such a task. Sometimes, even with this knowledge it becomes very difficult to clearly delineate schemes with clearly defined outcomes; in other words, some schemes may be contributing to more than a single outcome in which case, framing of subprograms poses serious problems. The international experience reveals that time allocation methods are used in accounting for expenditure. These are advanced techniques, which may be considered when we have had more experience of preparing program performance budgets. However, currently, the method adopted is to assign the scheme to a subprogram, under which the primary impact of the scheme is likely to befall.

Performance database: The critical factor for the success of any outcome focused budgeting framework is to have the necessary performance information relating to all programs and subprograms generated on a periodical basis, especially data relating to outcomes and most importantly used in the decision-making process. Unfortunately, the current availability of data for outcome indicators is very weak in Karnataka, and it is even more unfortunate that there is inadequate attention paid to identification of relevant performance indicators for many a program. Hence, effort has to be first in identifying the performance indicators collect the baseline data and to be followed up with a prescribed periodicity. It is also to be noted that the data collected from various districts are consolidated at the state level; there is a need to adopt a common methodology at various data collection points. Moreover, as far as possible, it would be better to give a break up across different social categories as it gives more meaningful information rather than presenting the information in a single average value.

In addition to this, the indicators identified by the department may change from time to time as the major thrust of a program or subprogram changes over the years. Therefore, there is a need to identify new indicators which meet the need of the community for which the program is targeted. Therefore, there is a need to develop additional performance indicators based on the performance of the program in the previous years and key community targets proposed to the community.

Numerous reporting formats: Currently, departmental performance is reported in numerous formats, often duplicative in nature. The departments produce annual reports; the performance budgets are prepared annually to report performance of plan schemes, and Departmental Medium-Term Fiscal Plans (DMTFP) are yet another reporting format that came into existence after the passing of the Fiscal Responsibility Act in 2003. Preparation of all these reports close to the budget time puts enormous amount of pressure on the officers preparing such reports. It has also been observed that very often the information is reproduced verbatim in all these reports. Hence, there is every need to review the need to continue with so many reporting formats and an important policy decision to discontinue some reports that would help in avoiding duplicating reporting

Task force members: In order to build the capacity of officers in the preparation of PPB, a core group of officers were identified for each department to undergo the required training and undertake the preparation of PPB. This initiative is good in view of the fact that budget officers have been traditionally preparing budgets in an incremental manner and new methods of preparing the same would require training. As a part of the PPB roll out in Karnataka USAID-REFORM, the officers in charge of preparation of the PPB document were trained by the REFORM team; however, they got transferred, and hence, it was difficult to ensure continuity to the work carried out under PPB. Despite the fact that respective departments constituted new task force, in the absence of earlier members, the pace of PPB progress suffered as the new set of officers had to get familiarized with the concept and the importance of introducing PPB. Resolving such problems in the long run would require an appropriate policy decision on creating technical expertise within each department. This could be by way of creating an exclusive cell within the department with earmarked staff who do not get transferred.

New schemes: Yet another key challenge that needs attention relates to the announcement of new schemes by the government from time to time in the PPB framework. A meaningful PPB framework is one that gets updated with the changes that occur in the government spending proposals from time to time. The new schemes that get announced from time to time need to be meaningfully grouped under an appropriate program based on the objectives of that scheme and also take into account the expenditure related to such schemes in the expenditure summary. Similarly, it becomes essential to identify appropriate indicators that explain outcome or achievement of the schemes.

Expenditure categories: Expenditure depicted by line items does not facilitate an economic analysis of expenditure. There is a need to understand the nature of expenditure by manpower costs, transfers, capital investment, operations and maintenance to analyze the economic significance of government spending. Components of expenditure also tend to vary from one level of government to another in a federal setup like India. For instance, at the district-level PPB, certain expenditures items such as transfer to local bodies, subsidies and debt servicing are not present at the district; hence, the casting of expenditure has to include the items that are specific to the lower level of government.

District-level PPB: Frameworks like PPB have worked very well at the lowest level of administrative units because they are the service providers and tracking the impacts is a lot easier. However, in a federal setup like India the district sector does not merely implement its own schemes but also the state sector and central sector schemes. In tracking the outcomes of programs, it is necessary to make sure that all schemes, be it state, center, or district sector are considered. Limiting the coverage of PPB framework at the district level to only those schemes implemented at the district level through ZP or those schemes which are given in the link document of the ZP that come under the administrative jurisdiction of the CEO will amount to a partial coverage. Certain departments like education, health and women and child development have state sector schemes implemented at the district level in addition to the ZP schemes. Hence, the impacts of all schemes in entirety need to be tracked.

6.2 Informed Decision Making

Results orientation to public budgeting has taken a number of forms (OECD 2008) like 'presentational performance budgeting', 'Direct performance budgeting,' performance-based budgeting'. While it is useful to have results orientation to government programs, a more important use of such frameworks is when the performance information is used in framing informed decisions. The routine incremental allocations without considering the progress achieved in a program intervention will only result in inefficient use of public resources and given the scarce public resources such application of funds will result in allocative inefficiency. Performance informed decisions will set right the priorities and enable an optimal use of resources. In the present times, both at the Central and State levels while there is experimentation with a number of frameworks, we are nowhere close to a proper application of such frameworks. The PPB framework used in Karnataka discussed above too is discontinued. In order to have these frameworks work, the government in the first place has to identify the relevant outcome indicators and generate data to verify progress in that direction. It is unfortunate that, there is no serious effort in identifying the right indicators let alone collection of data for the myriad programs run by governments at all the three levels. At this juncture, when there are a number of successful country cases that have put in place a meaningful performance orientation, India need not reinvent the wheel, the best practices can be carefully studied and adapted to our requirements. Such an effort, however, cannot succeed sans strong political will.

References

Gayithri K. (2014). Evaluation of State Finances of Karnataka, an unpublished report submitted to the Fourteenth Finance Commission. http://fincomindia.nic.in/writereaddata%5Chtml_en_files%5Cfincom14/others/11.pdf.

Gayithri, K. (2015). *Performance-based budgeting: Subnational initiatives in India and China*. ISEC Working paper, 334, Institute for Social and Economic Change, Bengaluru.

Gayithri, K. (2017a). Financing human development in Karnataka, a chapter in the Karnataka Human Development Report, Planning Department, Government of Karnataka (forthcoming).

Gayithri, K. (2017b). Karnataka State Fiscal transfers to local bodies: The current status and the state's fiscal Capacity, a research report submitted to the Fourth State Finance Commission, Government of Karnataka.

Ghosh, M. (2006). Economic growth and human development in Indian States. *Economic and Political Weekly, 41*(30), 3321–3329.

Kraan, D.-J. (2007). Programme budgeting in OECD countries. *OECD Journal of Public Budgeting, 7*(4), 7–46.

Shah, A., & Shen, C. (2007). A Primer on Performance. In Budgeting in Anwar Shah (Ed.), Budgeting and Budgetary institutions, The World Bank, Washington, D.C.

The World Bank. (1998). *Public expenditure management handbook*. Washington, D.C.

OECD. (2008). *Performance based budgeting: A user's guide*. OECD Policy Brief. https://www.oecd.org/gov/budgeting/Performance-Budgeting-Guide.pdf.

USAID. (2008a). *The expenditure planning and management practitioners guide*. USAID, New Delhi. http://fiscalwatch.org/Reform_volumes/VolumeII.pdf.

USAID. (2008b). *USAID/INDIA reform project compendium with practitioner's guide*. Vol. 1 USAID, New Delhi. http://fiscalwatch.org/Reform_volumes/VolumeI.pdf.

Chapter 9
Accrual Budgeting

S. K. Das

More than two hundred years ago, Thomas Jefferson, America's third President, had declared that he wished to see, the finances of the Union as clear and intelligible as a merchant's books, so that every member of Congress, and every man of any mind in the Union, should be able to comprehend them to investigate abuses, and consequently, to control them.[1] There was a reason why Jefferson wished so. Historically, governments have accounted on a cash basis, while private enterprises accounted on an accrual basis. It is true that, from time to time, some government agencies did adopt accruals for their operations. For instance, accrual accounting was introduced for UK local authority accounts in the mid-nineteenth century, and by the end of that century, it had been adopted by most of the larger municipal councils.[2] Ultimately, however, accrual accounting did not find favour with the government, and the UK Treasury officially accepted cash basis of accounting as a part of the major reforms introduced in 1866.[3] That is why cash basis was used by British colonies across the world for the next hundred years.[4]

It is only during the last four decades that a number of countries have moved away from the cash basis. This move has come about as a part of comprehensive public management reforms, which correspond to the agenda called "new public management (NPM)".[5] The NPM reforms, which emphasize transparency, cost-effectiveness and managerial flexibility, highlight the shortcomings of cash-based

[1] Rayegan et al. (2012), p. 525.

[2] Wynne (2003), p. 3.

[3] Ibid.

[4] Ibid.

[5] Hepworth (2002), p. 4.

S. K. Das (✉)
Bengaluru, India
e-mail: sisirdas2050@gmail.com

G. Karnam (ed.), *Public Budgeting in India*, India Studies in Business and Economics, https://doi.org/10.1007/978-81-322-3917-8_9

accounting and budgeting systems[6] and stress the usefulness of accrual systems for generating information on how to enhance decision-making, reflect accountability and ensure control over long-term consequences of government policies.[7] While a number of countries have changed over to accrual accounting systems, only two countries (New Zealand and Australia) have adopted for full accrual budgeting.

This article is organized into three parts. The first part offers an analysis of the limitations and benefits of cash and accrual systems. In the second part, we evaluate experiences of New Zealand and Australia with accrual budgeting in order to gain insights into how accrual budgeting has impacted in areas of public performance, sustainability and accountability. In the third part, we look at the prospect of introducing accrual accounting and budgeting in India, based on the insights gained from the experiences of New Zealand and Australia.

1 Cash and Accrual Systems

Cash and accruals are the two endpoints in a spectrum of accounting and budgeting bases.[8] In fact, there is more to cash and accrual systems than representing mere technical means of measurement—in the case of government accounting, they determine the extent of information that the accounting system can collect and therefore report, and in the case of government budgeting, they reflect fundamental choices about using the budget for a number of productive purposes.[9]

1.1 Cash-Based Systems

In cash-based systems, transactions are accounted for only when cash is received or paid within a reporting period. Most governments account on a cash basis. This is because it is relatively simple and easy to learn and implement. In addition, it provides a focus on cash management. Most governments also budget on a cash basis. This is due to the fact that the cash basis is well-adapted to the needs of budgetary control: strict budget control can be exercised by comparing sums authorized with those actually spent. Moreover, the cash basis is a widely used and traditionally accepted measure of the impact of the government on the economy since the cash-based deficit closely approximates the needs of the government.[10]

---

[6]US GAO (2000), p. 197.
[7]Das (2006), ix.
[8]World Bank (2002), p. 2.
[9]US GAO (2000), p. 193.
[10]US GAO (2000), p. 196.

A cash budget suffers from a number of limitations.[11] First, in the case of programmes such as credit, pensions, and post-employment benefits, the obligations of the government for the current year involve cash flows to and from the government for many years. The cash budget does not measure these obligations adequately. Second, social insurance programmes involve implied commitments or claims on future budgetary resources, and a cash-based budget does not capture these commitments or claims. Third, the cost of decisions that usually have a long-term impact, such as the cost of some tax expenditure, regulations or government liabilities for environmental clean-up, is not adequately reflected in a cash-based budget. A cash-based budget does not recognize the ultimate costs to be borne by the government at the time the commitments are made. Fourth, a cash-based budget does not provide adequate information or appropriate incentives for some important government activities. For example, in the case of capital assets and inventories, the actual use or consumption of the asset may be spread over a period of time. As a result, a cash-based budget is not in a position to properly align costs with the provision of goods or services. In other words, the true cost to the government as a whole and the specific costs of particular goods or services are either overstated in some periods or understated in others.

1.2 Accrual-Based Systems

An accrual system recognizes transactions and events when they occur rather than when cash is paid or received. It provides users with information about the resources of an entity, its revenues, the cost of services, and other information needed to assess the financial position of the entity and changes to it, and the means to assess its performance in terms of economy and efficiency.[12] In an accrual budget, the most important financial statements are the statements of financial position (balance sheet), the statement of financial performance (statement of income and expenses, profit and loss account) and the cash flow statement.[13] An accrual budget provides an important link between the statement of financial position (determination of assets) and the statement of financial performance (determination of the net result): there is thus a causal link between changes in equity (balance sheet item) in a particular year and the net result (profit and loss account item) for that year. This link between the statement of financial position and the statement of financial performance is not present in a cash-based system.

In accrual budgeting, the year of payment or receipt is not important. What is important is the year to which income and expenses are allocated for economic purposes.[14] Expenditure relating to more than one year is depreciated, and the cost

---

[11] US GAO (2000), p. 193.

[12] Das (2006), p. 8.

[13] Algemene (2007), p. 10.

[14] Algemene (2007), p. 11.

of capital expenditure is spread out over the budget for the years in which use is made of the investment. That being the case, accrual budgeting provides an insight into the annual cost of policy, and this insight can be used productively in budgeting, accounting and management.[15]

Accrual budgeting has generated a lot of interest in recent years. This is because an accrual budget offers a number of benefits. First, it improves the completeness and usefulness of the budget for decision-making by (a) better aligning cost with performance (b) providing information on all costs to encourage a longer-term management and policy focus and (c) improving the consistency and credibility of budget reporting.[16] On the whole, accrual information helps in ascertaining the full costs of government programmes and activities.

Second, it establishes a relationship between the services performed by the government and the cost of those services. This increases the efficiency and effectiveness of government programmes. Accrual budgeting makes it possible for choices and decisions to be based on economic considerations by translating expenditure into cost per period.[17] If both the budget and financial statements are accrual-based, it becomes easier to compare the amount requested for and appropriated in the budget to actual results reported in the financial statements and other financial reports.[18]

Third, an accrual budget incorporates a balance sheet perspective and that is how it is able to improve the information and incentives for supporting the government's stewardship role. Costs incurred during a fiscal year are reflected in accrual-based appropriations, and therefore, these appropriations are in a position to provide information similar to that found in an operating statement. An operating statement recognizes revenue and expenses of a period and reflects changes in the balance sheet. For example, the value of an asset is reduced by depreciation in the balance sheet, and a depreciation expense is recorded in the operating statement. This enables an assessment to be made of how the government has managed its assets and liabilities and also its longer-term financial health.[19]

Fourth, accrual budgeting is the best possible way to measure the potential cost of long-term commitments. This is because it allows the calculation of the likely cost of cash flows in the present values and anticipates measures in order to ensure that financial sustainability is not compromised.[20] In addition, it is in a position to identify budgetary effects on long-term sustainability as well as intergenerational equity issues.[21]

It has been pointed out that accrual budgeting has three limitations.[22] First, there is the concern that decision-makers in the government may find it difficult to understand

---

[15]Ibid.

[16]US GAO (2000), p. 203.

[17]Algemene (2007), p. 12.

[18]US GAO (2000), p. 204.

[19]Ibid.

[20]Meyers (2009), p. 216.

[21]Ball et al. (2000), p. 8.

[22]Ibid.

the complexities of an accrual budget because accrual measurements are based on technical issues and assumptions. In particular, it has been pointed out that legislators may find much of the information in the accrual format to be complex and inaccessible.[23] Second, because accrual measurements focus on recognizing the financial effects of economic events, they are dependent on interpretations of and judgements on when the economic effects would occur and what their ultimate costs would be. It is a fact that the accrual accounts require a number of professional judgements to be made on a variety of issues.[24] That is why it has been pointed out that accrual budgeting would open up many opportunities for 'creative accounting'.[25] Third, there are limits to an accrual budget, based on financial accounting standards, being able to address long-term accountability issues. A key limitation in this regard is that, in countries where it has been adopted, the accrual budget has failed to capture some key fiscal pressures, such as future costs associated with social insurance programmes.[26]

It will be useful to analyze these limitations and see if steps can be taken to overcome them. In respect of the concern that legislators would find much of the information in the accrual format to be complex and inaccessible, the format could perhaps be so designed that an accrual budget can actually help the legislators in the fulfilment of their duties. Admittedly, the legislators will be in a position to take better decisions if the information provided to them is clearer and is of better quality. Adoption of accrual systems would in fact generate good-quality information, particularly on the cost of policy and on assets, and if the information is presented to the legislators in an accessible manner, it would be of great help.[27] With regard to the concern that the accrual system, by requiring a number of professional judgements to be made, opens up opportunities for 'creative accounting', it actually depends on the role that the standards setters are called upon to play and their independence.[28] In New Zealand and Australia, it has been the practice to have only one professional accounting standards setter for both the public and the private sector and the governments abiding by the decisions of the standards setter. Such a practice has ensured the independence of the standards setter as well as precluding the possibility of any 'creative accounting' taking place.

There is also the concern that accrual budgeting has failed to capture the future costs associated with social insurance and healthcare programmes. There is an explanation for this. It is due to the fact that the concerned countries did not recognize these social insurance commitments as liabilities in their financial statement nor did they record the expense in their accrual budgets as such.[29] This was because these commitments did not meet the criteria of the financial accounting standards for being

---

[23] Algemene (2007), p. 12.

[24] Blondal (2004), p. 116.

[25] Ibid.

[26] US GAO (2000), pp. 216–7.

[27] Algemene (2007), p. 12.

[28] Blondal (2004), p. 116.

[29] US GAO (2000), p. 218.

recognized as liabilities. That being the case, it really depends on how the financial accounting standards define liability recognition.

At a more fundamental level, there is the concern that the budgeting needs of the government, which are premised upon the principle of democratic accountability, cannot be adequately served by a private sector-based accrual system that tends to concentrate on financial performance and profitability.[30] We need to recognize that, after all, the accrual basis is just a means or tool for decision-making and not an end in itself. Since the government has to play social and developmental roles, the accrual systems it adopts need to be adapted to the requirements of the social and developmental policies and commitments of the government. However, the bottom line is that the focus of accrual budgeting in the government should be to ensure that the output and outcome of its spending are commensurate with the inputs, and the long-term sustainability of government programmes is captured appropriately.[31] Another concern is about the need for valuing assets (such as museums, hospitals and military hardware) that produce no income stream and for which no market exists.[32] Governments, particularly those that operate in a democracy, are custodians of the money raised from their citizens, and they have a duty to ensure that assets created through such sources are looked after properly.[33] That being the case, it is important to record such assets in the books of accounts and to provide for depreciation even for entities that produce no income stream.

On the whole, the benefits that accrual system would bring to the government are substantial. By adopting accrual budgeting, the government will be in a better position to assess its financial performance and financial position. An accrual budget will help in preparing the position of assets and liabilities of the government, which is not possible under the cash-based system. It would also help in better fund management and evaluation of the performance of various departments. Further, accrual systems will help in estimating the cost of services more appropriately, which would be a critical input for managerial decision-making.[34] That being the case, accrual budgeting will be a useful tool to address concerns of performance, sustainability and accountability.[35]

As we noted, a number of countries have adopted accrual systems. The countries which have adopted full accrual accounting, but still follow cash-based budgeting are: Canada (while the federal government adopts cash budgets, several Canadian provinces have adopted accrual budgeting), Japan, the USA, Italy, the UK, Portugal, Azerbaijan and Uzbekistan.[36] Countries which have set in motion the process of moving over to accrual-based accounting systems are: France, Fiji Islands, Indonesia, Marshall Islands, Peoples' Republic of China, Philippines, Republic of Korea, Sri

---

[30]Shah (2007), p. 9.

[31]GASAB (2015), p. 10.

[32]Shah (2007), p. 9.

[33]GASAB (2015), p. 5.

[34]GASAB (2015), p. 10.

[35]US GAO (2000), p. 222.

[36]GASAB (2015), p. 6.

Lanka and Mongolia.[37] The countries which have moved over (or moving over) to accrual accounting and budgeting are: New Zealand, Australia, the Netherlands (in the process of introducing full accrual budgeting), Sweden (in the process of introducing full accrual budgeting) and Switzerland (in the process of introducing full accrual budgeting).[38]

2 Experiences of New Zealand and Australia

2.1 New Zealand

2.1.1 The Setting

The period from the 1960s to 1980s was a bad time for New Zealand's economy.[39] During this period, New Zealand suffered from two shocks. The first shock came with New Zealand being deprived of its assured market when UK joined the European community. The second shock was from the OPEC oil crisis which drove up the cost of energy. A currency crisis developed in the first half of 1984 when there was a substantial outflow of foreign exchange. There was also a parliamentary election in 1984, and the Labour Party formed the government. The foreign exchange market was shut down immediately after the election, and when it reopened, the New Zealand dollar was devalued by 20%. Inflation was soaring and so did unemployment.

The newly elected Labour government initiated wide-ranging reforms, driven mainly by financial and economic considerations.[40] It introduced a comprehensive agenda of financial reforms, by making performance the determining factor for all activities in the government. In order to reflect performance, the accounting and budgeting system had to meet several requirements. It needed to generate information to enable comparisons of efficiency and effectiveness of government activities across public and private sectors. It also needed to generate information to produce statements of service performance. In addition, the accounting and budgeting system had to generate aggregate financial information for the government as a whole. There was the need to produce cost-based information in order to manage for performance (outputs).[41] Budgets and accounts had to be prepared on an output basis, and service performance information had to be generated.

Only an accrual system was in a position to meet these requirements. The accrual system could accurately cost the resource use in producing outputs. It could help in assessing the performance in relation to output production, providing information

[37] Ibid.

[38] Ibid.

[39] Das (2006), p. 48.

[40] Algemene (2007), p. 66.

[41] Algemene (2007), p. 65.

to the legislature about the effectiveness and efficiency of resource use, comparing efficiency and effectiveness across governmental activities and between the government and private sector and assessing performance of government departments, and the achievement of the government as a whole.[42] It could also capture and measure both the ownership and purchase interests of the government.[43]

The Public Finance Act 1989 stipulated that all departments of the government should change over to accruals in both accounting and budgeting in three years' time.[44] The Act also stipulated that the financial statements of the departments and for the government as a whole should conform to generally accepted accounting practice (GAAP).[45] This was realized in 1991 (within 2 years). The first set of financial statements for the Government of New Zealand on an accrual basis was prepared for the six months ending 31 December 1991.[46] With this, New Zealand became the first country in the world to present Central government financial statements on an accrual basis.

2.1.2 The Budget

The accrual budgetary process in New Zealand reflects two key features:

- The need for the legislature to exercise effective control over the activities of government departments
- The requirement to reflect performance expectations arising from the government's purchase and ownership interests in the department.[47]

Appropriations in New Zealand are made for costs to be incurred in producing the outputs. Full costs are measured on an accrual basis, including depreciation and capital charge. Capital injections are appropriated and paid in cash in the year appropriated. Benefits and grants are appropriated on a cash basis, although it is now considered that there may be merit in accrual appropriations, as situations arise where an obligation to pay a benefit or grant occurs near the year's end, payment is not made until the following year.[48]

A department's budget is published in two documents: Estimates Appropriation and Departmental Forecast Reports and submitted to Parliament simultaneously by the Minister of Finance.[49] The Estimates contain the 'votes'—the seven categories of appropriations. The Departmental Forecast Reports contain (a) statement of objectives (b) forecast financial statements and (c) statement of responsibility.

---

[42] Das (2006), p. 53.

[43] OECD (1993), p. 40.

[44] Algemene (2007), p. 65.

[45] Das (2006), pp. 53–4.

[46] Das (2006), p. 56.

[47] Das (2006), pp. 63–4.

[48] Das (2006), p. 64.

[49] Algemene (2007), p. 67.

The statement of objectives contains performance criteria (for each class of output, including information on quantity, quality, delivery time and cost), expected revenue and cost (for each class of output) and financial performance forecast. The forecast financial statements contain estimated statements of financial position, operating statement, cash flow statement and the statement of accounting policies. The statement of responsibility is issued by the top level in the government.

The department's annual financial statement, together with the statement of service performance, forms part of the departmental annual report. The statement of service performance (including notes) presents efficiency indicators to indicate whether the organization has achieved its performance targets or not. The statement is also covered by the audit office's report. The other parts of the Central government—the Crown entities and state-owned enterprises—prepare similar financial statements. The financial year in New Zealand runs from 1 July to 30 June.[50]

Consolidation takes place when the overall budget (estimates of appropriations) is prepared for each budget year containing aggregate statements of appropriations and all votes. Annual consolidated financial statements for the government of New Zealand are also prepared. In fact, New Zealand Inc. publishes government accounts in a manner similar to those in a private company, the first government in the world to do so.[51] Since 1994, parliament has been authorizing the cost of services performed (outputs).[52] Formal appropriation takes place at the level of the 'votes', a group of one or more appropriations for which a minister is responsible and which are managed by a single department. Appropriation gives the minister the power to incur or enter into expenditures, costs and obligations.

2.1.3 Standards

The Accounting Standards Review Board (ASRB), a statutory body, is the standards setter.[53] NZ GAAP is set out in the New Zealand Financial Reporting Standards (FRS) issued by the Financial Reporting Standards Board and approved by ASRB.[54] Approval by the ASRB means that the standards have legal backing as they apply to the Crown, government departments, Crown entities, local authorities, issuers of securities and to all companies. A significant feature of the standards setting in New Zealand is that a common set of standards is established both for the public and private sectors.[55]

---

[50] Ibid, p. 67.
[51] Das (2006), pp. 68–9.
[52] Algemene (2007), p. 68.
[53] Das (2006), p. 54.
[54] Algemene (2007), p. 68.
[55] Das (2006), p. 54.

2.2 *Australia*

2.2.1 The Setting

During 1970s, Australia experienced declining international competitiveness and mounting fiscal deficits.[56] As a result, the country had to seek and negotiate substantial foreign and public debts. When the Australian Labour Party came to power in 1983, it embarked on wide-ranging reforms to improve the efficiency and effectiveness of the public sector and its accountability to government and Parliament.[57] The implementation of these reforms demanded better information in order to assess the effectiveness of programmes and ensure more efficient allocation of resources. More comprehensive information on revenues and expenses, and assets and liabilities was a subset of such information.[58] The idea of enacting these reforms was to ensure that the departments achieve maximum outsourcing, subject to value for money, efficiency and public policy considerations.[59] That being the case, comprehensive financial information was needed for evaluating programmes and proposals, determining prices for goods and services, lease-buy alternatives, and benchmarking and outsourcing.[60]

In 1992, the government appointed a federal-state working party to consider issues relating to government accounting, reporting and budgeting. The working party recommended that financial statements should be prepared on an accrual basis.[61] The Australian Accounting Research Federation also prepared an exposure draft on financial reporting by government departments, which recommended the adoption of accruals.[62] The Department of Finance initiated a pilot study in 1992 to assess the value of these two reports. The study endorsed the findings of the reports and recommended adoption of accrual accounting.[63] In November 1992, the Minister for Finance announced that federal government departments would move to financial reporting on an accrual basis for the financial year ending 30 June 1995.[64]

Following the successful introduction of accrual accounting, the need for an integrated resource management and accountability framework was emphasized by the National Commission of Audit in the Management Advisory Board's Beyond Bean Counting and also, in reports by parliamentary committees.[65] In addition, there was dissatisfaction in parliament about the mismatch between the budget and the

[56]Ibid, p. 70.

[57]OECD (1993), p. 26.

[58]Ibid.

[59]Ibid.

[60]Das (2006), p. 73.

[61]OECD (1993), pp. 27–8.

[62]Das (2006), p. 74.

[63]Ibid.

[64]OECD (1993), p. 28.

[65]Das (2006), p. 76.

accounts. The government decided to adopt accrual budgeting, and the first accrual-based budget was prepared for the 1999–2000 financial year.[66]

2.2.2 The Budget and Appropriation

The accrual budget in Australia contains (a) planned outcomes (b) planned outputs (c) a budgeted operating statement (statement of financial performance) (d) a budgeted cash flow statement (planned purchase and financing of assets by departments) and (e) notes.[67] The financial statements are part of the annual report. The other main component of the annual report is the report on performance (report on the realization of outcomes). The main components of the financial statements are:

- Statement of compliance (ministerial declaration that the financial statements provide a true and fair view)
- Statement of financial performance
- Statement of financial position
- Statement of cash flow
- Statement of commitments
- Schedule of contingencies
- Notes to and forming part of the financial statements.[68]

The budgets of the various parts of the Commonwealth are combined with the federal budget, which consists principally of three parts:

- Appropriations on an accrual basis
- Budgeted operating result of the financial year
- Budgeted fiscal balance

Since 1998, the financial statements issued by the various parts of the Commonwealth have been consolidated into the consolidated financial statements for the Commonwealth of Australia.

Appropriation is based on cost, which is presented in relation to estimated effects. There are two main appropriation bills. The first appropriation bill refers to the regular annual cost of the government organization itself. The second appropriation bill relates to the states and capital injections. Appropriated amounts and planned outcomes are included in a portfolio budget statement, disclosing the outputs and financial resources necessary for each outcome (planned performance). At the end of the financial year, the planned performance is compared with the actual performance set out in the annual report which considers the actual outcomes, outputs and financial resources.

---

[66] Algemene (2007), p. 71.

[67] Algemene (2007), p. 72.

[68] Algemene (2007), p. 73.

2.2.3 Standards

AAS31 was issued by the Australian Public Sector Accounting Standards Board in 1996, setting out standards for financial reporting by the federal, state and territory governments.[69] AAS31 requires the adoption of full accrual accounting, and it prescribes model, general-purpose reports that can be modified to suit the particular needs of a reporting entity.[70] The statements, which present whole-of-government accounts using GAAP, are usually audited by the auditor general. Australian budgets that are presented in accordance with the Accounts Uniform Presentation Framework are based on two different standards: AAS31 and the Accrual Government Finance Statistics (GFS) Framework of the Australian Bureau of Statistics (the national accounting system).[71]

2.3 Insights Gained from the Experiences of New Zealand and Australia

In order to gain insights from the experiences of New Zealand and Australia with adoption of accrual budgeting, we now evaluate the contribution of accrual budgeting in areas of public performance, sustainability and accountability in these two countries.

2.3.1 Performance

A report by the Government Accounting Office of the US Government, which analyzed the experiences of New Zealand and Australia, found that accrual budgeting had addressed performance management challenges in the following four ways:

- Reflecting and supporting decentralized and performance-based accountability systems
- Facilitating more competitive, business-like approaches to provision of government goods and services
- Fostering cultural change that heightens awareness of performance and financial management issues
- Encouraging more efficient and effective resource management, particularly in respect of capital assets.[72]

---

[69] Das (2006), p. 77.

[70] Ibid.

[71] Algemene (2007), p. 74.

[72] US GAO (2000), p. 209.

2.4 *Decentralized and Performance-Based Accountability Systems*

In New Zealand and Australia, adoption of accrual budgeting gave government managers considerable autonomy which included increased freedom over the use of resources. However, the government was also in a position to hold its managers accountable for delivering specified results within balanced costs. Because accrual budgeting offered a tool to match costs with the provision of goods and services, it could support decentralized management systems that promoted managerial flexibility as a means of improving efficiency and effectiveness.[73]

2.5 *Facilitating More Competitive Approaches*

In these two countries, adoption of accrual systems enabled the debate to focus on the nature of the various services being delivered by a department, what the government is paying for them and how effective is the management of the department delivering them.[74] This was instrumental in enhancing performance by enabling comparisons among alternative sources of provision of goods and services. This allowed better choices to be made about whether particular goods and services should be provided by a government department or by a private sector entity.[75]

2.6 *Fostering Cultural Change*

Adoption of accrual budgeting promoted a culture change for the people working in the government through an acceptance of the benefits it offers, an understanding of how to use the additional information generated by accrual budgeting and inducing an ownership of the budgeting reform.[76] The Australian National Commission on Audit was of the view that a full accrual framework, including accrual budgeting, was an essential component of the structural and cultural change the government was seeking for a more competitive, efficient and effective public sector.[77]

---

[73] Ibid.

[74] Das (2006), p. 69.

[75] US GAO (2000), p. 211.

[76] Das (2006), p. 196.

[77] US GAO (2000), p. 212.

2.7 *Encouraging Efficient and Effective Resource Management*

Accrual budgeting encouraged more efficient and effective resource management, particularly in respect of capital assets.[78] It improved resource management by providing an analytical base and incentives for assessing performance and managing costs. In particular, it provided information on the value of under-utilized assets; on the basis of such information, decisions were taken, leading to better management of assets.[79]

2.7.1 Sustainability

Accrual budgeting led to better understanding of the long-term sustainability of government policies by providing (a) better budget recognition of liabilities and (b) a more complete set of information to assess the country's financial health. Adoption of accrual budgeting in these two countries helped to improve decision-making by providing more complete information in order to understand how particular decisions could affect the country's financial health. It provided a more comprehensive measure of the total activity of the government and the long-term effects of current policy, thereby bringing about sustainability and sound fiscal management and providing policymakers with information about the financial effects of current policies on future generations.[80]

2.7.2 Accountability

New Zealand's Fiscal Responsibility Act and Australia's Charter of Budget Honesty asked for the release, at the start of the budget process, of fiscal strategy statements setting out the broad strategic goals of the government. This is now being done in these two countries and this was made possible because of the adoption of accrual systems. The process of releasing fiscal strategy statements at the start of the budget exercise improved transparency. It also helped in setting of priorities, both within areas of expenditure and across them, by reference to the broader strategic goals of the government.[81] In addition, accrual budgeting based on accounting standards increased the consistency and credibility of the budget information because the accounting standards are independently developed, well documented and more readily understood.[82]

---

[78] Ibid.

[79] Das (2006), pp. 146–7.

[80] Das (2006), p. 86.

[81] Das (2006), p. 69.

[82] US GAO (2000), p. 219.

On the whole, the experiences of these two countries with accrual budgeting indicate that it has been a useful tool in addressing concerns about public performance, sustainability and accountability.[83]

3 The Indian Context

Budgeting in India involves the presentation of an Annual Financial Statement, which is a requirement mandated by the Constitution in Articles 112 and 202. The Annual Financial Statement is a statement of estimated receipts and expenditures of the government which needs to be laid before the legislature for every financial year. The revenue budget consists of the revenue receipts of the government (tax revenues and other revenues) and the expenditures (payments) met from these revenues. The capital budget consists of capital receipts and payments.

Governments in India have historically accounted and budgeted on a cash basis. The cash system was established in colonial India by the Regulation Act of 1773, which required Indian accounts to be consolidated and presented to the British Parliament.[84] A system of annual budgeting was introduced in 1861–2, and by the year 1865, a system of monthly consolidation of accounts had been established in place of annual consolidation.[85] In 1884, a Comptroller and Auditor General was appointed and made responsible for conducting appropriation audit and supervising government accounting. After independence, the office of the Comptroller and Auditor General was continued and invested with both accounting and audit functions. Article 150 of the Indian Constitution stipulates, "The accounts of the Union and of the States shall be kept in such form as the President may, on the advice of the Comptroller and Auditor General of India, prescribe." The Comptroller and Auditor General created the Government Accounting Standards Advisory Board (GASAB) in August 2002 and charged it with the responsibility of formulating standards relating to accounting and financial reporting by the Union, the States, and the Union Territories with legislature.

As we noted, accrual systems have been adopted by countries across the world for government accounting during the last four decades. Taking note of this development, the Twelfth Finance Commission suggested in December 2004 that accrual accounting should be introduced in India for government accounting.[86] The Commission recommended[87]:

- The Central Government should gradually move towards accrual basis of accounting (para 14.16).

---

[83] US GAO (2000), p. 222.

[84] Das (2006), p. 17.

[85] Ibid.

[86] Kothari (2013), p. 2.

[87] Ministry of Finance (2005).

- In the interim period, additional information in the form of statements should be appended to the present system of cash accounting to enable more informed decision-making. The additional information may relate to subsidies; expenditure on salaries; expenditure on pensions; committed liabilities; maintenance expenditure; segregation of salary, non-salary portions and liabilities; and repayment schedule on outstanding debts (para 14.16).
- The definition of revenue and fiscal deficit may be standardized and instructions for a uniform classification code down to the object head may be issued to all the states (para 14.17).
- A National Institute of Public Financial Accountants should be set up by the Government of India and its charter should be decided in consultation with the Comptroller and Auditor General (para 14.18).

In 2005, the government accepted the recommendations of the Twelfth Finance Commission in principle and asked GASAB to prepare a detailed roadmap and an operational framework for adoption of accrual accounting.[88]

As we can see, the recommendation was for a stage-by-stage approach to adopt accrual systems. The Thirteenth Finance Commission endorsed this by asking the government to move cautiously in the matter of changing over to accrual accounting.[89] The Commission, in fact, suggested the adoption of a 'bubble-up' approach in which local bodies like large municipalities and Panchayati Raj Institutions would choose accrual accounting, given the fact that the National Municipal Accounting Manual integrating the principles of accrual accounting had already been prepared with guidance from the Comptroller and Auditor General of India.[90] The Second Administrative Reforms Commission also asked for a cautionary approach to be adopted in the matter. It recommended that, before implementing the change to accrual systems, training and capacity-building requirements of accounting professionals and stakeholders in the decision-making process should be addressed in accordance with the roadmap of implementation.[91] It also recommended that prior to the adoption of accrual accounting, there should be appropriate alignment between the plan, accounts and budget and also, a more feasible financial information system.[92]

As mandated by the government, GASAB has prepared a roadmap, and it has been accepted by the Government of India.[93] GASAB's roadmap specifies the activities and milestones to be completed for migration to the accrual system. It envisages a transition period of five to six years in three stages.[94] The stages envisaged are:

---

[88]Jena (2013), p. 7.

[89]Sasidharan (2011), p. 275.

[90]Ibid.

[91]Ibid.

[92]Ibid.

[93]Rai (2011), pp. 5–6.

[94]Sasidharan (2011), p. 277.

1. In the first stage, value addition to be made by adding separate statements on salaries, subsidies, interest, pension, etc.
2. In the second stage, value addition to be made in the extant system with greater disclosures such as arrears in revenues, committed liabilities, etc.
3. The final stage to consist of conversion to accrual-based accounting.[95]

GASAB has also developed a detailed 'Operational Framework for Accrual Basis of Accounting in Governments in India', which provides an overall architecture of the accounting model consistent with constitutional reporting needs.[96] The process involves the creation of adequate database necessary for implementation of accrual accounting, identification of assets and liabilities, and creation of asset registers.[97]

Considerable progress has been made in the matter. The National Municipal Accounting Manual which incorporates the principle of accrual accounting in a stage-wise approach has been prepared by the Comptroller and Auditor General.[98] Twenty-one state governments have agreed in principle to move to accrual accounting.[99] Several urban local bodies have already introduced accrual accounting. A number of state governments have adopted a double-entry accounting system for their rural local bodies.[100] GASAB has approved two accrual standards: IGFRS-2 (property, plant and equipment) and IGFRS-5 (contingent liabilities and contingent assets: disclosure requirements).

Central government entities like the Railways and the Department of Posts have conducted pilot studies on migration to accrual accounting, and some pilot studies have also been conducted in states like Madhya Pradesh, Haryana, Gujarat and Rajasthan under the aegis of GASAB.[101] The idea is that these pilot studies would be the precursor to a national rollout of changeover to accrual accounting. These studies have been conducted by teams drawn from the office of the Accountant Generals of the concerned states with guidance from national and international consultants and with the support of respective state governments. The funding for these pilot studies has been provided by the World Bank.

These pilot studies provide two important insights.[102] The first one is about the criticality of a robust IT system for maintenance of accurate, reliable, valid and integrated data and generation of accounting and financial information. That being the case, it has been suggested that there is need for constituting Enterprises Resource Planning (ERP) systems like SAP across the country, both at the Centre and the States.[103] The other insight is that there should be an assessment of training needs

[95]Ibid.

[96]Rai (2011), p. 6.

[97]Ibid.

[98]Jena (2013), pp. 7–8.

[99]Rai (2011), p. 7.

[100]Jena (2013), p. 8.

[101]Rai (2011), p. 7.

[102]Ibid.

[103]Ibid.

in terms of capacity building for managing the transition, implementation and management of accrual systems.

The pilot studies suggest that the transition to accrual systems can be expensive, mainly because of the requirement of substantial investment in IT infrastructure.[104] There are two recent government initiatives which are relevant in this context.[105] One is that several state governments are computerizing their treasury systems. The second initiative is the Government of India scheme of computerizing treasuries on a mission mode in 626 districts at a cost of about 600 crores. It makes sense to take advantage of these two computerization initiatives to build in the required IT capacity by providing appropriate accrual heads of accounts.

The National Round Table Conference on Accrual Basis was held in Delhi on 7 May 2009. The conference, convened by GASAB, deliberated on measures required for migration to accrual accounting and laid down the roadmap for the process. In addition, on 21 June 2011, there was a day-long National Conference of state finance ministers on "Accrual-Based Financial Reporting in Government". Inaugurating the conference, the Union Finance Minister sounded a note of caution by stating, "I understand that some pilot studies have been undertaken in selected government departments and other entities. Based on the knowledge gained through these pilot studies and the experience of other countries, it is clear that introduction of accrual accounting is not going to be an easy task. In fact, we need to clearly identify the critical and the preparatory steps which need to be taken…there are many challenges in view of the complex nature of administration and accounting in a diverse nation as India and these have to be carefully factored in."[106] However, the Comptroller and Auditor General was more confident and told the conference, "since reforms are always evolved over a period of time, and it could take a preparation time of 5 years, I would look forward to active participation from all the participants present here today to flag issues to be addressed to make the process of transition smooth. If we want to retain our position among the global leaders, we must move with a definite timeframe to achieve the transition towards accrual based financial reporting."[107]

Based on the deliberations of the conference on "Accrual-Based Financial Reporting in Government", the following timeline was assigned for the implementation process.

- In the first phase of implementation, the government would expand the IT sector in the country and revamp the existing norms and procedures to make way for accrual accounts. The time period covering 2011–2013 is identified as the first phase.
- In the second phase of implementation, financial reforms that are needed for effective functioning of accrual accounting system will be taken up. This phase will extend from 2013 to 2015.

[104]Rai (2011), p. 9.

[105]Ibid.

[106]Ministry of Finance (2011), p. 1.

[107]Rai (2011), p. 12.

- The third phase of implementation will finally result in an accrual system of accounting in India. This phase starting in 2015 will see the ultimate switch over of the current Indian financial accounting system into the all-new accrual method.[108]

In furtherance of the implementation schedule, a number of steps have already been initiated. In September 2011, an apex committee for implementation of and transition to accrual-based accounting systems in government was constituted. In 2012, the Union Finance Minister stressed the need for strengthening the process of developing accounting standards to keep pace with other countries in the world. GASAB is engaged in developing the version 1.0 for financial statement formats, based on the findings of the pilot studies. Work on a comprehensive migration manual is being done by GASAB in order to facilitate entry-level implementation. A workshop on experience-sharing of transition to accrual accounting in the Railways and Department of Post was held on 24 March 2014. However, there is an impression that doubts regarding costs and benefits, complexities and risks involved while adopting accrual accounting and administrative preparation and key requirements of capacity building weigh heavily on the transition path.[109]

It is very likely that migration to accrual accounting may take more time than has been estimated. But we need not worry about the delay of a few years in the migration process because most countries which have moved to accrual accounting have taken at least seven to ten years for the transition.[110] New Zealand, which made the fastest transition, took nearly five years to come to the stage of producing the first accrual budget.[111] Canada which is a country similar to India in terms of the federal structure and complexity took about eight years for completing the transition.[112] Considering the size and complexity of India, it is estimated that the transition process may take about ten to twelve years.[113] Of course, India has the advantages of a late-developer: it can learn from the experience of other countries which have successfully transitioned to the accrual regime.

There is also the question of the additional time that would be taken to implement an accrual budgeting system. Full accrual budgeting would require at least three to five years from the time the transition to accrual accounting is achieved. In the ultimate analysis, a delay of one or two years here and there does not matter much; what matters is that India should move over successfully to the full accrual regime consisting of accounting, financial reporting and budgeting. Since economists and accounting authorities generally attribute the sovereign debt crisis including the Greece effect to opaque government accounting and practices,[114] it would make sense for India to migrate to clear, efficient and timely accrual accounting, reporting and budgeting.

---

[108] Adwaith (2011), p. 1.

[109] Jena (2012).

[110] GASAB (2015), p. 8.

[111] Das (2006), pp. 56–7.

[112] GASAB (2015), p. 8.

[113] Ibid.

[114] Ramakrishnan and Sivabalan (2011), p. 1.

References

Adwaith. (2011). *The concept, mechanism and advantages of accrual accounting in India.*

Algemene R. (2007). *Accrual budgeting and accounting in central government: Budgets and accounts in balance.* The Hague.

Blondal, J. (2003). *Accrual accounting and budgeting: Key issues and recent development*. Paris: Organization for Economic Cooperation and Development.

Blondal, J. R. (2004). Issues in accrual budgeting. *OECD Journal on Budgeting, 4*(1), 103–121.

Das, S. K. (2006). *Rethinking public accounting: Policy and practice of accrual accounting in government*. New Delhi: Oxford University Press.

Ehsan, R., Parveizi, M., & Nazari, K., et al. (2012). Government accounting: An assessment of theory, purposes and standards. *Interdisciplinary Journal of Contemporary Research in Business, 3*(9), 521–531.

GAO, A. B. (2000). *Experiences of other nations and implications for the United States*. GAO-AIMD-00-57, pp 193–222.

GASAB (Government Accounting Standards Advisory Board). (2015). *Primer on accrual accounting.*

Hepworth, N. (2002). *Changing to accrual accounting in Central Government (with special reference to the experiences of the United Kingdom).* Norway: Institute of Public Finance Limited.

Jena, P. R. (2012). *Public financial management in India: Reforms and scope for innovations.*

Jena, P. R. (2013). *Improving public financial management in India: Opportunities to move forward*. Working Paper No. 2013-123.

Kothari, S. S. (2013). *Government accounting—Accrual is the way to go.* The Hindu Business Line, 8 September.

Meyers, R. T. (2009). Ball of confusion' in federal budgeting: A shadow agenda for deliberative reform of the budget process. *Public Administration Review, 69*(2), 211–233.

Ministry of Finance. (2005). *Main recommendations of the twelfth finance commission.* Government of India.

Organisation for Economic Co-operation and Development. (1993). *Accounting for what? The value of accrual accounting to the public sector.* Paris: Organisation for Economic Co-operation and Development.

PIB. (2011). *Identify steps necessary for introduction of accrual accounting*. FM Inaugurates Conference of State Finance Ministers, 21 June.

Ramakrishnan, V., & Sivabalan, S. (2011). In search of a Kautilya. *The Hindu Business Line*, February 16, 2011.

Sasidharan, K. P. (2011). Reforms in government accounting and financial reporting. *The Chartered Accountant 60*(2), 274–277.

Schick, A. (2007). Performance budgeting and accrual budgeting: Decision rules or analytic tools? *OECD Journal on Budgeting, 7*(2), 109 (World Bank, Washington DC).

Shah, A. (Ed.). (2007). *Budgeting and budgetary institutions*. Washington DC: World Bank.

World Bank. (2002). *Accrual accounting and budgeting: Key issues and recent developments*. Washington DC: World Bank.

Wynne, A. (2003). Do private sector financial statements provide a suitable model for public sector accounts? *European Group of Public Administration,* 1–22.

Chapter 10
Revisiting Financial Accountability

A. Premchand

During recent years, there has been a growing demand from the people, their elected representatives and the democratic institutions for increased accountability of governments. In part, this was an expression of a severe discontent with the way in which governments have been functioning at various levels in the country and the perceptions that the actions of government have been contributing to the emergence of cronyism and several oligarchies that seem to have gained a strong hand in directing the policies of the government and the use of public resources, not for public benefit but for advancement of personal interests of the dominant personalities in politics, in industry and practically in all other spheres. This growing perception has morphed into a single demand for greater accountability. At this stage, the idea of accountability is variously interpreted by the different groups demanding actions. Some consider that greater accountability is the panacea for all societal and governmental ills and that it provides a comprehensive remedy for the record **levels** of corruption prevalent in the country. Others contend that improved channels of accountability would put the governments on a leash and that with gradual improvement in the system of governance, there would be a new dawn and the beginning of a new era. In reality, however, the hopes of the people would appear to be pegged at a somewhat less realistic level and inevitably there would be disappointments. Available evidence does not lend much support to the realization of the community's hopes.

In this chapter, an attempt is made in the first instance, to consider the historical evolution of the concept of accountability. Inevitably, it is more in the nature of a synoptic sketch and no attempt is made to be comprehensive. Rather, it is the milestones that receive recognition and discussion.

Financial accountability, as it has come to be interpreted, revolves around four elements, all of which represent the important elements of the financial cycle of operations of governments. These include appropriation, the first stage under which

A. Premchand (✉)
82, Whisper Valley, DARGA, Hyderabad 500008, India
e-mail: premchandarigapudi@gmail.com

G. Karnam (ed.), *Public Budgeting in India*, India Studies in Business and Economics, https://doi.org/10.1007/978-81-322-3917-8_10

the people's representatives approve the appropriation of funds to be spent by the government. The amounts to be spent and the purposes for which they are to be spent from part of a compact between government and the society. The spending authority is limited to a period of one year, (although some exceptions have been made), and a new beginning is made for the next year. This stage reflects the legislative approval and also is the stage where legitimacy is provided for governmental actions. To ensure compliance, the legislature attaches various conditions for controlling the government actions. The second element is what is called reappropriation which reflects an element of the framework of delegated power to governments permitting them to change the appropriations in minor ways so that the overall aim of the primary appropriation is not materially and unilaterally changed by governments. The third element, which also underscores the constant need for vigilance, is misappropriation of funds. The funds approved by the representatives of the people may be embezzled or used for wrong purposes. The fourth element represents the record of amounts spent and the status of excesses and balances, if any. These are called annual accounts which are needed to be audited and thus be held accountable. These four stages have evolved over a period of time reflecting the pulls and pressures between the two major domains of government, viz. the executive and the legislature.

1 Accountability in Ancient Times

The experiences relevant for purposes of discussion here—are Greece and Ancient India. The former was the oldest democracy, while the latter is recognised now as the biggest democracy in the world although the form was very different in prewritten times. The experience of the former is relevant for the simple reason that the foundations of public accountability in general and financial accountability, more specifically, were laid there. Countries in the western world later built elaborate edifies on those foundations. In Greece, the accounts of the public bodies were read in the Senate and the councils, and the process of listening to these financial accounts came to described as audit. From the act of listening, the term was later elaborated to include verification of accounts. Accountability was the basis for calling it an audit, a term that has gained an institutionalised and independent form as government audit agencies organised themselves into an International Organisation of Supreme Audition Institutions (INTOSAI). It is an organisation based in Vienna, and all Supreme Audit Institutions are members of the organisation which is also responsible for formulating audit protocols and standards.

The beginning made in Greece did not gain many adherents until centuries later. Even in Greece, it went through periods of discontinuities as the form of government was changing from time to time. In India, (the India of that period had empires, kingdoms, urban councils, and Jaanpads or rural communities), there was no Central government then and the only empire of note was the Mauryan Empire. The political and administrative philosophy of the empire was provided by Kautilya in his famous work 'Arthashastra'. Kautilya's philosophy was a contrast to the Greek approaches in that the pivotal authority, to him, was the all—supreme, and divinely blessed and guided King. Whatever the King did was for the benefit of the people; the people trusted him to do just that—nothing more and nothing less. So, the issue of accountability did not arise. The people were the willing subjects of the King. Also, the properties and wealth of the territories belonged to the King. The key tenet for Kautilya was the strength of the kingdom's treasury. Kautilya's advice was very simple—look to the treasury for it is the key to all. To maintain that treasury, Kautilya provided architectural blueprints as to how they should be built (moats and all) and protected at all times by the army which guaranteed protection from invaders. Kautilya was also anxious to ensure that the money, not to mention the precious stones, were not stolen from the treasury. So, he advised that the King should first meet with his auditor, every day morning before moving to other matters.

What is of importance is the fundamental difference between the two approaches of Greece and India. It was also the difference between the rule by royalty and rule by the elected (although the Greek franchise admittedly was very small and far from egalitarian at this stage as it excluded women, immigrants, slaves and the poor). Although called a democracy, it was essentially a rule by the elite/representatives of the people. More significantly, it established the goal of accountability to the people. This theme became the fight in Great Britain between the crown and the members of parliament (not all of them were elected at that time. People with money could buy estates or boroughs and on that basis could become members of parliament). For the first few centuries in the Christian era, the struggle was between the parliament which tried to establish that the power to impose taxes could only be exercised with the consent of the people. Up to the sixteenth century, the legislative fight was to acquire that power to levy taxes. There was not much debate about the items of expenditure, which gradually come to be vested in the parliament. Meanwhile, the British economy went through major changes and London became the Centre of Trade. The trading guilds looked for information about the activities that were being financed by the government, but that information was not available as the British Government was not systematically well organised to compile government accounts. So, the trading guilds organised their own accounting cells to compile data on the expenditure operations of the government. Over time, however, the strategy of the guilds changed in that the accounts of the government came to be comprehensively collected and laid before the House. Later, it was felt that the accounts so compiled should be reviewed by a committee of the House. Thus, a committee on Public Accounts (now better known as PAC both in the UK and in India) came to be set up. It was charged with the duty of maintaining oversight on the annual accounts of the government. In a way, these events presaged what was to come in the Colonial India. Most legislative practices in India including the Standing Committees and Consultative Committees that came into being toward the end of twentieth century were essentially the long shadows of the practices of the House of Commons. Whether as a colony or as an independent secular and socialist republic, India always looked, whether on its own initiative or under pressure, to the Conventions in the UK.

During the eighteenth century when vast dominions in India came under the administration of the honourable company, a kind of centralised financial administration came to be introduced. There was, however, no legislature, nor any idea of setting up a watchdog until the company yielded place to the crown. Within a decade after the change of power from the Company to the crown, however, an idea was mooted not by Indians, but by the Colonial Government to establish an audit department. The idea had both opponents and supporters. The former contended that the working of an audit agency might not reflect well on the Colonial Government as each failure and lapses were likely to be pointed out by the audit department. The supporters were keen, however, that an agency should function as a countervailing power. In the event, the proponents had the final decision in their favour in that an audit department was established in 1866.

But it was a flawed arrangement whose effects continue to dominate the Indian accounting scene. The opponents to the scheme also won part of the arguments in that audit were not formed as a separate agency. The new department combined both the functions of accounting and auditing which also meant that the audit agency was auditing a set of accounts that were compiled by itself. But nobody could be an objective auditor of the accounts compiled by himself, so the compromise of having a single agency won the day and the practice continued for all intents and purposes for another century. This does not mean that there were no critics of the system both within and outside of the system. During the 1920s, based on the recommendations of the Auditor General (he was not a Comptroller then. It was a title added in the Indian constitution. It remains, however, a title only as the function of exchequer control was never introduced in India), a pilot scheme of separation of accounts from audit was introduced in, what was then called United Provinces. But the separation movement (if it was one) did not get much traction. It stopped where it started. After Independence, however, some more half-hearted attempts to separate the two functions were made and separate Pay and Accounts offices came to be organised in selected central departments. The practical consideration stalling the separation effort was the expense involved. But that consideration which held away for many decades was swept aside, when in a sudden move, and for reasons that were never specified, the audit function at the centre was separated and a separate civil accounts department came to be established in the mid-1970s. As always, however, the decision to separate the two functions was not a full one as it was limited to the Central government only. At the levels of state government, the Accountant General or its modern equivalent, Director General, continued to be both an accountant and an auditor as well. So, the anomaly, a vestige of the Colonial administration, continued in one form or other. Whether this has affected the quality of audit, in contrast to the Central government, is an issue that remains to be explored in detail. Meanwhile, the self-styled conscience keeper of the nation continues to be an odd creature in that he is an auditor of the Central government and an accountant and auditor of the twenty-nine state governments.

There were other institutional developments, however, particularly since the beginning of the demand for reforms to introduce a form of self-government. What was sought was greater participation in the making of policies that shaped the financial future of as yet a colonially administered nation. While the Public Accounts Committee continued to review the annual accounts for onward transmission of the central legislature, there was no participation of the Indian political leadership in budgetary decision making more specifically, in the determination and approval of specific expenditure proposals. So, the British Government decided to make an experiment through the organisation of a Standing Finance Committee, comprising members of the central legislature. But it was not a full legislative body in that the Secretariat of the committee was provided by the Finance Department. The committee's proceedings were printed and were widely circulated and the participation in decision making came to be welcomed, as one of the many steps in self-rule, even if the views of the committee were subject to the final approval of the Finance Member of the Council. But that did not stand in the way of enthusiastic participation of the members who relished their new role as decision makers. The committee was in existence until independence and yielded place to what came to be called as Estimates Committee.

2 Post-independence Morphing

The legislative programme of the parliament has not gone through any transformation after independence. For all intents and purposes, the financial and legislative procedures specified in the 1935 Act continued to operate during the transition between the independence and the establishment of a Republic, and even later as most of the legislative process continued as before. The firm dividing lines between the three domains—executive, legislative and judiciary continued to be maintained. Executive policy management, viz. the maintenance of the country's—governance—identification of needs, formulation of policies aimed at addressing them, allocation of financial resources for an year at a time of implement the approved policies—acquisition of man, materials and money for implementing the policies, maintaining accounts for the moneys received and spent, and approval of the annual accounts after the financial year, continued to be the main task of the executive, while the role of the legislature consisted of approval of proposed policies, appropriation of needed funds, monitoring of progress and a review of the finances at the end of the year. The last two stages were essentially taken care of by the Public Accounts Committee, while the first two stages were sought to be addressed through parliamentary debates in the Houses.

In due course, the absence of the Standing Finance Committee, which was abolished after the new constitution became operational, made the members of parliament feel that they were missing some levers of control. The parliamentary debate on budget which though extensive and for that reason appears to lack coherence was not entirely satisfactory to the members. It appeared that they were seeking a more—hands-on approach and deeper involvement in policy management. As a consequence, and following the procedure of House of Commons, an Estimates Committee came to be established. Ostensibly, as the name implied, its function was expected to be a deeper analysis of the budget estimates for each agency for the next year. But this appears to be too late a stage to have the imprint of the parliament on policy management. So, the mandate of the Estimates Committee come to be a review of the current activities (a grab all approach that was also very flexible) of government in general and specific activities of individual departments selected for study. Accordingly, the annual programme of committee included the review of horizontal themes, e.g. budgetary reform, as well as specific themes engaging the attention of ministries. The study did not focus on the economy and efficiency of departments. Rather, it was hoped that they would undertake such an effort, although in retrospect, it appears that there were no such efforts.

The Estimates Committee, together with the Public Accounts Committee became the two eyes of the parliament to secure financial accountability. It is a separate question whether this hope of a system of full-fledged system of legislative accountability was ever fulfilled, an aspect that is considered further on. Regardless of the gains, the two committees provided a good deal of stability and coherence to legislative operations. Meanwhile, as an integral part of the socialistic pattern (the constitution of India did not as yet proclaim India as a socialistic republic. It came much later with the usual zeal and exuberance associated with such proclamations. In due course, that fizz subsided and a stage has been reached where the government now needs to be reminded that it is even now a socialist republic) the state expanded considerably with many forays into the ownership and management of enterprises. Public enterprises or public-sector undertakings as they were technically called became a massive component of public sector operations. As a consequence, and with a view to afford an opportunity to the Houses to look into the operations of the enterprises, a committee on PSUs came to be set up. The two eyes now became three and seemed adequate for securing financial accountability to the legislature. The new set up continued for almost five decades, i.e. into 1990s, when the members of parliament began to feel restive as they recognised that even with three committees, the impact of the legislature on the functioning of the executive was barely discernible. The executive, it appeared to them, was not merely growing in size but was also becoming assertive as administration through the issue or ordinances, rather than through newly enacted legislation became a regular feature. If it was a tussle for turf, the legislatures recognised that they lost the argument and the battle. Meanwhile, as in the UK, the backbenchers began to press for opportunities to have their voices felt both inside and outside the Houses. The result of this clamour was the establishment of Standing and Consultative Committees for each or groups of ministries. The Standing Committees were to review the annual financial programme of each ministry and submit their findings to the full Houses—a process of furnishing meaningful inputs into budget discussion. The Consultative Committees were expected to provide an opportunity for the members to share their thoughts with the ministries. Neither the reports of the Standing Committee nor the advisory inputs of the members were binding either on the full Houses or on government. To be sure, however, they expanded the scope of legislative participation in policy making and gave a feeling of assurance to the members.

It is debatable, however, whether more of this type of legislative expansion was contributing to enhanced financial accountability of the governmental system or whether it was a case of less being adequate.

3 Changing Trends and Demands

The substantial expansion in the role of the legislatures and the role of their committees needs to be seen in the context of changing trends and demands on democratic functioning and on addressing the public needs. These changes are several and are both structural and political, and some of them are examined to assess the meaning and utility of the preceding system of financial accountability.

Structurally, the shape of the government itself has been changing in that the functioning of the Central, State and local governments has become a seamless web in which the boundaries and demarcation lines between the various governments are severely blurred. The resource transfers from the Central government to the other levels are so extensive that approximately more than 60% of the national resources are passed on to the State and Local governments. This has contributed to a situation where the roles of the respective governments in administrative decision making are far from clear. The financial relationships have contributed to a new web of dominance and dependence. There has also been a growing shift of financial decision making from local governments to the Central government, its ministries and autonomous agencies, and commissions. The transfers of money from the higher levels to the subnational governments are ring fenced with numerous conditions that provide an apparent picture of infinite detail of accountability for the levels where the moneys are spent. In turn, this has contributed to a complex picture of vertical accountability in which the local actions are said to be regularly monitored and evaluated as a part of the comprehensive computerised monitoring systems introduced during recent years. It is also the conventional belief that this improved vertical accountability is supplemented by a system of horizontal accountability where the elected representatives at the state and local government seek and receive accountability through their own inspection and audit agencies, and legislative committees that for the most part mimic the system of accountability in the Central government. The fulfilment of the goal of overall accountability in the country is dependent on the functioning of the vertical and horizontal system of accountability.

This traditional picture of accountability has come to be severely skewed in the context of the development during the last few years which contributed to a delinking of service provision and its financing. In the traditional system, the services provided to the public, such as education and health, were both funded and provided directly by the government or under its supervision. The new system of public–private partnerships changed this relationship in that services are provided by the private sector while the funding continues to be within the responsibilities of the government. This has contributed to the emergence of a third-party provider of services where the providing is not a part of the governmental system and where the receivers of services are as remote as the providers of services. The third-party payment system has converted the government into ATMs, where the providers are many, each with its own operational system, and the receiving public is as extensive as the community itself. This substantial change in the provision of services remains, however, to be supplemented by a new framework of regulations and a well-developed system of vertical and horizontal accountability.

In addition to the above structural changes that have and continue to take place, there have also been significant changes in the behavioural patterns of government on the one hand and the voting public, on the other. A major change is to be found in the nature of democratic functioning itself. More than four decades ago, a well-known political leader, Lord Hailsham, in the UK pointed out that there are in effect two democracies, the one is promised and the other one actually found in practice (See his, The Dilemma of Democracy, Collins, London, 1978). His view was that once a party is elected into power for a period of five years, it starts becoming less democratic and more autocratic. They impose new regimes that are of questionable democratic inclinations and tend to rule through ordinances and manipulative measures. He wrote 'we are in fact governed by a bureaucracy of mandarins and their subordinates imposing (emphasis added) on a people partisan policies devised by a government of amateurs who have achieved their position by a minority of votes under on unfair voting system, bringing into parliament candidates elected by local caucuses of activists or outside bodies and have little else to commend them but their loyalties' (pp. 160–161). This led, as the Indian system of governance conclusively show to the growth power centres, both within and outside the governments that tend to impose their own political preferences, ignoring the parliamentary consultation process, all of which raise leading questions on the nature and utility of the system of political accountability. At each level, the issue is examined in political terms and even routine financial transactions are legalised or regularised on the basis of voting taking place under a party whip.

Yet another aspect with a pervasive impact on the functioning of democracy itself relates to the practices of government which not merely appear to but in reality, stray away from the professed ideals. The world of democracy, people find, is very different from what was aimed at or what was intended to be. Every democracy develops its own set of values that govern the functioning of its institutions and that go beyond the electoral process. These values keep changing from time to time reflecting the changing goals and priorities of the people. Values are of importance as they tend to influence the views of the decision makers as well as those of the people who are at the receiving end. These values could be and indeed are different from what the political leadership would like the people to believe. There are many aspects of civic life where the democracy in practice is different. One such significant value that dominated public aspirations and discourse related to equality for all. After independence, it was recognised that the hierarchically structured, Hindu society could be a major obstacle for securing equality. So, beginning with the constitution, a slew of legislative measures was enacted to bring about equality. Further, in the name of protective social discrimination and affirmative action, political participation was assured through reservation of seats; advancement of backward classes was sought to achieve through reservation of quotas in educational institutions and government services. These measures have ended up creating new and privileged classes (the later because the benefits of a number of programmes are aimed at them) that have led to the creation of new power blocks. The end of all political ambition is now to get elected as many times as possible so that they continue to be in power. The use of power, legitimate or otherwise, has become the dominating theme. But as sociologist R. S. Khare points out (p. 68, *Culture and Democracy*, 1985) 'democratic use of power is at once attractive as well as alien to the people'. The political class is contributing to the spread and perpetuation of power both within and outside of government. Thus, power is centralised in government or proxy centres of power outside government. Along with government processes, there are also traditional processes, such as the caste-based *Khap* systems that dispense justice further along with the judicial institutions. Elections take place, for the most part in a fair way, as specified by the objective Election Commission of India, but the informal systems have their own ways that defy both equality and representation. Often, politicians would appear to prefer non-democratic means to achieve their objectives. Thus, the government engages in extra judicial killings (otherwise known as encounters), imprisons people for long periods without bail, procure land for public purposes that are often disguised to serve personal enrichment, evolve laws and procedures, that confer additional privileges and thus power on themselves. Thus, any enquiry into the allegations of corruption requires the approval of the President or the Governor, and in the case of officers from selected services, from the Union Home Ministry. The state-owned agencies such as Air India are expected to provide special privileges to the honourable members of parliament and true to nature all of them insist on equality while craving for special treatment. Their attachment to democratic value appears to be skin deep. While they have no hesitation to grant special powers to armed forces and thus create, in effect, two systems of administration—one run by the armed forces and another by the civil authorities; the armed forces are also given large amounts of money to be distributed to the political class (no part of it is public) and thus play a political role, if only discreetly, in India's life. Their professed attachment to democratic power does not extend to establish democratic governance to their own political parties. Pursuit of power, based on caste, has contributed to a proliferation of political parties (there are more than 400 political parties registered with the Election Commission of India) with each one intended to further the personal/caste interests of a local leader.

There are any number of complex layers of functions both within and outside the government that often have the effect of subverting the constitutional intent or more important is end of all efforts, the establishment of a just society. Democracy in India is judged in terms of experiential adequacy, justificatory adequacy and explanatory adequacy. It is considered to be experientially adequate when it is viewed as adequate for practical reasons and is an improvement on the previous conditions. From this limited point, Indian development comes out with high marks as democracy offers a practical system of governance in a society that continues to be hierarchical and that is divided by religions, race, language, not to mention political ideology. These add to the moral, legal and cultural justifications for adequacy and point out that a caste member getting some benefits because of his caste then democracy is adequate for him. But, it also becomes a basis for legal discrimination that ceases to be democratic. Since this criterion does not satisfy all, it may not offer satisfaction from the second adequacy test, viz. justificatory adequacy. What is more, this becomes context dependent and what is offered as a political justification by the leaders. This also leads to issues about explanatory justification when democracy is considered as equivalent to government in its various manifestations, then some issues arise and democracy end up as a melting pot in which many layers, contradictions and compromises emerge as regular features and each one plays out in its own way, sometimes violently and often times, with luck and fortitude, peacefully. The contradictions and tensions become everyday's regular feature, and the common man accepts it. There are some elements which oppose the system and oppose the whole institutional framework, which they want to be replaced. These rebels are also a part of the society and are frequently suppressed by brutal force deployed by the government. This too is a part of democratic functioning although the means deployed may be anything but democratic. In such situations, the tenor and focus of accountability itself may become a victim of democracy, as it did, for a brief period in the early 1970s. The content of accountability also changes when form has the better of substance. Thus, in a context where there was only a single member in the legislature from the opposition party, as was the case in Sikkim, a few years ago, the member may take less interest in matters of accountability even if he was the Chairman of the Public Accounts Committee. He may be indifferent to the process and may not even convene meeting for extended period, as was indeed the case for a few years. Democracy poses infinite challenges and offers as many compromises and reconciliations, and each of them affects the content of political discourse and civic life. These aspects have, however, not received much attention in the literature as there have been few studies into the social anthropology of governance in general, and accountability, in particular.

Finally, one major development that has had major impact on the entire system of governance needs to be considered. Hitherto, the voters have been distant or often mute spectators of what was being played out in the national and state capitals. Now, it takes less than a minute, for him to receive information on the political developments, warts and all, in the country. Although positive developments may not always get noticed (they may not remain long in the memory of the viewer), the follies, and there are many, remain on the radars of the people. This has been the result of the electronic media and the impact of more than 800 television broadcasting stations, out of which a little over 400 stations are exclusively devoted to news. The viewer in the picture now forms his own reaction. This also had a transformational impact in two ways, on the viewer, or voter, as was pointed out by the British Political Scientist, David Marquand, in his book, The Unprincipled Society (Jonathan Cape, London, 1988). He says that ambiguities and discrepancies they cloak 'were not probed'. But 'once the convention come under critical scrutiny, once the population outside the club will ask what principles they embody and why their principles should be accepted, arrangements of this sort are bound to run into trouble. Regard for the rules of the game will gradually ebb away' (p. 198). He also points out another political feature that has emerged, and to make his point, he offers the powerful example of British Football, a national pastime, both for playing and betting. Marquand observes that the spectators are no longer content with watching the game; they now want to come out on to the field and play. The era of participatory democracy has dawned, among others because of this growing awareness, in particular the yawning gap between promise and performance, and the inadequacy of the systems that were designed a long time ago to address the concerns of long ago and have therefore become less relevant than before. The time has come when they have to prove their relevance. This mode of enquiry has also contributed to a widening of the concept of accountability.

4 Framework of Accountability Now

The overall framework of accountability may be seen at a nexus between the people, on the one hand, and the service providers on the other. The term people represents several interests and include the investing and consuming classes, as well as those classes that are dependent on the government and those who have benefits from governments in the form of entitlements. If, hitherto, accountability was a matter between the government and the legislatures, the developments in the theory and practice of democratic functioning have taken the scope of accountability beyond their conventional boundaries and now reflect a direct relationship between the citizen and the large variety of service providers. The services may be provided by corporate firms but their obligations to the consumer are sought to be specified as an integral part of regulatory framework. The regulatory framework is also a part of the accountability framework, and a part of the citizens' rights. The accountability to the citizen to be provided by the corporate world is specified by the various government agencies that have been entrusted the task of protection of the consumer. Some institutions such as commercial banks are expected, by law, to display prominently the rights of the client. In much the same way the television viewing public can send their feelings and views about the content of the broadcasts to the Broadcasting Authority of India. This segment of the information world has witnessed enormous progress, indeed a sea change, over the last few decades and now data streams into the telephone mobile sets of the individual users. The changes are taking place at such a fast chip that it is impossible to describe the coming shape of the world, even when assisted by established commentators such as Allen Toffler and his ilk.

For purposes of discussion here, these groups of users who seek and obtain accountability may be identical. There are, (i) the individual—whether called a citizen, or a common man or a client or a consumer or any other similar description, (ii) the social group, which are any number and which can be found at all levels and having a certain dream of social legitimacy in the form of an association, an organisation or institution, or (iii) a short-term, specific purpose-oriented groups, and the legislatures at the Central, State and local levels, as well as the Union Territories that have their own legislatures.

The service providers include governments at all levels, their publicly owned enterprises and financial institutions, public–private partnerships, non-governmental organisations including faith-based organisations that may be partly or fully funded by the general government as well as contractors, funded by the government and engaged in the provision of public services funded by governments. The regulatory tasks, for the sake of convenience, are not taken up here.

The needs of the individual and thus of the society are sought to be addressed through a variety of means including the channels through which data and information are supplied to the legislatures. Thus, government departments now have websites describing their charters and the activities undertaken by them. More detailed information can be obtained through intensive internet forays. As of now, to describe the information so provided is more than ample for purposes of the ordinary citizen. Frequent reports on progress made also appear on the websites. Not too long ago, people who were interested in knowing the status of public finances could get that information only at the end of the year when the consolidated accounts were published, inevitably, after a long gap. Now, monthly and some weekly data are made available through the media, with a view to addressing the concerns of the investing public. Governments have invested huge sums to operate the computerised system and make available the data at regular intervals. The secrecy hitherto attached is no longer an impediment.

In addition, since 2005, the citizen has been conferred the right to obtain information from government agencies. Toward this end, a whole bureaucracy has been organised and any issues experienced in getting information can be taken up for resolution with higher authorities, and they are specified appeal procedures for the purpose. There are more than eighty counties who are implementing the right to information legislation. This process has opened up a whole new world that was hitherto deemed to be dark and surrounded in mystery. It is no longer the case. The citizen has his rights, and the public authorities are obliged to be at his/her service. It represents an immeasurable leap in progress. The practice, however, is a different matter and is considered below.

Social audit, which remains to be institutionalised, is mostly context dependent. It may be undertaken to evaluate the claims of benefits of a project or programme or may focus on specific aspects of a programme, such as muster rolls. In fact, what seems to have brought social audit and sparked a growing awareness of the likely benefits of social audit, related to the experiences of auditing the muster rolls in local governments. They found, not to anyone's surprise, that among those said to have received wages for casual labour included people who have long since left the village or in a few cases, are no more alive. As anyone who knows something about the implementation about public works, also know that muster rolls have also been the traditional money spinners for the engineering staff. It is presumably for this reason that the British system envisaged for India, the appointment of Divisional Accountants to ensure greater reliability. Manipulation of records, however, has always been a common trick to make more money, and in this regard, the government employees have never been disappointed. Muster rolls continue to be an easy and regularly employed technique in government accounts. It is only the discovery by the public, and their revelations through the media brought a new-found recognition among social activists for getting a semblance of accountability or a medium of truth in the accounts of public bodies. Much of social audit is dependent on the enthusiasm of the local activists or the institutions undertaking this effort, which they do at their own expense and time, and therefore has no specified timetable. It is an initiative that depends on the attitudes and priorities of the society.

The final element of public accountability is that one which is designed and consequently managed by the elected representatives of the people. Reflecting the long struggle of the people on the actions of the crown, the first major achievement of the people was the signing of Magna Carta in 1275 in what the UK is now. Since then efforts at various stage have yielded further progress, and finally, the scrutiny and acceptance of public accounts by the elected members came to be institutionalised in the form, as discussed earlier, of a committee on Public Accounts. The primary task of the committee is to undertake with the assistance and active participation of the national audit office (the actual titles of these offices may vary from country to country as is the scope of audit undertaken by them). In general, the audit undertaken by the audit department is of three types: (i) appropriation audit—the primary purpose of this audit is to ensure that the legislative authority has not been violated. The scrupulous adherence to the approval limits of appropriation is a cornerstone of this audit. Accordingly, the supplementary demands, whether they have been taken in time, and whether have been fully utilised before the year and any unavoidable excess expenditures have been incurred are also matters that are examined as a part of this audit; (ii) accountancy audit—the focus of this audit is to examine whether the outlays have been properly classified, whether the amounts have been spent by the competent authorities for the purposes specified by the legislature; and (iii) performance audit—this audit was not a part of the traditional examination undertaken by the audit department. It does not figure in the approved duties of the audit department. Reflecting the growing concerns, however, an agreement was reached in the late 1970s between the Union Ministry of Finance and the Comptroller and Audit General of India, permitting the latter to undertake performance audit which evaluates the overall performance of a selected programmes or an agency, without, however, getting into an examination of the policies of the agency. The choice in the pursuit of policies is the task of the executive; it becomes legitimate whenever money is appropriated for those policies by the legislature. These three functions recognise the supremacy of the legislature in all financial matters.

The above processes are replicated for the most part by the state legislatures and their Public Accounts Committees. At the local level, audit is conducted by the local fund audit divisions attached to the State Finance department and by the Chartered Accountants appointed for the purpose.

While the types of accountability, which had since become conventional, continued, if only by force of habit, new forms of accountability emerged since 1970 reflecting the changing circumstances and changing policy goals of the government and society. Governments began to experience severe fiscal stress particularly after 1973 following the increase in the price of oil. It seemed, both for industrial and developing countries, that it was very difficult to manage the national economy. Governments began to borrow heavily from the national and international markets and trips to Washington to borrow from the International Monetary Fund for short and medium period to tide over the growing balance of payments difficulties became routine. There was a growing recognition that governments were living beyond their means and were mortgaging the future generation. The borrowing from the domestic markets crowded out needs of the corporate sector. The growing budget deficits contributed to rising levels of inflation. There was also the reality that entitlement programmes and similar welfare commitments created a whole category of uncontrollable outlays. Fiscal slippages became too common, their occurrence became regular and the contours of fiscal policy began to change. These developments contributed to demands for the restructuring of government operations, for scaling down the growth of public expenditures and for the introduction of a new management philosophy. There was also a recognition that the governments had grown in all directions as it was no longer possible to fix responsibility and thus secure accountability. It was a situation that was rightly believed to be ripe for severe surgery and for the reorientation of government operations.

The above concerns reached a stage by late 1980s that concerted international action was no longer an option but an imperative of the times. A general conclusion shared by all was that government operations needed to be transparent and accountable. Although neither theme was bold or totally new, they offered a hope that these two measures would provide the much-needed reorientation in the operations of the government. New policies for reorienting and revitalising the operations of the public agencies included privatisation, contractorization and decentralisation of government operations. The rallying cry was for a demand for the introduction of competitive forces and related market tests to determine the ways in which government operations were to be carried out. They were also needed to be supplemented by structural changes in the government. The government departments were too many and seemed to be engaged both in policy formulation and implementation. Inevitably, in those situations, accountability too became diffuse and lacked focus. To overcome this type of structural bottlenecks in the systems of governance, various government tried different reforms. Thus, as a part of the 'Next Steps' programme, task-oriented, and thus fully accountable agencies were created in the UK. In New Zealand, non-departmental bodies were created. As in the corporate sector, heads of departments in governments were replaced by Chief Executive Officers, who were appointed for specific period, usually five years, and were given specific terms of reference, tasks and goals to be achieved. These steps were deemed essential for achieving greater efficiency and accountability for government agencies. These developments also contributed to the growth of a new composite form of accountability that had three elements in addition to the financial accountability that was a part of the inheritance of most British Commonwealth Countries. They included the following: (a) programme accountability: the focus of the legislative committees shifted from how much was spent, although it continued to be a major element of the overall system of accountability, to the fulfilment of programme results. What was spent was important, but the results and their impact on the system and welfare of the community were far more important and needed to be reviewed; (b) economic stability: the experience of the 1970s was too familiar and needed to be avoided. Thus, self-imposed limitations, if necessary in the form of constitutional amendments, were deemed to be essential. Limitations on the size of fiscal deficits, and public borrowing as a percentage of GDP, or on the permissible rate of inflation, became part of the new policy structures. It was as an extension of this approach that the Union Government and many state governments in India enacted Fiscal Responsibility and Budget Management Legislation. It was yet another step in the long journey toward attaining full accountability; and (c) policy accountability: there was a general recognition that the traditional form of financial accountability eschewed the consideration of underlying policies and concentrated only on regularity aspects of expenditures. It was too narrow for purposes of knowing what the operations have contributed to. What was more important was the outcome and how those outcomes helped the country. It was toward this end that outcome budget was introduced. But its place in India was more to supplement the budget demands than as a piece for the assessment of the overall success or failure of government policies. In short, these three components, and the traditional financial accountability formed the four-legged accountability framework in governments. That these forms are generally found in political and academic discussions does not mean that all the precedent steps are indeed found in practice. Practice in government is always another world, often entirely different from the conceptual world. A consideration of the practical world is essential to know the state we are in and the benefits or limitations of such a state.

5 Praxis: Illusion and Reality

How did the system work in practice, and has it achieved the goal of securing full accountability for the nation? These are vital questions that need further exploration. Before moving into the details, some features of the experiences of the Government of India may be noted so that they may provide some perspectives about the history of the system. It is clear, however, that the Government of India and the administrative classes that perform the functions never viewed the concept and content of accountability in its totality, albeit, the totality was changing from time to time. Even now, accountability is understood by the people and the governing institutions in different ways. For some, it is an issue of addressing corruption in the use of the massive public resources. To some, it is a matter of addressing the grievance of the people in their capacity as consumers, clients and the participants in the public market where democratic institutions provide goods and services that cannot normally be provided by the conventional marketplace. To some, particularly those who serve in the government ostensibly to address the public needs, it is a matter of providing detailed audited accounts of the money collected from the public and spent for them. Accountability has always been much larger than what these facile but popular impressions convey. If governance is what governments do, accountability is a process or a combination of several converging processes that aim at revealing what governing agencies have done for the people during a given period. It is inherently much wider and larger than being interpreted as a part of a legislative function of approving the annual accounts. For much of Indian history, however, the narrow view prevailed because that was the only function that was carried out by the Colonial government after the beginning of the series of reforms which culminated in the enactment of 1935 Act.

It did not cross the implicit Lakshman Rekha (notional boundaries but based on the legendary Ramayana) and was very much within the boundaries indicated by Ernest May, and later refined by Ivor Jennings and others. Even after a century since the establishment of the audit department, the first Administrative Reforms Commission which authored a series of reports but not a single overall report unveiling its own philosophy of governance in general, and more specifically, the broad relationships, which are necessarily reciprocal, between the society and its governing institutions, did not pay more attention to this theme. These aspects did not receive much attention even when the constitutional amendment in the form of Art. 56A, about the duties of the citizens (a unique feature that no other country has) was availed during the 'scoundrel time' of the emergency. Rather, the commissions of enquiry moved into the consideration of specific aspects, often influenced by the contemporary topical themes and foreign experiences. The commissions did not really endeavour to look within and find out where the faults were and how the governing institutions can be taken closer to the people and made accountable to them as was vaguely dreamt, by the founders of the nation and the luminaries that drafted the constitution. Even the adviser, Sir B. N. Rao, an eminent Jurist in his own right, who was specifically asked to study the constitutions of other countries, would appear to have missed the woods for the trees. The segmented look, or what economists call partial equilibrium analysis, became the well-treaded path for the subsequent endeavours.

The first report of the Administrative Reforms Commission was on citizens' grievances and how they may be addressed. Some of the institutions recommended by it took decades for being implemented. The institution of ombudsman, a practice found in the highly democratic, socialistic and thinly populated Nordic countries were sought to be replicated through the establishment of Lok Pals and Lok Ayukts. Apart from looking into individual grievances brought to their notice, these institutions were implicitly assumed to be addressing the root causes of corruption and the frustrations of the common man. Even with the passage of time, and even after the introduction of e-governance, the frustrations and corruption continue unabated. To some extent, this was sought to be corrected through the introduction of an on-the-spot redressal of grievances. The legislation drafted for the purpose remains to become formal and operational. The experience suggests that the lags in the formulation of remedial policies and design of related institutions are admittedly long. Longer, however, are the legislative lags in the approval for the requisite legislation. People on the street, to whom the governments are accountable, wonder why these lags persist and why efforts to improve end up being counter-productive. In this preoccupation with citizens' grievances, the larger purposes of accountability came to be side-lined. It remained a rallying cry for enthusiasts for civil society system and other professional agitationists. The benefits to the people continue to be elusive. Most importantly, what has been lost sight of is the fact that a clear approach to accountability could have strengthened the sinews of democratic functioning, despite the embedded derisive factors that have and continue to be exploited for electoral purposes, and the society as a whole could have had a sustainable purpose. But what the government did not have could not be conveyed to the people and the thought process on accountability reached the comfortable zone of stagnation.

It is in the above broader context that the content of the existing framework of accountability, fragile and inadequate as it is, needs to be considered. Taking into account, first, the vertical accountability, it was expected even as early as the mid 1950s; given the extensive involvement of the Central government and the related transfer of financial resources to the state governments (the picture of the local governments was totally different from that which emerged after the 73rd Amendment to the constitution), there was a demand that the activities financed by the Central governments, at the level of subnational governments should be made more accountable to the Centre. The honourable members, who are otherwise strong supporters of federalism, were keen that the accountability to the centre be strengthened in every possible way. But the Finance Minister (C. D. Deshmukh) was not troubled by the demand. To him, in a federal set up (he believed the country to be federal through that word is not found in the constitution), the roles of the then two levels of cognate powers were independent and had their own specified channels of accountability. In this, he was influenced by his own long experiences, part of it as a Finance Secretary in the then Province of C.P. and Berar, and in the revision of the Niemeyer award of the divisible resources between the Centre and the States. In the later years, all that the Central government needed then was a utilisation certificate from the state governments that the thoroughly ring-fenced transfers were utilised for the purposes specified. The vertical accountability came to be dependent on this utilisation certificate or UC for short that was in any event, a formal if thoroughly routine affair. The certificates were routinely demanded, were furnished equally routinely and were routinely filed in the central papers. More or less, the same process continues to date. The routine continues, and it is believed that vertical accountability, such as it is, is fully operational. The Public Accounts Committee in the state governments does take up these matters when they have a political interest and when prodded by the Accountant General of the State. The 73rd Amendment, however, changed the situation in that a third layer of government has come into existence in most states. There are new complex financial arrangements relating to the third layer in that the state governments are obliged to appoint Finance Commissions of their own, like the Central Finance Commission to review periodically the status of the finances of local governments and their needs. Also, the Central transfers to the third layer for developmental purposes do not go through, any longer, the state budgets but are transmitted directly and the third layer is directly answerable to the Central government for such transfers. Unlike the state governments, the accounts of the local government are neither compiled nor audited by the audit department as is the case with the state governments. These are complied by the local governments' own staff and are audited by the Chartered Accountants from the private sector, who are appointed for the purpose. In so far as is known, the accounts so maintained are not in conformity with generally accepted accounts principles (GAAP) nor have any audit standards been specifically set up for the purpose. There are also no requirements for the review of accounts and audit certificates, except they are subjected to some scrutiny by the periodic Finance Commissions. If this process is deemed as adequate for purposes of vertical accountability, then it must be conceded that there is an apparent full accountability. The reality is, as always, very different.

It is a process that meets the purposes of a form. In substance, it is a procedural ritual that does not come anywhere near fulfilling the tenets of accountability.

Vertical accountability also includes the relationships between ministers or the departments, be it the Central or State governments, and the Secretaries of their respective departments. Both under the conventions and the rules of business of the respective levels of government, the minister is responsible for the policies of his department. These policies are vetted by the respective cabinets, but it is the minister who is answerable to the legislature for the policies. The finances of the department are administered by its Secretary, who is the administrative head of the department and is also its Chief Accounting Officer. These conventions have come to be questioned in a recent case which is technically still under investigation in the former State of Andhra Pradesh. The case involves grant or heavily subsidised sale of public lands to selected private parties in deals that allegedly involve *quid pro quo* investments by the private parties in the companies owned and managed among others, by the family of the then Chief Minister, who has since died in a helicopter crash. The defendants, viz. the minister of concerned departments and their departmental heads, countered that they were not responsible for these deals as they were approved by the cabinet, or that the ministers and departmental heads were pressurised or directed by the then Chief Minister to approve the deals, although every participant in the deal knew full well the financial implications for the public exchequer. In this thick and impenetrable fog of mutual recriminations and finger pointing, the respective boundaries of each levels, responsibilities and their jurisdictions are being debated. The organised unions of the civil servants have not lost any time to point out that the responsibilities of the ministers include the policy management of their spheres of activities. These types of cases once again illustrate the fact that the responsibility of policy management may be indivisible; it can be argued that the responsibilities of ministers and their civil servants are symbiotic and the lines between them can never be formally delineated. What happened in the informal realm between the two levels in the approval of the crony deals is yet to come out. The CBI, for its part, has presumably as a precautionary measure and to ensure that the evidence is not tampered with, arrested both the minister and some civil servants and remanded them into custody for extended periods (they have since been released). Regardless of the final outcome, the case provides yet another illustration of the difficulty in determining the person(s) responsible for the policy caper. It also shows that vertical accountability is as complex as any other sphere of government accountability. The informal motto of the government has been, and is, that when in doubt, spread or diffuse the responsibility to as many as possible.

Another component in the overall scheme of accountability relates to individual grievances, and the general complaints that an individual might have toward the public bodies on behalf of the community. These grievances and complaints have their origins in the individual's dealings with the government. With a view to adding additional justification to his grievances and complaints, the individual seeks to know how a particular policy decision came to be made in the first place. The background and the material relating to that decision are not usually available in the public domain and have to be obtained, through formal requests from the government itself.

Since, however, the grievance or the complaint is ostensibly against the government, the latter is generally unwilling and non-cooperative in providing that information. The seeds of an adversarial relationship are sown in the process. The government servant is likely to treat the grievance as against himself or against his class. Although there were complaints boxes set up, even during the Colonial regime, the fate of the complaints dropped into the box was generally known in that action was most unlikely. So, after years of prolonged agitation, and following the developments in the Western democracies, it was deemed essential to endow a right in the individual member of the society to obtain information from the government. It was also seen as an opportunity to open the secret and private world of the government, while most democracies enacted the right to information legislation and the measure was welcomed by the people's representatives, the administrative classes were not entirely enthusiastic about it as the complaints were about them. Their discontent remained a private matter in the first stages as they also recognised that the new machinery organised for the purpose of considering the complaints was also a part of the administrative machinery, which meant that the usual tricks of administration could be played in this area too. Thus, the stalling technique came to be deployed with the usual effect that information was not available as it was not traceable in the records or was lost in a fire that took place in the offices years ago, or when information came, parts of it were inked out, a familiar technique used by the FBI in the USA and what was made available proved to be inadequate for the purposes in view. From this stalling posture, the next set of aggressive steps came to be initiated what became controversial was the scope of 'public bodies' to whom this legislation was sought to be applied. While all bodies financed by the Consolidated Fund of India were naturally determined to be a part of government or public bodies whose activities are of interest to the public, less clear was the position of some institutions such as the political parties in the country. The information commissioners took the view that political parties were part of the overall democratic fabric, and therefore, within the ambit of the legislation, the political parties have so far resisted to be so included. Thus, there are areas of darkness where the rays of information legislation have not penetrated thus far. Meanwhile, some more aggressive steps were taken in that the public activists who were actively engaged in getting and publicising the information were found dead. Who was responsible for this 'final solution' remained unclear. But its impact became clear in that the activists now know that their own lives are in danger. Furthermore, it began to be argued, that information legislation has an adverse effect on the decision-making approaches of the administrative machinery in that the fear that one day in the future their actions could become questionable and their reputations could be besmirched, might alter their behaviour. More significantly, they all, as a class, could become risk averse. This does not however, mean that they were willing to take risks before. Rather, the experience both in the Central and State governments conclusively shows that there was often a collusion between the political and administrative classes and that it worked to advance the interests of both classes.

The important issue, however, is whether the information legislation has advanced the cause of public accountability. To think that it has may be delusional, not merely because of the operational issues discussed above, but because of the inherent limitations in the scope of the legislation itself. It deals primarily with the issues affecting the careers and lives of individuals often arising from the situation in which an individual is placed. It is not concerned with 'public' issues, and therefore, actions taken in pursuance of the legislation do not confer any externalities or spill-over effects, on the general public. Thus, the utility of the legislation, valuable though it is in making an opening into the hitherto closed world, its overall contribution to the saga of public accountability is at best limited.

So, it is, in the case of social audit as well, while the technique has immense potential in exposing the rot at the core of the governmental system, it lacks a definitive focus, in the choice of projects, methodology and in the conclusions reached. More significantly, it does not have the persuasive power to move the implementation agencies to mend their ways. The agencies, for their part, are deeply allergic to the social audit reports and do everything possible to stynch them. The social audit agencies have only the will-o-wisp attitudes of the public as their support system and that is not much. It can certainly be a major instrument in the hands of the public, but those who undertake it should also recognise the fact that they are up against the powers that be.

Financial accountability, on the other hand, has several structural limitations which have not thus far been recognised, and therefore, those limitations continue to persist despite the long history. These include the following: (1) the work of the audit agency, which is also the fundamental base for the operations of the Public Accounts Committee, does not include the normal budget items such as the world of contingent liabilities stemming up from the *quasi*-fiscal operations of guarantees, or land grants. Both these areas have become major instruments of patronage and cronyism and a significant abuse of power. In some cases, where there has been a public furore separate audit reports were submitted on land grants, and subsidised sales but this has not become a regular feature of the annual appropriation audit for the simple reason that they do not require legislative appropriation. Similarly, public debt operations, which form part of charged expenditure and are significant in transfers were a part of the territories neglected by the audit for a long time, though attention is being paid to that now; (2) the work of the PAC does not cover the role of tax expenditures although they have become as important as regular expenditures. Their budgetary and social impacts are of considerable importance. The grant of these incentives suggests the discretionary powers of the executive and can be arbitrary. But there is no regular coverage of these transactions; (3) equally important are the content and operations of the public–private partnerships which are stated to gain more importance in the future. The audit of these partnerships varies and is dependent on the enabling providers included in the original contracts between the government and the private parties vary from one to another and would appear to be dependent on the political and negotiating power (the private parties are richly endowed and their pockets are large enough to enable them to hire the biggest names among lawyers) of the parties. The audit of the grant-aided bodies is ad hoc at best, and therefore, the receiving organisations have learnt the tricks of the trade to receive grants even when the accounts of the previous years have not been compiled let alone submitted to the government, but continue to receive the generous help from the government; and (4) the financial sector, i.e. nationalised banks, is subjected, if only to regular commercial audit. The growing size of the non-performing assets of these institutions, however, attests to the political power and the extent of corruption prevalent. The losses of the banks are regularly socialised in that the people, viz. the shareholders end up bearing the burden.

Apart from the above structural issues, there is a major feature of the PAC which raises a judgmental issue about the social utility of the committee. The committee is there primarily to provide legitimacy to the findings of the audit department through the legislative garb. It is primarily a show of the audit department, and the members are not known to have made any major contribution except to make political scores when the sleaze of the ruling party is exposed. The appropriation audit reveals the dysfunctional nature of the budget system that regularises excess expenditures, and routinely processes supplemented demand thrice a year. If their features are removed from the system (and these are no place for them in a disciplined and well organised financial system), then there is not much of an appropriation audit.

Does the PAC's work contribute to the might of legislature? In all fairness, it has to be conceded that there is not much that the Public Accounts Committee contributes, apart from concluding the cycle of annual budgetary operations. As a system, it continues because it is a relic of the past and thus carries a good deal of history. The main reason for its continuance is its history, not its utility. Most of its recommendations are routinely 'noted' by the government and routinely the action taken reports are submitted to the legislature. In a context where the bulk of the budget is approved without any discussion, it is difficult to imagine that the power of the PAC would add any weight. It is an illusion maintained that it is fulfilling accountability. Social and political realities demand a new beginning to be made to render accountability, not in the form but in substance, to the people. Formation of more committees is not the answer. Designing effective means of control and accountability is a task that remains to be addressed. If the existing system does not fulfil the expectations of the society, then it is time that a new beginning is made to reform the system. This is a story with a simple truth, that legislatures are ensuring accountability is a myth. The reality needs to be addressed and that is what the society is demanding.

Chapter 11
Public Financial Accounting and Auditing: Principles and Practices

C. Vijaya Kumar

1 Background

Public financial management (PFM) includes all phases of the budget cycle encompassing the preparation of budget, expenditure and revenue management, internal control and audit, procurement, monitoring and reporting and external audit (The World Bank 2010). Government accounting is the process of systematically recording financial information relating to government receipts and expenditure. Under Article 150 of the Indian Constitution, the President of India prescribes the form of Accounts of the Union and States on the advice of the Comptroller and Auditor General (CAG). Uniformity in the heads of accounts for budgeting and accounting of the Union and States is to be ensured. In this regard, the Government accounting rules, 1990[1] prescribe that 'Every year, from the accounts compiled by the authorities authorised to maintain the accounts of Central Government, State Governments and Union Territory Governments, accounts showing under the respective heads the annual receipts and disbursements for the purpose of Union of each State and of each Union Territory having a Legislative Assembly (including Appropriation Accounts) are to be prepared and got certified by the Comptroller and Auditor General of India. According to the government accounting rules, 1990, the reports of the Comptroller and Auditor General relating to these accounts shall be submitted to the President or the Governor of a State or the Administrator of a Union Territory having a Legislative Assembly, as the case may be, who shall cause them to be laid before the Houses of

[1]This chapter contains excerpts from the GOVERNMENT ACCOUNTING RULES 1990. The entire report can be downloaded from the CGA website http://www.cga.nic.in/DownloadPDF.aspx?filenameid=3. See (CGA 1990).

C. Vijaya Kumar (✉)
Comptroller and Auditor General of India-Field Office, Bangalore, Bangalore, India
e-mail: chadal56@gmail.com

G. Karnam (ed.), *Public Budgeting in India*, India Studies in Business and Economics, https://doi.org/10.1007/978-81-322-3917-8_11

Parliament, Legislatures of the States and of Union Territories respectively'[2] (GOIp 2). The government accounts need to be classified and reported both in their aggregate and disaggregated forms. Government financial operations need to be tracked and recorded in as detailed, systematic and accurate manner as possible to enable reliable and efficient management of public finances. Government accounting is expected to serve a number of purposes. It aids in the conduct of financial business of government in a timely, efficient and reliable manner such as to make payments, settle liabilities, collect sums due subject to the necessary financial controls. Government transactions tracked and systematically accounted for help in understanding the behaviour of financial status from time to time and a meaningful analysis helps a great deal in the framing of informed financial decisions that ultimately help in efficient public financial management. These records also serve well in ensuring budgetary control both for internal control and the needs of external auditors.

The basic requirements to enable the effective use of government accounts is to make sure that the accounting system is comprehensive and well documented, relatively uniform, simple to learn and operate, easy to consolidate and comparable across levels of government and over time. Any changes brought about in the classification and recording need to be well documented and provide necessary explanatory information.

Following are the major components of government accounting system:

- Record of evidence of transactions
- Accounting of payments and receipts through banks or other bodies
- Maintenance of accounting records (cash book, ledgers, etc.)
- Controls and checks
- Aggregation of accounting data
- Internal accounting reports
- External accounting reports (financial statements)

Discussing the importance of financial reporting systems, the World Bank, states 'High-quality financial reporting in the public sector is the basis for accountability and transparency in Public financial management. The institutional framework for public sector accounting should include adherence to international accounting standards and use of qualified accounting staff to provide the timely, relevant, and reliable financial information that is needed to support fiscal and budget management, decision-making, and reporting processes. If financial statements are to be useful and contribute to transparency, they must be understandable to the reader and must deal with transactions, assets, and liabilities in a transparent and consistent manner. This is the purpose of financial reporting standards. Some countries have their own public sector financial reporting standards, set by government or by another authorized body' (The World Bank 2010, 7).

On the contrary, inadequate accounting systems cause considerable difficulty in carrying out day to day transactions in an effective manner. This could be in the nature of lack of authentic records coupled with their inaccessibility. Under such

[2]http://www.cga.nic.in/Book/Published/4.aspx.

situations pinning responsibility on those alleged to have carried out corrupt activities becomes hard and also causes hardship in achieving budgetary and internal control. Government accounting could be either cash based or accrual based; the current thinking is to switch to the accrual base. Cash basis is the predominant basis due to the ease with which it can be carried out, and there is no need to have any special accounting skills. It is also well-adapted to the needs of budgetary control. Payment is definite and strict budget control can be exercised by comparing sums authorised with those actually spent.

2 Budget

Government budget is a financial statement of the government presenting the financial proposals relating to the revenue to be raised and the spending to be incurred for a prescribed period of time pertaining to the Financial Year (FY). In the case of India, it is from 1 April to 31 March.

The list of Budget documents presented to the Parliament, in addition to the Finance Minister's Budget Speech, include the following: (GOI 2018)[3]

- Annual Financial Statement (AFS)
- Demands for Grants (DG)
- Finance Bill
- Statements mandated under FRBM Act include the Macro-Economic Framework Statement, Fiscal Policy Strategy Statement and Medium Term Fiscal Policy Statement
- Expenditure budget
- Receipts budget
- Expenditure profile
- Memorandum explaining the provisions in the finance bill
- Budget at a glance
- Outcome budget

While the AFS, demand for grants and the Finance Bill are mandated by Art. 112,113, and 110(a) of the Constitution of India, respectively, there are some statements like macro-economic framework statement, Fiscal Policy Strategy Statement and Medium Term Fiscal Policy Statement mandated by the FRBM Act and the others listed above are explanatory statements.

The structure of the Annual Financial Statement (AFS) as provided under the Aricle 112 of the Constitution includes in it the budget proposals for the ensuing year, revised and budget estimates of the previous FY and actual receipts and expenditure for the year before. In other words, the budget for 2018–19 will include budget estimates for 2018–19, revised and budgeted estimates for the FY 2017–18 and actual receipts and expenditure for the FY 2016–17. The statement will include the

[3]Government of India 2018, Key to Budget documents, The Union Budget 2018–19.

details under the Consolidated Fund, Contingency Fund and the Public Account. The Union government's AFS will include the budget proposals for the receipts and expenditure of the Union Territories without Legislature. The AFS which is the main budget needs the approval of the Parliament/Legislature for the Executive to have the required authorisation to execute the budget.

3 Accounting Structure

A standard Accounting structure is prescribed for the government accounts and is presented below as detailed in the Government Accounting Rules, 1990.[4] (Government of India, pp. 14–16) Government accounts are presented in three parts.

Part I Consolidated Fund
Part II Contingency Fund
Part III Public Account.

3.1 The Consolidated Fund

There are two main divisions under the Consolidated Fund, i.e. Revenue and Capital. The Revenue division (Revenue Account) deals with the proceeds of taxation and other receipts classified as revenue and the expenditure met there from, the net result of which represents the revenue surplus or deficit for the year. Surplus in the revenue account are welcome as it augments the resources available for capital investments. Currently, while most of the subnational governments in India have revenue surpluses after the framing of Fiscal Responsibility Legislations, the Central government has huge revenue deficits, often close to 70% of fiscal deficit, an issue for serious concern.

In the capital division, the section 'Receipt Heads (Capital Account)' deals with receipts of capital nature. The section 'Expenditure Heads (Capital Account)' deals with expenditure met usually from borrowed funds with the objective of increasing concrete assets of a material and permanent character. The budget head 'Public Debt, Loans and Advances', etc. includes in it the loans raised by the government and their repayments made by Government. The Budget Head 'Loans and Advances' relates to the amount of loans and advances given by the government to the lower levels of government (states and local bodies, respectively) and loans and advances given to government staff.

The Consolidated Fund includes in it certain items of expenditure such as Salaries of the Constitutional Authorities, loan repayment, etc., that are in the nature of 'Charged' expenditure and are not subject to 'Vote' by the Parliament/Legislature. All other expenditure has to be necessarily voted by the Parliament/Legislature.

---

[4]http://www.cga.nic.in/Book/Published/4.aspx.

3.2 The Contingency Fund

In the Contingency Fund, the transactions connected with Contingency Fund established under Article 267 of the Constitution of India are recorded. The Constitution under Article 267 authorises the existence of a Contingency Fund of India. This is an imprest (corpus) placed at the disposal of the President of India to facilitate meeting of urgent unforeseen expenditure by the government, pending an authorisation from Parliament. Parliamentary approval for such unforeseen expenditure is obtained, ex-post-facto, and an equivalent amount is drawn from the Consolidated Fund of India to recoup the Contingency Fund. The limit on the imprest was very small at Rs. 50 crore from 1976 but has been revised to Rs. 500 by the Central government in 2005 after the Tsunami. States too have contingency fund to enable to meet emergency expenditure. The Contingency Fund for Karnataka for the year 2016–17 was Rs. 80 crore.

Public Account of India accounts for those transactions where the government is merely acting as a banker. This fund was constituted under Article 266 (2) of the Constitution. In the Public Account, the transactions relating to 'Debt' (other than those included in Part I), 'Deposits', 'Advances', 'Remittances' and 'Suspense' are recorded. The transactions under 'Debt', 'Deposits' and 'Advances' in this part are those in respect of which Government incurs a liability to repay the moneys received or has a claim to recover the amounts paid, together with the repayments of the former ('Debt', and 'Deposits') and the recoveries of the latter ('Advances'). The transactions relating to 'Remittances' and 'Suspense' in this part include merely adjusting heads under which appear such transactions as remittances of cash between treasuries and currency chests, transfers between different accounting circles, etc. The initial debts or credits to these heads will be cleared eventually by corresponding receipts or payments either within the same circle of account or in another account circle.

Sector and Heads of Accounts: Within each of the sections in Part I, i.e. the Consolidated Fund mentioned above, the transactions are grouped into sectors such as 'Tax Revenue', 'Non-Tax Revenue' and 'Grants-in-aid and contributions' for the receipt heads (Revenue Account), and 'General Services', 'Social Services', 'Economic Services' and 'Grants-in-aid and contributions' for expenditure heads. Specific functions or services (such as Education, Sports, Art and Culture, Health and Family Welfare, Water Supply, Sanitation, Housing and Urban Development, etc. in respect of Social Services) are grouped in sectors for expenditure heads. In Part III (Public Account) also, the transactions are grouped into sectors, such as 'Small Savings', 'Provident Funds', 'Reserve Funds', etc. The sectors are sub-divided into major heads of account. In some cases, the sectors are, in addition, sub-divided into sub-sectors before their division into major heads of account. The structure of Union and State budgets are presented in charts 11.1 and 11.2, respectively.

The budget presentation is prescribed in the government accounting rules and hence the following discussion on the classification is largely from Government Accounting Rules, 1990.[5] The major heads are divided into sub-major heads in some cases and minor heads, with a number of subordinate heads, generally known as sub-heads. The sub-heads are further divided into detailed heads. Under each of these heads, the expenditure is shown distributed between charged and voted. Sometimes major heads are also divided into sub-major heads before their further divisions into minor heads. Apart from the sectoral and sub-sectoral classification, the Major Heads, Sub-Major Heads, Minor Heads, Sub-Heads, Detailed Heads and Object-Heads together constitute a six-tier arrangement of the classification structure of the Government Accounts. The major, minor and sub-heads prescribed for the classification of expenditure in the general accounts are not necessarily identical with the Grants, sub-heads and other units of allotments which are adopted by the Governments for Demands for Grants presented to the Parliament or Legislatures but in general a certain degree of correlation is maintained between the Demands for Grants and the Finance Accounts.

The major heads of accounts, falling within the sectors for expenditure heads, generally correspond to the functions of Government, while the minor heads, subordinate to them, identify the programmes undertaken to achieve the objectives of the function represented by the major head. The sub-head represents the scheme, the detailed head represents the sub-scheme and object head represents the purpose/object level of classification.

[5]http://www.cga.nic.in/Book/Published/4.aspx.

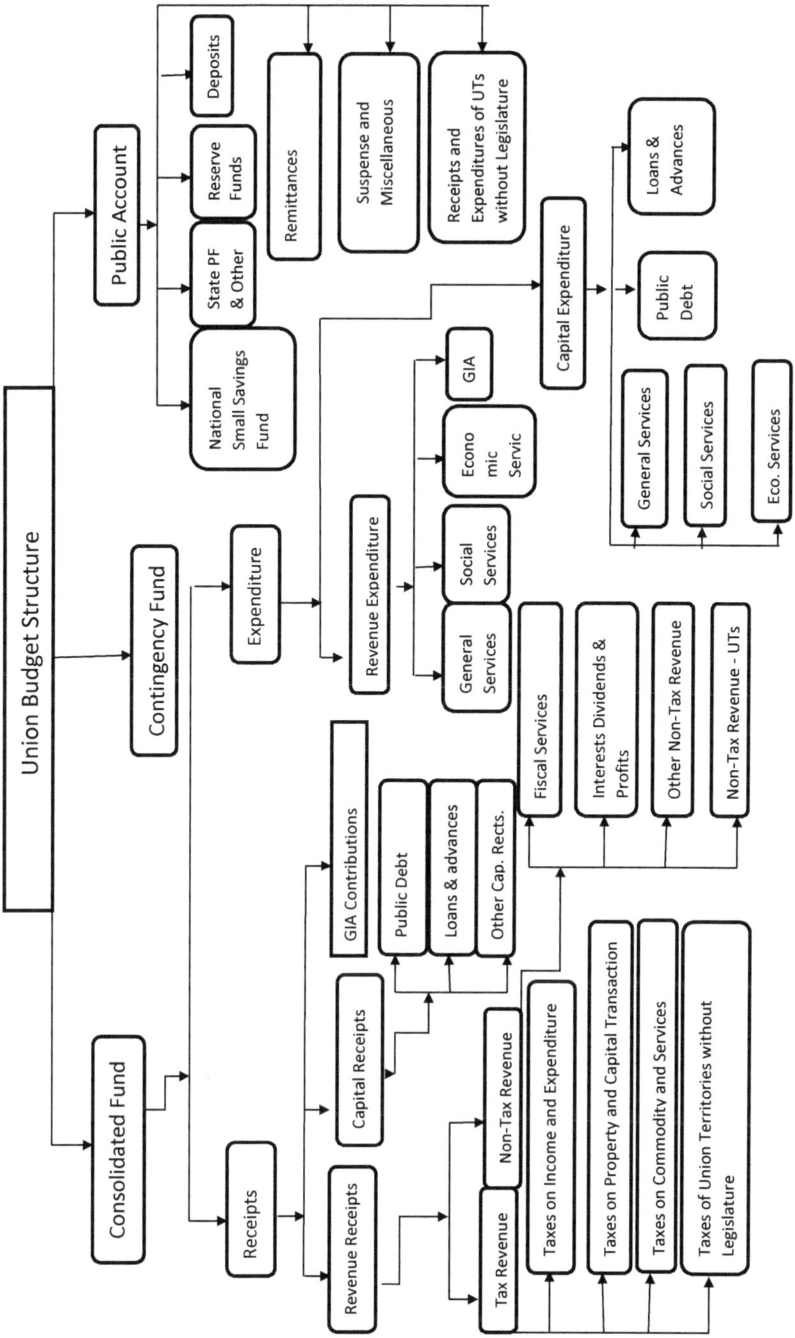
Union Budget Structure
Public Account
Contingency Fund
Consolidated Fund
Deposits
Reserve Funds
State PF & Other
National Small Savings Fund
Remittances
Suspense and Miscellaneous
Receipts and Expenditures of UTs without Legislature
Expenditure
Revenue Expenditure
Capital Expenditure
General Services
Social Services
Econo mic Servic
GIA
Public Debt
Loans & Advances
General Services
Social Services
Eco. Services
Receipts
Revenue Receipts
Capital Receipts
GIA Contributions
Public Debt
Loans & advances
Other Cap. Rects.
Fiscal Services
Interests Dividends & Profits
Other Non-Tax Revenue
Non-Tax Revenue - UTs
Tax Revenue
Non-Tax Revenue
Taxes on Income and Expenditure
Taxes on Property and Capital Transaction
Taxes on Commodity and Services
Taxes of Union Territories without Legislature

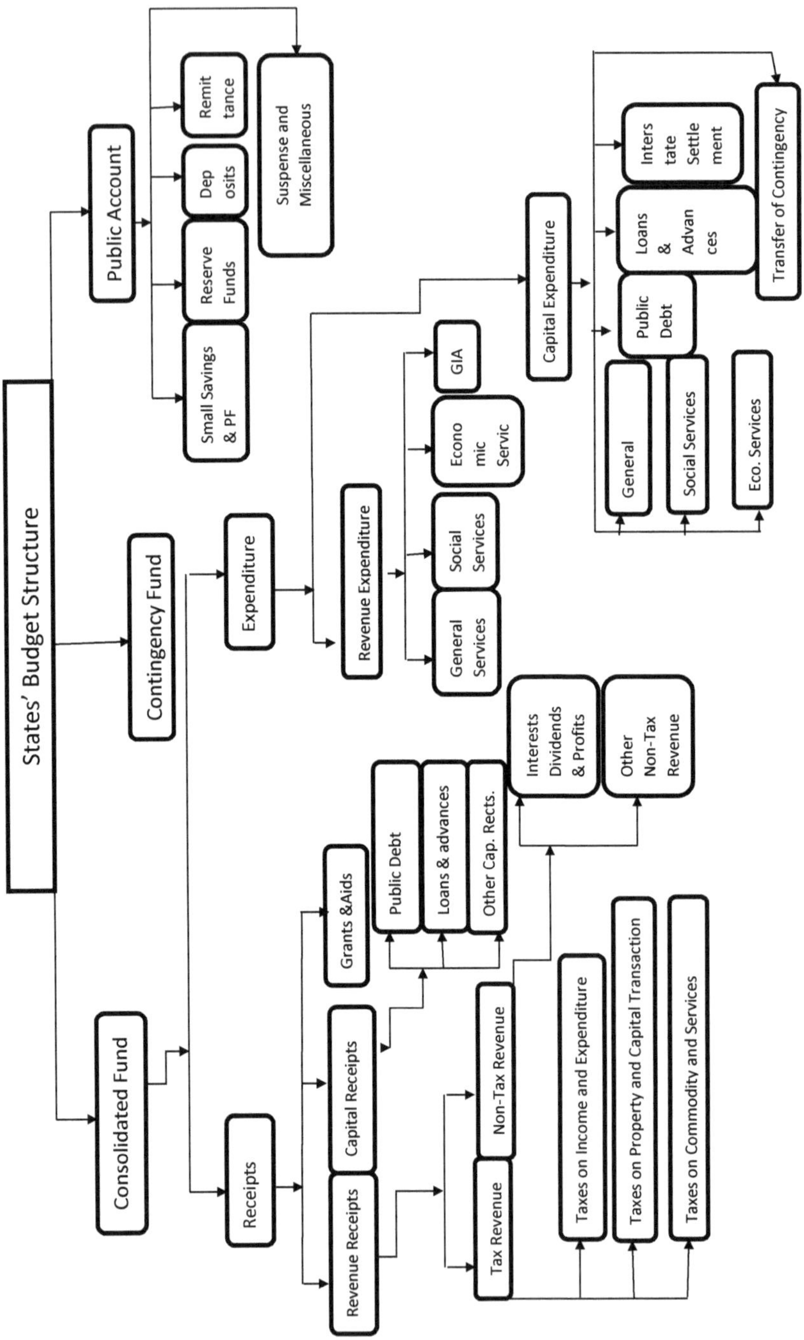
States' Budget Structure
Consolidated Fund
Contingency Fund
Public Account
Small Savings & PF
Reserve Funds
Dep osits
Remit tance
Suspense and Miscellaneous
Receipts
Expenditure
Revenue Receipts
Capital Receipts
Grants &Aids
Tax Revenue
Non-Tax Revenue
Taxes on Income and Expenditure
Taxes on Property and Capital Transaction
Taxes on Commodity and Services
Interests Dividends & Profits
Other Non-Tax Revenue
Public Debt
Loans & advances
Other Cap. Rects.
Revenue Expenditure
General Services
Social Services
Econo mic Servic
GIA
Capital Expenditure
General
Social Services
Eco. Services
Public Debt
Loans & Advan ces
Inters tate Settle ment
Transfer of Contingency

Coding pattern: A four-digit code has been allotted to the major heads with effect from 1 April 1987; the first digit indicates whether the major head is a Receipt head or Revenue Expenditure head or Capital Expenditure head or a Loan head.

The first digit of code for Revenue Receipt head is either '0' or '1'. Adding 2 to the first digit code of the Revenue Receipt head will give the number allotted to corresponding Revenue Expenditure head; adding another 2, the Capital Expenditure; and another 2, the Loan head of Account. For example, for Crop Husbandry code 0401 represents the Receipt head, 2401 the revenue expenditure head, 4401 the Capital Outlay head and 6401 the Loan head.

Such a pattern is, however, not relevant for those departments which are not operating Capital/Loan heads of account, e.g. Department of Supply. In a few cases, where receipt and expenditure are not heavy, certain functions have been combined under a single major head, the functions themselves forming sub-major heads under the Major head.

Sub-Major heads—A two-digit code has been allotted, the code starting from 01 under each Major head. Where no sub-major head exists, it is allotted a code '00'. The nomenclature 'General' has been allotted Code '80' so that even after further sub-major heads are introduced the code for 'General' will continue to remain the last one.

Minor Heads—These have been allotted a three-digit code, the codes starting from '001' under each sub-major/major head (where there is no sub-major head). Codes from '001' to '100' and few codes '750' to '900' have been reserved for certain standard minor heads. The coding pattern for minor heads has been designed in such a way that in respect of certain minor heads having a common nomenclature under many major/sub-major heads, the same three-digit code is adopted as far as possible.

Under this scheme of codification, the receipt major heads (Revenue account) are assigned the block numbers from 0020 to 1606, expenditure major heads (revenue account) from 2011 to 3606, expenditure major heads (capital account) from 4046 to 5475, major heads under 'Public Debt', from 6001 to 6004 and those under 'Loans and Advances', 'Inter-State Settlement' and 'Transfer to Contingency Funds' from 6075 to 7999. The code number 4000 has been assigned for Capital receipt major head. The only major head 'Contingency Fund' in Part II 'Contingency Fund' has been assigned the code number 8000. The major heads in the Public Account are assigned the code number from 8001 to 8999.

The transactions included in these accounts represent mainly the actual cash receipts and disbursement during the financial year April to March as distinguished from amounts due to or from Government during the same period. The cash basis system is, however, not entirely suitable for recording the transactions and presenting the true state of affairs of Government commercial undertakings run on commercial principles. The detailed accounts of this class of undertakings are, therefore, maintained outside the regular accounts in proper commercial form and are subject to test check by the Indian Audit and Accounts Department.

The figures of actuals shown in these accounts are net, after taking into account the recoveries, although the Demands for Grants presented to Legislature and the

Scheme of codification

Consolidated fund	Major head code numbers
Section 1 receipt heads-revenue account	0020–1999
Expenditure heads: revenue account	2011–3999
Section 11; receipt head capital account	4000
Expenditure heads-capital account	4046–5999
Section 111 public debt loans and advances	6001–7999
Part 11—contingency fund	8000
Part 111—public account	8001–8995

Source Government accounting rules, 1990

Appropriation Accounts are for gross expenditure and exclude credits and recoveries which are otherwise taken as reduction of expenditure.

4 Role of Treasury

Department of Treasuries, one of the divisions in the Finance Department, is the backbone for the financial transactions related to expenditure and revenue of the government. Treasury functions are the mechanism through which effective financial control is exercised over public spending by various government departments of the State. Treasury offices are the basic unit and fiscal point for recording the financial transactions of the government and are the starting point of public accounts. While in general, the functions of treasury at the sub-national level are the same, this discussion is based in particular on treasury operations in the state of Karnataka and is largely drawn from the Government of Karnataka Treasury department website.[6]

The broad objectives of the Department of Treasuries are:

1. To pass Government bills and cheques correctly and promptly
2. To prepare accounts of receipts and payments correctly and promptly
3. To maintain the budget and control over expenditures
4. Timely disbursement of pension
5. Safe custody of valuables.

The function of the treasuries starts with budget finalisation and effectively ends with submitting of accounts to the Accountant General. The entire budget is shared with the Department of Treasuries after completion of department wise allocation. It is also responsible for monitoring expenditure against the allocated budget. Once Treasuries receive the final budget figures, the jurisdiction of treasuries over the payments and control over the expenditure based on the budget allocation begins. The Treasuries interact with different entities, while fulfilling their objectives with respect

[6]Government of Karnataka, http://karnatakatreasury.gov.in/.

to the monitoring of the financial operations in the State Government. Monitoring of the spending and receipts at the treasuries start with the process of Drawing Disbursing Officers (DDOs) of respective departments submitting their bills (Abstract Contingency, Detailed Contingency, Salary, Travel Allowance, etc.), for processing and payments. The treasury processes these bills as per the rules laid down by the State Government and funds available with the particular department out of its budget allocation. Treasuries issue cheques or transfer payment to the person/entity whose bill is found to confirm to the existing rules. Treasuries and Finance Department keep a check on the cash position while making payments. The revenue earning departments remit money through banks to the treasuries. Treasuries receive the related figures from the agency banks. Banks submit statements of deposits and payments on a timely basis to the treasuries. Treasuries carryout reconciliation of the payments and the receipts with their own records and submit monthly statements to the Accountant General Office for Audit and Evaluation. Organizational structure of the Treasury consists of a Head Office at Bangalore (in the case of Karnataka, other states too will have similar structures) headed by the Director of Treasuries (DoT), which is the administrative centre for the department. Actual treasuries that conduct transactions are, the treasuries at Bangalore called the State Huzur Treasury and the Pension Payment Treasury. Every district has a treasury headed by the District Treasury Officer (DTO), and further on, in the talukas are the Sub-Treasuries. These offices interact with DDOs and other stakeholders for discharging the functions set out in the treasury code.

4.1 Treasury Reforms

Reforms in treasury management have been attempted by a number of Indian states. There have also been efforts to move to an Integrated Financial Management Information System (IFMIS) with Human Resource Management System (HRMS) to have a common reliable database. However, there is need to further strengthen these processes, and in this context, it is stated 'these reform exercises are being pursued by states individually and in complete isolation, interaction between them to learn from each other's experience and knowledge is rare. There is little visibility that states have done in this area'. (Government of Andhra Pradesh and the World Bank 2014, 5) The report states that Andhra Pradesh and Karnataka are in the process of implementing next generation of Financial Management Information System where Maharashtra is attempting complete automation of its major revenue department. An important observation that is made in the report relates to the reinvention of wheel by each state that is attempting to introduce reforms and emphasises on the need for support by Government of India in providing the necessary capabilities. It is felt that a model code can be developed which can be adopted by the states, in view of the fact that Treasury code is similar in many ways across states.

An attempt is made to discuss the reform features of Karnataka in the following section as presented in the reports of the Treasury Department, Government of Karnataka.[7]

4.2 Reform Initiatives Undertaken by Government of Karnataka

Department of Treasury initiated the process of automation of its core processes in the year 2001. During this process, a computerised system named 'Khajane' was put in place. This system has been in operation ever since, and the state has introduced Khajane II to improve the system further, the processes continue to be reformed.

The existing Khajane system implemented to automate the treasuries was a substantial leap from the pre-existing manual system with features like:

- Each of the treasuries in the state would have in place system-based clearance of bills backed by a proper verification for budget availability. Online funds transfers help reduce delays in fund release to the agencies.
- Network all the treasuries in the state and have all the transactions monitored online by the central server.
- Generate automated monthly accounts.
- Enable better cash management, budget control and monitoring.
- Provision of accurate real-time data on receipts and expenditure to the departments to facilitate better management of their schemes.
- The computerised treasury system to eliminate the systemic deficiencies emanating from the manual treasury operations such as misclassification of expenses, excess or fraudulent withdrawals and the delays due to duplicative processes.

Khajane system was a pioneer in automating treasury functions and had many advantages over the manual system, won several awards like the Silver Icon in the 9th e-Governance conference in 2006 and the CSI-Nihilent overall runners up award in 2005–06. However, there were the following limitations.

1. Automation was limited to the functions of the Treasury department.
2. Duplication of data entry that gets done at multiple levels.
3. Delay of 5–10 days in generation of account statements with enormous manual effort.
4. It is developed on a Client–Server technology and till recently operated on a limited bandwidth resulting in higher maintenance costs.
5. It has serious security gaps like inability to have of audit trails, possibility of modification of data at the database level, easy access by use of only passwords, unencrypted management of passwords, etc. due to lack of guidelines on data security.

[7] Government of Karnataka, http://karnatakatreasury.gov.in/.

6. It works on outdated hardware and system software, which are not supported any longer.

In the year 2008, PwC was given the task to conduct an audit of the system. The audit found serious lacunae within the Khajane system and recommended series of changes and modifications. Further, it was also observed that with the passing of time, the hardware meant for supporting the Khajane was becoming old and irreparable. Under these circumstances, it was felt that the old Khajane should be phased out, both in terms of software and hardware, and replaced with a new system, which can cater to the requirements of the department for the next 10 years.

The Government of Karnataka has been working on Khajane II with the following objectives (GOK)[8]

1. Generation of daily accounts of the State, prepared with a high degree of accuracy and generation of accurate monthly accounts within 2–3 days of month end;
2. Generation of daily cash position of the state including the payments and receipts that are in the pipeline;
3. Online system for release of funds;
4. ECS payments for a substantial number (over 90%) of payments;
5. Online visibility of Personal Deposit (PD) accounts to PD account holders and facilitating direct payment from PD accounts;
6. Online tax and non-tax payment facility any bank payment option for citizens;
7. Centralised pensioners database;
8. Eliminating manual data entry or double data entry for a large proportion of transactions.

This will involve

1. Online bill submission by Drawing Disbursing Officers;
2. Integration with Human Resources Management System;
3. Incorporation of e-Scrolls from Agency Banks;
4. Releases to be electronically incorporated directly through inputs from Finance Department or Line Departments;
5. Changes to the budget (appropriations, additionalities, supplementary) to be electronically incorporated in Khajane II system.
6. Real-time information regarding receipts, fund releases, scheme-wise expenditure details to both finance and stakeholder departments;
7. Comprehensive management information system reports and decision support systems;
8. Business process engineering to ensure that the financial decision outputs and the database updating take place simultaneously;

---

[8] http://karnatakatreasury.gov.in.

5 Government Auditing

Auditing primarily aims at ensuring public accountability of the Executive to the Legislature and in turn the Legislators to the citizens of the country.

5.1 Role of Accountant General

The office of the Comptroller and Auditor General (CAG) is created by the Constitution with several provisions to provide and safeguard an independent status. Independence of the CAG is guaranteed by prescribing that he shall be appointed by the President of India and shall not be removed from office excepting on the ground of proved misbehaviour or incapacity. Further, the salary and allowances of the CAG, the pension and other benefits payable on retirement, etc., are 'charged' on the Consolidated Fund which means it will not be subject to the vote of parliament. The Constitutional duties of CAG are compilation of accounts of the states and audit of the accounts of the Union and State governments. CAG's audit is conducted in two stages, the first, appropriation audit at the macro-level verifying unspent funds and excess expenditure over the budget provisions, status of supplementary provisions, etc. The Appropriation Accounts record the grant wise gross expenditures against provisions approved by the State Legislature and offer explanations for variations between the actual expenditure and the funds provided. Secondly, audit of budgetary process and controls in the departments at the micro-level. CAG plays a very important role in enforcing accountability on the part of the Executive to the Legislature and also aids in adherence to financial rules and regulations. More recently, the performance audit undertaken for select programs has been helping in a critical review of translation of outlays into outcomes.

The organisations subject to audit include:

- All Union and State government departments and offices as well as departmental. Commercial undertakings
- All public commercial enterprises controlled by the Union, State and Union territory governments
- Noncommercial autonomous bodies and authorities owned and controlled by the Union, State, and Union territory governments
- Authorities and bodies substantially financed from Union, State, Union territory government revenues.

Accounts are 'Statements of facts relating to money or things having money value'. The 'facts' that are incorporated in accounting records are transactions.

The sources from which accounts along with the supporting documents flow to the Office of the Accountant General are many. In his office, The Accountant General examines these transactions and also the documents supporting them, posts them in appropriate manner to produce intelligible, readable and usable monthly accounts and annual accounts.

The accounts of the Union Government were departmentalised (i.e. maintained by the departments concerned) in stages from 1 April 1976 to 1 April 1977, relieving the Comptroller and Auditor General from the responsibility for compiling the accounts. The compilation of accounts of the Union Government has now been entrusted to the Comptroller General of Accounts. As of now, the Comptroller and Auditor General is responsible for maintaining the accounts of the State Governments and of Union Territories, (except that of the States of Goa and Sikkim and the Union Territory of Pondicherry) as per Article 150 of Constitution of India.

5.2 Sources of Initial Accounts

The sources from which accounts along with supporting documents flow to the Accountant General are:

a. District Treasuries;
b. Public Works Divisions, Forest Divisions and other departmental accounts offices like Karnataka Bhavan, New Delhi, which are authorised to make payments through cheques and receive moneys and which render compiled accounts. In Karnataka, the transactions of Public Works and Forest are routed through treasuries, only residuary accounts are sent directly to the Accountant General.
c. Inter-State Suspense Account from other Accountants General;
d. Clearance memos advising Inter-Government Adjustments in the books of the Reserve Bank and the statement of monthly balances from the Reserve Bank;
e. Adjustments carried out in the office of the Accountants General, which include Inter-Government transactions, book transfers for inter-departmental supplies and services, periodical adjustments and rectification of misclassification.

Public Works divisions, Forest Divisions and departmental accounts officers render to the Accountant General monthly fully compiled accounts classifying the receipt and payment transactions of the month under appropriate heads of account duly supported by vouchers and other documents. In Tamil Nadu and Andhra Pradesh and Karnataka, the treasuries render the fully compiled accounts to the concerned Accountants General.

The initial accounts of State Government transactions are prepared by the authorities through whom the transactions occur, such as Treasuries, Public Works Divisions, Forest Divisions and other Departmental Accounts Offices, Inter-State Suspense accounts received from other Accountant General etc. From these initial accounts the Indian Audit and Accounts Department compile, under different heads prescribed for Government Accounts, and bring out monthly civil accounts and annually the Appropriation Accounts and the Finance Accounts, showing the result of all the transactions, which occur during that period.

The main checks that are undertaken in AG are:

1. Classification of transactions.

2. Checking of high-value vouchers.
3. Drawal from Contingency Fund.
4. Periodical Adjustments.
5. Annual adjustments (only during end of the Financial Year).
6. Govt of India loans and repayments under major head 6004.
7. Transactions of internal debt under major head 6003.
8. Transactions of Govt of India Grants under major head 1601.
9. Interest payments under major head 2049.
10. Transactions under major Deposit heads.

After the compilation of accounts, the accuracy of the monthly accounts is verified by comparing abstract of Major head totals (Source-wise totals) with that of Disbursers account (destination wise totals). The cash balance arrived at will be checked with cash balance of the State maintained in Central Accounts Section (CAS) of RBI at Nagpur. The differences are reconciled subsequently. The differences crop up due to the fact that Agency banks and local RBI rectify the errors after the closure of monthly accounts at the treasuries. Treasuries close the accounts on the last of the month, the agency banks and local RBI get additional 10 to 12 days for rectification of errors before sending the final figures to CAS/Nagpur.

6 Effectiveness of Government auditing: Issues in India

There are a number of issues that are hindering an effective public financial accountability both at the Centre and State government levels.

6.1 Corrective Action on audit reports

Reports of the CAG get referred to the Public Accounts Committee (PAC) for their scrutiny. Audit effectiveness is largely dependent on the functioning of the PAC/COPU. Audit reports provide legislatures with performance reports of the executive to enforce accountability. Public Accounts Committees examine the audit reports and make recommendations. PAC adopts a selective approach by choosing some important audit paras for an in-depth examination. The action taken notes (ATN) on all the paras of CAG should be furnished to the PAC through the Ministry of Finance within a period of four months from the date of laying of the reports on the Table of the House. The issue of delays that are occurring in addressing the audit paras/reports by the administrative departments by way of Action Taken Notes has been addressed and corrective action initiated by the Public Accounts Committees from time to time which has resulted in a decline in the number of pending cases. While such numbers were 4216 in 2010 the number has come down to 806 cases pending as on 31-7-2016 and 781 by 30-09-2016 (GoK, PAC 2017) It has been

Table 1 Action taken notes pending as on 30-09-2016

Number of reports/paras on which ATNs have not been received even for the first time	151
Number of reports on which revised ATNs were awaited from Ministry	338
ATN s finally vetted by Audit but pending with Ministry/Monitoring Cell for submission to PAC	86
Number of ATNs with audit for vetting	206
Total	781

Source GoI, PAC, 2016–17

Table 2 Year-wise position of outstanding UCs

Year	No of UCs awaited		Amount involved (Rs. in crores)	
	Maharashtra	Karnataka	Maharashtra	Karnataka
Up to 2012–13	60920	NA	35632,06	NA
Up to 2013–14	NA	44	NA	34.31
2013–14	5390	NA	7307.78	NA
2014–15	15567	14	18209.03	51.07
2015–16	NA	66	NA	402.43
Total	81877	124	61148.87	487.91

Source Finance accounts of respective states

observed that there is a huge pendency, although on the decline due to the corrective measures initiated by the PACs from time to time, details are provided in the Table 1.

Getting a complete picture of the status of compliance with the audit paras and the timelines has been a Herculean task especially at the subnational level. While there has been some improvement in states like Karnataka, considerable delays are occurring in many states. It is observed that due to failure of submission of explanatory memorandum by the departments and for other reasons, arrears in discussion of audit reports have reached staggering proportions. In several major states, discussions are confined to paras of old reports on a piecemeal basis. Some of these audit paras are more than a decade old and have lost relevance. In some states, a series of audit reports were passed over entirely by the PAC due to huge backlog (Government audit in India: Is and ought, CAG 2004).

Non-submission of utilisation reports has been yet another serious problem faced in a number of states. Financial rules stipulate that utilisation certificates (UC) should be obtained by departmental officers from the grantees and on verification should be forwarded to the AG within 18 months from the date of sanction. Karnataka and Maharashtra, the two states for which year wise data on outstanding Utilisation certificates reveals that the latter has huge arrears (Table 2). In Karnataka while it is mainly the Health and Family welfare department which is not producing utilisation certificate, in Maharashtra more than ten departments are involved. The large pendency in submissions of UCs indicates lack of monitoring of grants and loans by the departments.

Such poor response from the departments despite well-established scrutiny and controls will not augur well in ensuring public financial accountability. The World Bank report (2010, 6) states 'This calls into question the ultimate usefulness of having well formulated and comprehensive budgets, when they are executed with inadequate controls, insufficient reporting, and limited scrutiny by parliament and audit institutions.... Given the interconnected nature of the PFM system, it is crucially important to address any gaps in applying the international accounting and auditing standards'.

References

CGA. (1990). Government accounting rules 1990, controller general of accounts, government of India, New Delhi; available at http://www.cga.nic.in/DownloadPDF.aspx?filenameid=3.

Government of Andhra Pradesh and the World Bank. (2014). *Workshop on treasury reforms in states and transition to IFMIS: Challenges and opportunities—A Report.* HTTPs://collaboration.worldbank.org/docs/DOC-11619.

Government of India, http://www.cgaindia.org/html/book3/chapter3.htm

Government of India. (2017). *Sixty sixth report, public accounts committee (16 Lok Sabha, New Delhi).*

Government audit in India: Is and ought, Comptroller and auditor general of India, (prepared by Ashwin Attri, et.al) https://www.cag.gov.in/.

Government of India. (2018). Key to budget documents, The Union Budget 2018–19.

Government of Karnataka, http://karnatakatreasury.gov.in/

The World Bank. (2010). *Public sector accounting and auditing in South Asia: A comparison to international standards* (Report Number 54606-SAS). South Asia Region Financial management unit.

Chapter 12
Public Provisioning of Infrastructure Changing Strategies: Empirics of India

Gopalkrishniah Nagesha

1 Introduction

It is not an overemphasis when we say that a solid infra base forms the backbone of economic growth of a country, considering that an adequate provision of infra services and regular maintenance of such services are absolutely essential in sustaining economic growth and harvesting the full potential of the various sectors of an economy. In the contemporary context of globalization and liberalization, it has become increasingly difficult for governments, particularly in the developing world to meet the rapidly increasing infra demand. Hence, as part of addressing this growing infra gap (difference between supply and demand), public–private partnerships have emerged as an effective alternative strategy across the globe since the 1990s.

In brief, public–private partnerships (PPPs) are broadly an alternative to the public budgeting in the provision of infra services. Under this mode, government investment in infra services is replaced by private investment for the creation of a new infra base as well as maintenance of such infra services. Typically, the infra services are created, maintained and operated partially or fully as an alternative to the traditional public budgeting.

Against this backdrop, the present study deals with theoretical strands of argument related to PPP as an alternative to public budgeting of infra services in Sect. 2. Section 3 explains briefly the various policy initiatives undertaken by the Government of India towards enhancing infra investment through PPP mode. Section 4 traces the growth of public and private sector investment and trends and patterns with respect to various infra sub-sectors in India. Section 5 comes up with a performance analysis of infra PPPs in India, followed by a summary of the study in Sect. 6.

G. Nagesha (✉)
Post Graduate Department of Economics, Government First Grade College, Yelahanka, Bengaluru, India
e-mail: nageconmics@gmail.com

G. Karnam (ed.), *Public Budgeting in India*, India Studies in Business and Economics, https://doi.org/10.1007/978-81-322-3917-8_12

2 Theoretical Expositions for an Alternative to Public Budgeting of Infra Services

Infrastructure sector is traditionally a public good, typically provided through the mode of public budgeting. However, massive infra needs, fiscal constraints, increasing public debt and fiscal consolidation, and many more factors have led to the development of an alternative to the traditional public budgeting strategies with respect to the provision of infra services. The following section describes briefly the important theoretical support for an alternative to the public infra budgeting as far as infra provision is concerned.

2.1 *Infrastructure as an Impure Public Good*

The routing of infrastructure services partially through the private sector lies in the impure characteristic of a public good, i.e. rivalry a situation of (one person's consumption limiting the consumption of others) and excludability (restricting/excluding others from using it when being used by one or more). These characteristics provide a fair scope for the private sector in terms of providing infrastructure services.

But the impure public good[1] nature of infrastructure, welfare aspect and its basic needs character, long gestation, and lumpy investments can make it almost impossible for the private sector to participate. However, the present state of governments' finances, technical and managerial expertise, etc., does not permit the government/public sector organizations alone to overcome these infrastructural bottlenecks. This can give rise to the amalgamation of both the public and private sectors in providing infrastructure services.

Dailami and Klein (1997), in the empirical study, explain the necessity of opting for private sector participation by governments in the developing countries in the creation of an infra base in the view of the debt crisis faced by the developing countries in the early 1980s that significantly restricted public borrowing for averting the debt crisis projects. The authors argue that governments can attract private sector funds in infrastructure provision in two ways: first, by way of providing financial assistance in the form of grants or guaranties or cheap loans and, second, by way of rendering the required policy support. This, they argue, protects the private investor concerns by ensuring macroeconomic stability and sound regulatory setups for facilitating and ensuring private sector investment in the infrastructure build up.

Besley and Ghatak (2001), while developing a framework with regard to the role of the state and the non-governmental organizations (NGO)/voluntary sector in the public projects, argue that incomplete contract results are subject to delays in investments and also that the ownership of public goods should rest with the party that cares most for the project. Their framework, while explaining how the private

[1] Impure public good—varying levels of rivalry and excludability principles are applicable.

sector can be involved in the provision of public goods, elucidates that the degree of impurity associated with goods or services determines the extent of private sector participation.

Francesconi and Muthoo (2004), in their theoretical work, while examining the non-rival and non-excludable nature of pure public goods, argue that most public goods are impure and that their ownership depends on the degree of impurity (i.e. rival[2] and /excludable[3]) associated with goods or services; i.e., when the degree of impurity is high in respect of public goods, then the ownership should be with the private sector and vice versa. They propose a joint ownership in respect of two cases, i.e. first, when differences exist in the valuation of impurity of public goods and, second, in the context of similar productivities of both the public and private sectors.

These two theoretical strands of argument arrive at an identical proposition that the level of private sector participation in infrastructure projects is determined by the degree of impurity, i.e. rivalry and excludability and the nature of technology required with regard to those goods or services. The present study presumes that one of the grounds for differing PPP types/models is the varying levels of public good characteristics present in various types of infrastructure services such as transport (roads, railways, airports and ports), urban infrastructure, health, and education sectors. Further, this difference of impurity of public good character may differ within the sector too and is project specific based on the geographic and demographic factors. Hence, there exist different PPP models that are employed within the same infra sub-sector.

2.1.1 Efficiency Grounds

Leibenstein (1966) empirically verified the argument that a monopoly situation in the provision of goods or services may lead to welfare loss and that competition in providing goods or services enhances the efficiency. PPP model, that enables a competitive provisioning of infrastructure services with the participation of private and public sectors, is expected to enhance efficiency. More importantly, this process of PPP infrastructure provision may eliminate the natural monopoly power of the public sector. The entry/participation of the private sector in the infrastructure provision expands competition which, in turn, leads to an improvement in various economic efficiencies. A lower degree of competition facilitates a greater allocative efficiency, while a higher degree of competition results in an increase in X-efficiency. Leibenstein specifies three important elements, namely intra-plant motivational efficiency, external motivational efficiency and non-market input efficiency for determining X-efficiency.

Lindberg study (cited from Leibenstein 1966) argues that in respect of industries, a sub-optimal disequilibrium (with respect to technology and utilization of capital

[2]Rivalry—refers to a situation where a good consumed by 'X' person is not available to 'Y' person.

[3]Excludability—refers to a situation where, in providing a given service to 'X' person, there is a possibility of 'Y' person getting excluded from accessing the given service.

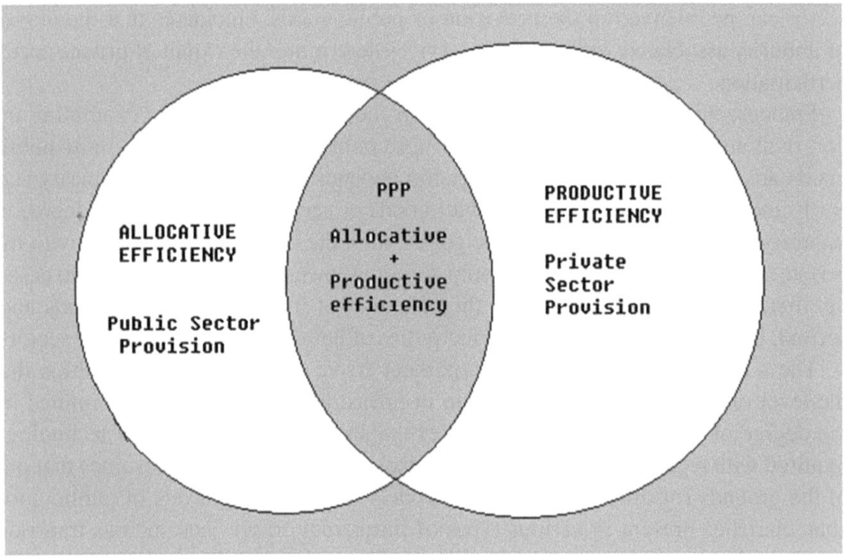

Chart 1 Efficiencies in various forms of infra services provision. *Source* Nagesha (2015)

stock) occurs mainly because of under-motivated managers and workers and that this situation motivates employees to move further away from an optimal equilibrium. While supporting this view, Fredrick Harbison (cited from Leibenstein 1966, p. 8) points out that the absence of motivation on the part of the management of one of the petroleum refineries in Egypt resulted in the operation of the nearly half of the other refineries for several years. However, an improved motivation (on the part of the new management team in the respective company with the same employees) tremendously enhanced its productivity. Thus, what the above case implies that managerial efficiency can result in an optimal growth. PPPs may be one of the strategies wherein private managerial efficiency can increase the potential use of input productivity with dynamic changes in the infrastructure sector in the long run.

The private sector is efficient in technological, managerial and risk managing aspects, while the public sector is efficient in allocative and financial aspects; i.e., the cost of public sector financing is less as compared to the private sector financing. Therefore, a blend of these two sectors may result in an efficient provisioning of infrastructure services.

Schmidt (1996), while supporting the X-efficiency theory, defines the trade-off between public and private ownership as follows: "Although the private sector provision generates a higher productive efficiency, the public sector provision generates a greater allocative efficiency. Both allocative and productive efficiencies increase simultaneously under PPPs. The public and private sector combination increases the total efficiency of a project". This is graphically explained in Chart 1.

PPPs function as co-producers between the government and private sectors under which the goal is achieved by the surplus value. Erik-Hans et al. (2005) explain that a mere partnership between government and private sectors will not create any surplus value, but a proper synergy between government and private sectors creates positive externalities, resulting in "*metaphorical formula* ***1 (public) + 1 (private) > 2***" (cited from Yin 2009, August 20, p. 1).

Hammami (2006) argue that inefficiencies prevailing in the public sector organizations led to the emergence of the new public management mechanisms in the UK and other countries towards improving the management of the public sector, having been prompted by the need to reduce public spending and to overcome the lack of managerial skills and efficiency associated with the public sector organizations.

2.1.2 Principal–Agent Theory

The mixed economy character of the Indian economy provides an opportunity for the existence of both the public and private sectors in providing infrastructure facilities. Under PPPs, the public sector is expected to perform as a regulator, facilitator, guide and philosopher to the private sector for the purpose of providing adequate infrastructure services.

Hence, the public sector needs to behave like a principal or a regulator in order to look after the welfare aspect of the general public by ensuring a ready accessibility to infrastructure facilities, while at the same time, ensuring minimum rates of return on investments and a favourable investment climate for the private sector.

If both the public and private sectors are able to function in tandem as the principal and agent, then one can expect a smooth and adequate provision of infrastructure services.

2.2 Public Debt: A Major Factor

With the nature of governments changing, their natural monopoly status came under an increased scrutiny, demanding a change. The debt crisis forced the governments to look for alternatives. The public debt crisis of the early 1980s in the developing countries significantly restricted public borrowing, forcing them to look to private infrastructure projects, as a possible alternative option, so as to avoid a major macroeconomic crisis (Dailami and Klein 1997). The study suggests that governments can attract private sector funds in infrastructure provision in two ways: first, by way of providing financial assistance in the form of grants or guaranties or cheap loans and, second, by way of extending the required policy support. This could protect the interests of private investors by ensuring macroeconomic stability and sound regulatory setups for facilitating and ensuring private sector investment in the infrastructure build up.

3 Government Policies Towards the Promotion of Infra PPPs

India has emerged as one of the leading nations with the largest number of infra PPPs in the world. As part of addressing the various infra bottlenecks and promoting PPPs, both the Central and State Governments have initiated many policy measures at the aggregate and sectoral levels.

Box 1: Timeline of Important Policies, Committees and Institutions for Promotion of PPPs

1996 – Rakesh Mohan committee on infrastructure financing

1997-2002 – 9th Five year plan - exclusively focussed on infrastructure- private sector participation through PPPs

Committee on Infrastructure (COI) - August 2004

Cabinet Committee on Infrastructure (CCI) – July 2009

To address the construction time and cost overruns – all NHAI's from phase III started development through BOT PPPs

2005 -Public Private Partnership Approval Committee (PPPAC)

2006- VGF- Viability Gap funding (VGF)

Empowered Institution (EI) / Empowered committee – To approve VGF

2006- India Infrastructure Finance Corporation Limited (IIFCL) - for innovative, cost effective methods of financing infrastructure projects.

Public Private Partnership (3Ps) Institute proposed in the 2014 union budget for promoting PPPs in the county by the Finance Ministry, GoI

Vijay Kelkar committee to revisit and revitalise the infra PPPs (May 2015)

Source Nagesha (2015)

The present section makes an attempt to track the policy impacts of governments and to critically analyze various vital policies both at the national and sub-national levels.

GOI has introduced, from time to time, many fiscal measures through formulation of special policies, establishment of institutions to address issues related to various infrastructure inadequacies and also (briefly specified in text Box 1) to encourage the private sector participation in this sector.

3.1 Fiscal Incentives to Infra Investment

In this direction, the GOI, in the 1996–97 budget, had announced several incentive measures regarding infrastructure promotion. These included mainly fiscal incentives like 'five-year tax holiday' for companies engaged in developing, maintaining and operating infrastructure facilities such as roads, bridges, new airports, ports, railway tracks/lines, and water supply, sanitation and sewerage projects. Secondly, income tax exemption was extended to dividend, interest or long-term capital gains earned by funds or companies set up to develop, maintain and operate infrastructure facilities. Thirdly, to augment resources, the government enhanced tax rebate limits so as to help channelize domestic savings into debentures and shares of infrastructure companies in the specified sectors. Fourthly, to provide long-term finance for infrastructure development, the government established Infrastructure Development Finance Company (IDFC) on 30 January 1997 with an authorized share capital of Rs. 5000 crore. Fifthly, the government relaxed many legal administrative procedures related to foreign investments in the infra sector by allowing foreign equity participation up to 74% in key infra sectors. Sixthly, the government obtained a loan of $300 million from ADB to help develop a long-term debt market and to support private sector infra investment projects.

With respect to sector-specific reforms, the GOI (1997) initiated the following vital measures. First, the GOI extended all the fiscal incentives to telecom projects by treating telecom sector as part of the infrastructure base. Secondly, it allowed the private sector into electricity transmission by amending the Indian Electricity Act 1910 and Electricity Supply Act 1948. Thirdly, the government introduced the Build-Own-Lease-Transfer (BOLT) and Own Your Wagon Scheme (OYWS) as part of facilitating the private sector participation in railways.

Viability Gap Funding (VGF): In order to support socially important, but economically unviable infrastructure projects, the GOI initiated a special scheme called VGF in 2006. For projects which are justified by socioeconomic returns, but do not pass the standard thresholds of financial returns, VGF is inevitable. Under VGF scheme, grant assistance up to 20% of the capital cost is provided by the Central government to PPP projects undertaken by any Central government ministry, state government, statutory entity or local body. An additional grant of up to 20% of the total project cost can also be provided by the sponsoring ministry, state government or project authority. For the national highway projects, the entire VGF is provided by National Highway Authority of India (NHAI) from the cess revenues transferred to it by the government.

Viability Support Fund (VSF): In the 12th FYP, it was envisaged that VSF financing both capital investment (capex) and recurring costs (opex) incurred by non-governmental agencies in the delivery of services to economically weaker section (EWS) families be reimbursed by the Central and State governments through VSF, based on the terms of concession agreement between the government and non-governmental entities.

Model Concession Agreements (MCAs): The GOI has evolved elaborate guidelines with a view to facilitating a hassle-free implementation of various infra projects. These include specific MCAs for the various infrastructure sector and sub-sectors, model bidding documents, project handling toolkits, standard concession agreements and regulation guidelines. These documents are meant to guide project initiating departments at various stages of project formulation and execution as also to avoid unnecessary disputes and to fix responsibilities for various tasks, etc., over the entire lifespan of the projects.

3.2 Infra Policy Measures for Sectoral and Regional Inclusion

As part of achieving the objective of a 'sustainable, faster and more inclusive growth,' the 12th FYP envisaged the adoption of PPPs in many sectors including social infrastructure.

Chart 2 specifies briefly the infra sub-sectors chosen for PPPs both by the national and sub-national governments. In addition to the traditional sectors (mainly transport), the government intends to promote PPPs in the social sector. This is discussed in the following paragraphs.

PPPs in the Social Sector: The 12th FYP lays a special emphasis on the social sector development in that it aims at reaching the fruits of development to the underprivileged sections of the society. The plan highlights that the limited available public domain resources are insufficient to achieve the physical targets envisaged and that the participation of the private sector is essential to bridging the resource gap. The private sector investment in the social sector under PPPs is aimed at '*reduction in time*

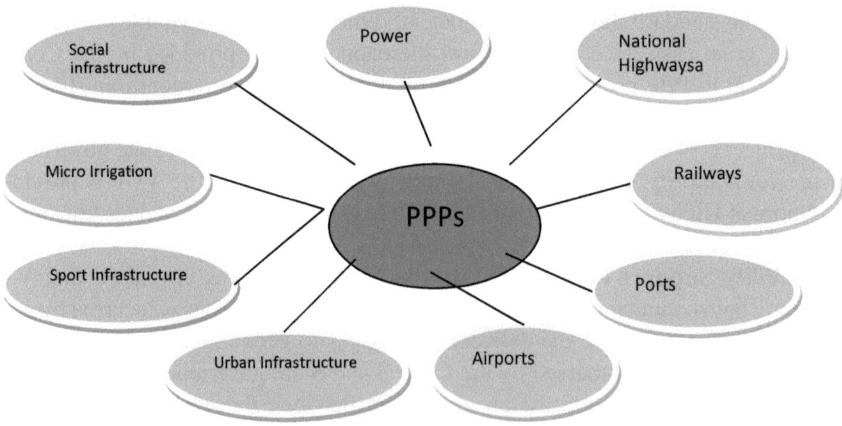

Chart 2 Infra PPPs across various sectors in India. *Source* Nagesha (2015)

and cost over-runs, improvement in efficiencies and better quality of performance' (GOI 2013a, p. 96).

PPPs in Education: The government plans to set up 2500 schools under PPPs during the 12th plan. The main objective of this program is to provide quality education to the underprivileged children (who cannot afford to pay fees charged by 'good' private schools). This scheme has a vision of providing quality education to 40 lakh children, including 25 lakh children belonging to the underprivileged sections of the society.

Government initiative in terms of adopting PPPs in education is very much timely as it is in line with its vision of providing world class quality education to the low-income families. The guidelines under the scheme make it clear that the government's policy formulation for improving the quality of education by identifying schools (under the respective scheme) is based on the previous track record of applicants, not on financial bidding. The mode of payment for such schools is also very clear. Hence, one has to wait for the actual implementation of the government initiative in this direction and its potential impact in terms of providing quality education to the hitherto marginalized sections.

PPPs in Healthcare Services: The objective of this scheme is "to create a health care delivery mechanism comprising multi-specialty hospitals to meet the growing health care needs of the poor, and for supplementing human resources in the sector by setting up nursing schools and medical colleges" (GOI 2013a, p. 97).

Under this program, the government aims at creating secondary and tertiary care hospitals through PPPs at the district level. A 200-bed district-level hospital would serve a catchment area of about 8–10 lakh population (20 lakh for a 300-bed tertiary care hospital). This scheme envisages providing a ready access to quality health care to the economically disadvantaged groups through tertiary/referral hospital setups.

PPPs in Sports Infrastructure: The objective of this initiative is "to utilize the existing facilities optimally throughout the year and also generate revenues for their operation and maintenance" (GOI 2013a, p. 95). The Planning Commission has also developed a model for operation and management of sports infrastructure through PPPs in consultation with Ministry of Sports and Youth Affairs. It is proposed to take up the sports infrastructure already existing as well as new stadia.

PPPs in Food Grains Storage: The government has also initiated steps to enhance 'food security, reduce wastage and to improve the quality of stored food grains' through PPPs. Under this program, the government plans to create 2 metric million ton (MMT) of modern storage facilities in the form of silos in the first phase. Silos will be constructed and operated through PPP mode in various states across India. The government also intends to contribute up to 20% of the cost of construction of storage silos to private entities under the concession agreement. The concessionaires are entitled to receive recurring storage charge, for assuring a required performance and maintenance standards.

Green Highway Policy: The GoI recently (29th September 2015) announced the green highways policy 2015. The policy broadly aims at developing eco-friendly national highways through plantation, transplantation, beatification and maintenance of trees across the national highway corridors. The policy also aims at making these roads more user-friendly by way of reducing the adverse impacts of air, dust and noise pollution and also making roads glare-free in the summer. The policy also aims at an investment of Rs. 1000 crore every year besides bearing one percent of the total project cost with respect of the implementation of the respective scheme. In addition to tree plantation, a regular monitoring of them will be taken up with the help of ISRO's Bhuvan and GAGAN satellite systems. This policy is expected to encourage the participation of local communities, farmers, private sector, NGOs and government institutions in the implementation process.

4 Sectoral and Regional Spread of Infra PPPs

The entire world including India has come to adopt PPPs as a mode of infra provision. This typically includes the maintenance of already existing infra services or a new creation and operation of various economic and social infra services. And as such, it is vital to analyse the trends and patterns in infra PPPs at the national and sub-national levels to understand the basic factors underlying such a development.

In India, 1437[4] PPP infrastructure projects with a total investment project cost of Rs. 9,27,819.5 crore have been developed by both the Central and State governments. These projects[5] include broadly five infra sectors, namely transport, energy, communication, water and sanitation, and social and commercial infra sectors. These infra sectors are further categorized into roads and bridges, ports (excluding captive), inland waterways, airports, railway tracks, tunnels, viaducts, bridges, while the urban public transport comprises transport sector category. Secondly, energy sector projects include electricity generation, renewable energy, electricity transmission, oil pipelines, oil/gas liquified natural gas (LNG) storage, gas pipelines and city gas distribution. Thirdly, communication sector includes telecommunication towers. Fourthly, water and sanitation sector consists of solid waste management, water supply pipelines, water treatment plants and sewage collection, treatment and disposal system, irrigation, storm water drainage. Fifth and finally, social and commercial infra sector includes common infrastructure for industrial parks, special economic zones (SEZs), cold chains and PPP only projects in the sub-sectors like hospitals and educational institutions and tourism sector infra projects.

4.1 Public and Private Infrastructure Investment in India

In India, prior to the 1990s, infra services were provided by the government through its budgetary sources. However, an insufficient government funding for the creation

[4]GoI (2015), As on July 23 2015, https://infrastructureindia.gov.in/project-list.

[5]These include construction, operation and pipeline stages of infrastructure projects. Accessed from https://infrastructureindia.gov.in/faqs.

of an adequate infra services base, lack of commitment towards maintenance of the respective existing infrastructure, enormous time and cost overruns of the proposed infra projects and many other aspects have resulted in serious obstacles to the infra growth.

A conducive environment provided by the government through its market-friendly policy initiatives as part of promoting infrastructure PPPs in the country both at the Central and State levels has resulted in a rapid growth of the private sector investment from a mere 20% of the total investment in the tenth plan (2002–07) to 30%[6] in the eleventh plan (2007–12), revealing evidence of a positive response from the private sector and is expected to increase further to 50% of the total infrastructure investment in the twelfth plan (2012–17).

The private capital share in the core infrastructure sectors during the 11th plan[7] was 82% in telecoms, 80% in ports, 64% in airports and 4% in railways. This is expected to increase further during the twelfth plan period.

Infra investment as percent of GDP for the period 2002–2017 is displayed in Chart 3. The chart shows a gradual increase in the infrastructure development in the view of an increased investment by the private sector over the reference period. This was very insignificant prior to the 1990s. Later, with a substantial private sector participation in this sector, the chart shows a steady increase in investment over the period 1999 to 2003–04, and for the subsequent years, a rapid increase in private investment due to the policy initiatives undertaken by the government. Although there has been a discernible growth observed in the rate of infrastructure investment and also development, it becomes evident that infra investment still remains below the expected 9% per annum required for harvesting the full potential of the available resources and achieving a high sustainable GDP growth. To realize this target of 9%[8] (per annum) growth in infrastructure investment, the government needs to streamline its various policy initiatives from time to time in order to lure the unwilling private sector into investing in infrastructure.

The public sector investment has remained stagnant over the entire reference period and is expected to decline from 4.85% of GDP in 2002 to 4.04% by 2016. While with respect to the same reference period, the private sector investment shows a gradual increase from 0.81% of GDP to a peak of 3.73% of GDP, particularly for the financial year 2009. This increasing private sector investment trend is expected to surpass the public sector investment by the end of the 12th plan period. While the sharp increase in the private sector investment is a welcome development, the aggregate realized investment of both the private and public sectors for up to 2011–12 shows how inadequate it has been when it comes to catering to the required infrastructure needs, while the required investment being 9% of GDP.[9] It is only in the event of the Planning Commission's projected figures for the 12th plan being realized that India's infra investment will reach 9% of GDP by 2016–17.

---

[6]GOI (2013a) 12th plan, volume 1, p. 87.

[7]GOI (2013b) 12th plan, Vol. 2, p. 212.

[8]GOI (2007) 11th Plan, Planning Commission.

[9]Rakesh (1996) and GOI (2007).

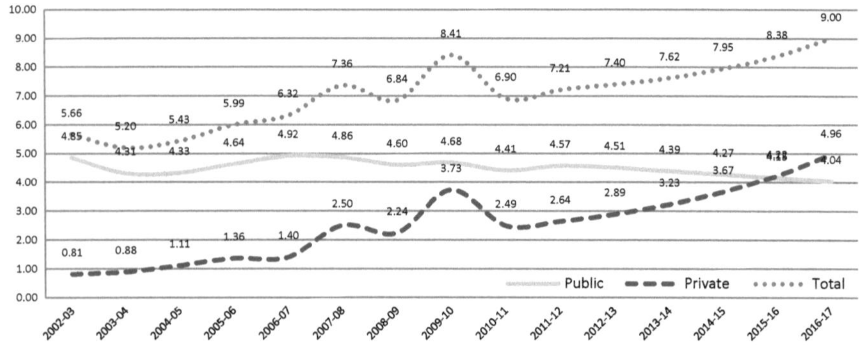

Chart 3 Infra investment as percent of GDP. *Source* Nagesha and Gayithri (2014). *Note* (1) Figures are expressed as percentage of GDP (2) 2002 to 2011–12 figures represent realized investment (3) ** for 2012–17, figures represent the Planning Commission projections

The growth trajectory of PPPs reveals that there has been a sharp increase in the number of PPP projects over the years contributing greatly towards enhancing the regional and sectoral infrastructural availability. However, these projects seem to have been concentrated in certain sectors and regions, both globally and domestically, despite the fact that there exists a sufficient scope for a wider dispersal of PPP projects. The energy sector accounts for the highest number of PPP projects at the international level.

The pattern of growth and distribution of PPP projects in India reveal that the growth of Indian PPPs is more discernible in infrastructure sectors coming under states than in the central infrastructure sectors. Further, the growth pattern of projects reveals that both in the state and central sectors, only a few infrastructure sub-sectors are being developed through PPP mode and that the projects so executed are mainly in the transport sector including roadways, airports, urban infrastructure and seaport sectors with urban infrastructure projects being large. A very few projects in other sub-sectors like health, education and rural infrastructure are also being executed through PPP mode. However, the government's policy as outlined in the 12th FYP vision document of creating social infrastructure through PPPs needs to be adhered to.

The study has also analysed the sectoral and regional concentration of projects in India. The concentration of projects can be seen only in the transport sector. Within the transport sector, national highway projects account for the largest share. Under these projects, only a few PPP models such as BOT toll and annuity methods are mainly used.

The regional concentration of projects has resulted in interstate disparity as far as the spread of PPPs is concerned a few economically developed Indian states account for more than 50% of PPPs. Many states have PPPs undertaken that remain below the national average both in terms of the number of projects and the total investment value. Some states like Himachal Pradesh, Jammu Kashmir, Goa and seven northeastern states, other than Assam, do not have even a single PPP project undertaken. There exists an intrastate disparity too; i.e., some urban epicentres have cornered a major share of PPPs, leaving rural areas lagging far behind. This regional disparity in the spread of PPPs is widespread across the world. The factors responsible for the sectoral and regional PPP preferences need to be explored in order to evolve suitable policy frameworks for channelizing PPP investments into other sectors and regions that are currently facing a serious deficit in investments. Since, infrastructure is a universal requirement for harnessing the development potential of a nation, there is an urgent need for addressing the infrastructure inadequacies, either through the PPP medium or direct provision by the public sector.

The present study cites the possible reasons for a skewed distribution of projects across the infra sub-sectors and regions in the Indian context: first, differences inherent in the political will on the part of national and sub-national governments with respect to the promotion of infrastructure PPP policies; second, the failure of governments' various infrastructure executive departments including PPP nodal agencies in identifying, executing and coordinating various departments; third, absence of commitment in the promotion of policies for facilitating a hassle-free investment environment; fourth, inordinate delays in the implementation of projects as part of redressing the various differences; fifth, lack of financial assurances to the concessionaires regarding their investments; sixth, lack of availability of land and other incentives like tax concessions and capital grants (viability gap funding); seventh, lack of awareness regarding the nature of project risks and a poor degree of private sector risk management capacity; and eight, inadequate consultations with end users, etc. These are some of the important factors that need to be explored in greater details.

5 Performance of Infra PPPs

GOI's shift from item rate contract to turnkey projects, i.e. a modified EPC or PPP mode of development, has certainly helped address time and cost overruns specific to most of the NH projects. This was one of the major impediments to the government traditionally, due to its limited budgetary sources, as also technological and managerial constraints.

In India, there has been a greater emphasis observed on encouraging competition and regulation with respect to various infrastructure services since the early 1990s. One of the milestone recommendations of the Committee on Infrastructure[10] was to introduce an element of competition and transparency in this sector. The committee recommended that a sufficient room be provided for private investment (both domestic and foreign) in various infrastructure projects as part of increasing accessibility and ensuring enhanced quality in harvesting potential benefits from growth and development. The reform process is oriented towards bringing private domestic and

[10]Rakesh (1996), Government of India (1996).

foreign investment into this sector. In fact, private investment in a few infrastructure sub-sectors like telecommunication, financial institutions, roadways and a few metro airports has resulted in an enhanced competition ex-ante and ex-post in the provision of these services.

5.1 Ex-ante Competition

By ex-ante competition, we mean bringing in an element of competition into the selection process of the private concessionaire through an open competitive bidding for provision of infrastructure services. The degree of competition present in respect of PPP projects can be captured through an analysis of the competitive bidding process, used for awarding infrastructure projects. Demsetz (1968)[11] observes that an ex-ante competition helps provide innovative, low-cost and better quality assured services. A private developer failing to provide such assured services may result in either a penalty/reduced annuity/toll payments or even the elimination of the developer by the respective government authority. Hence, a transparent competitive bidding process in respect of PPPs is the key element in achieving the objective of creating a cost-effective and quality infrastructure base.

The present study has examined the element of competition at the procurement stage of the PPPs by verifying the role of ex-ante competition in determining the aggregate cost of the selected PPP projects with regard to four infra sub-sectors, namely national highways, airports, ports and urban infra of India. In addition, the study also has examined the 'economies of scale' effect of the select national highways (NH)-239 PPP projects (by way of analyzing the concessionaire-wise number of projects handled) on the project cost.

An analysis of 55 Indian NH PPP projects reveals that the level of competition has remained very low, over the entire reference period. As can be seen from Chart 4, the number of single-bidder projects amounts to three that of two- and three-bidder projects 36 (18 each), and so on. A large number of projects account for two and three (number of) bidders. This clearly indicates the presence of duopoly and oligopoly conditions in the participation process of bidders or potential developers in respect of the national highway projects (refer Table 1).

The degree of ex-ante competition across 55 NH PPP projects is not uniform (see Table 1). The study attempted to analyze the association between the level of competition and the cost per lane km of road by employing Spearman rank correlation. In normal circumstances, an increase in competition should be accompanied by a decrease in the TPC and vice versa. However, the correlation results presented in Table 1 reveal a negative correlation between the estimated cost and the number of bidders, irrespective of the number of bidders/developers participating in the bidding process for the 55 projects under review. However, if we ignore the single and two-bidder projects, the results are found significant and robust in that the average cost

[11]Cited from Rathi Vaibhav (2013).

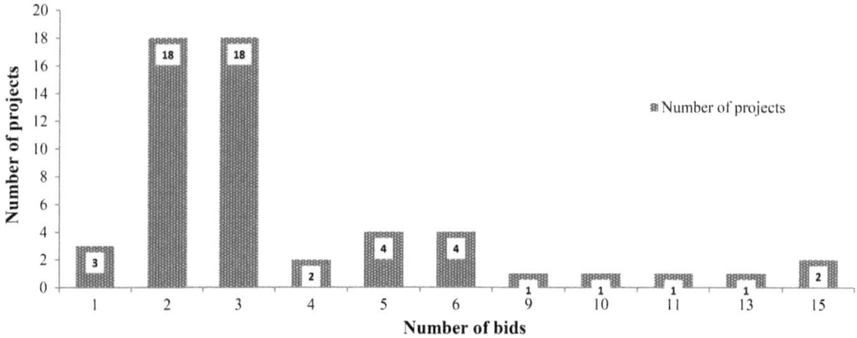

Chart 4 Nature of competition among the select NH PPP projects. *Source* Nagesha (2015)

Table 1 Correlation between competition and cost of NH PPP projects

Number of bidders	Number of projects	Cost per kilo metre (Rs. crore)	Spearman rank correlation	Market type (based on the number of bidders)
1	3	2.25	−0.35	Monopoly
2	18	2.11	−0.15	Duopoly
3	18	4.77[a]	0.35	Oligopoly/monopolistic
4	2	1.23	0.643**	
5	4	1.35	0.46	
6	4	1.52	0.31	
9	1	1.83		
10	1	1.29	1*	
11	1	1.57	1*	
13	1	1.58	1*	
15	2	1.62		
Average	**1.92**			
Minimum	**1.23**			
Maximum	**4.77**			
Median	**1.58**			

Source Author's estimation database on PPPs from Department of Economic Affairs, Ministry of Finance, GoI (2013c)

[a]Cost per kilometre is very high author's compilation under this category due to the presence of BOT annuity projects

*Significant at one percent level, **significant at five percent level

per km is high in respect of single-bidder projects, indicating at a very high monopoly price. Further, the cost decreases in respect of two-bidder projects to Rupees 2.11 crore per km as compared to Rs. 2.25 in respect of single-bidder projects. However, if we consider the projects with more than two bidders together, it becomes clear that the average cost is lowest as against the single and two-bidder projects.

In respect of 18 three-bidder projects under review, the average cost per km works out to Rs. 4.77 crore (refer Table 1) due to the fact that many projects under this category happen to be BOT annuity type projects unlike the other BOT toll projects. The study finds PPP toll projects cheaper than annuity projects.

The study empirically finds that the per unit cost of PPP roads under review is significantly associated with the level of ex-ante competition existing in the market. In addition to ex-ante competition, the study cites many other factors also as responsible in determining the cost of roads which include the type of a given PPP project, i.e. BOT annuity/toll, psychology of bidders and the prevailing political environment, among others. However, it needs to be explored further.

Opting for PPPs might be advantageous to the government as compared to the EPC projects because of their superior managerial and technical expertise and also the fact that they do not involve additional operation and maintenance risk and cost over the lifetime (20–25 years) and also no-interest payment burden on the part of the government. In addition, the performance record of PPP national highway projects for the past fifteen years reveals that the percentage of on-time completion of construction is higher in respect of PPP than EPC projects.

5.2 *Value for Money (VfM)*

Value for money, in the present context, refers to the financial and non-financial savings to the government and the public/users. It is highly advisable that governments venturing into PPPs make appropriate cost-benefit advantage methodologies available and that they make use of one of the methodological tools, i.e. VfM analysis, as it enables governments to find out whether PPP method of infra service provision can create any positive/additional benefits quantitatively (both financial and non-financial) and qualitatively.

Nagesha and Gayithri (2015) find quantitative VfM to the government positive in respect of the randomly selected three national highway projects to the tune of Rs. 1040 crore; i.e., the government has been able to save money by executing the respective road projects through PPP mode. Further, the authors empirically prove the presence of qualitative VfM in respect of the select national highway projects, based on a road user survey with indicators such as a substantive reduction in travel time, improved fuel efficiency, consistency in reaching the destination and a reduction in vehicle O&M costs, considered construction of better quality roads, followed by a regular operation and maintenance of the same with respect to the average road roughness, guaranteeing of zero potholes, installation of road barricades and all other road furniture and a proper maintenance by the concessionaire, etc., are regularly monitored by an independent consultant in conformation with the PPP contract.

6 Summary

The present study primarily focusses on the theoretical expositions in favour of an alternative to the public provision of infra services through PPPs. Various studies mentioned in the present study prove that PPP mode of infra provision enhances the overall efficiency of services in addition to reducing the fiscal burden governments.

Further, the study highlights the various policy measures undertaken by the government of India towards enhancing the infra base of the country, both at the national and state levels, such as sectoral policies, model concession agreements, exclusive institutional arrangement, etc. These measures have enhanced substantially the infra investment in the country. Presently, India is one of the largest infra PPP countries in the world.

The study, while tracking the growth of PPPs and their relevance, observes a massive increase in the number of infra PPP projects and the volume of investment at the international, national and sub-national levels over time.

Further, the study reveals that there has been a reduction in the cost of provision of infrastructure services, which could be readily attributed to the presence of ex-ante competition. Lastly, the study brings out that value for money to the government and road users is positive.

From the above analysis, one can follow that PPPs have both theoretical and empirical support as an alternative strategy for the provision of infra services vis-a-vis the traditional public budgeting. On the whole, the study results indicate, in brief, that PPP, as an alternative infra provision strategy, could be very effective in addressing issues like efficiency in public budgeting, fiscal consolidation, intergenerational liabilities of public debt and provision of services.

References

Besley, T., & Ghatak, M. (2001). Government versus private ownership of public ownership of impure public goods. *The Quarterly Journal of Economics,* 1343–1372.

Dailami, M., & Klein, M. (1997). *Government support for private infrastructure projects in emerging markets.*

Dailami, M., & Klein, M. (2014, September 1). http://elibrary.worldbank.org/doi/pdf/10.1596/1813-9450-1868.

Francesconi, M., & Muthoo, A. (2004). An incomplete contracting model of ownership of impure public goods. Unpublished, University of Essex, England.

GOI. (1997). *Economic survey 1996–97*. New Delhi: Ministry of Finance, GoI.

GOI. (2007). *Eleventh plan document*. New Delhi: Planning Commission, Ministry of Fianance, GoI.

GOI. (2013a). 12th five year plan document. New Delhi: Planning Commission.

GOI. (2013b). *12th plan document* (Vol. 2). New Delhi: Sage.

GOI. (2013c). *RTI response "PPP project detatails of India"*. New Delhi: Department of Economic Affairs, Ministry of Finance.

GOI. (2015, July 23). *Infrastructure India.* Retrieved from https://infrastructureindia.gov.in/project-list.

Hammami, M., et al. (WP 99, 2006). *Determinants of public private partnerships in infrastructure*. Washington DC: IMF.

Leibenstein, H. (1966). Allocative efficiency vs. X-efficiency. *The American Economic Review, 56*(3), 392–415.

Nagesha, G. (2015, December). Ph.D. thesis. *"Public Private Partnerships (PPPs) in the Promotion of Infrastructure in India" Supervisor Dr K Gayithri, Mysore, India: University of Mysore.*

Nagesha, G., & Gayithri, K. (2014). Research note on public private partnership of India's infrastructure development. *Journal of Infrastructure Development, 6*(2), 1–19.

Nagesha, G., & Gayithri, K. (2015). Performance analysis of National Highway PPPS. *Public Works Management and Policy, 20*(3), 264–285.

Rakesh, M. (1996). *The India infrastructure report policy imperatives for growth and welfare*. New Delhi: Ministry of Finance, Government of India.

Rathi, V. (2013). *Competition concerns in public private partnerships: An economic perspective*. New Delhi: Competition Commission of India.

Schmidt, K. M. (1996). The costs and benefits of privatization: An incomplete contracts approach. *Journal of Law Economics and Organization*, 1–24.

Teisman, G. R., & Klijn, E.-H. (2005). http://onlinelibrary.wiley.com/doi/10.1111/j.1540-6210.2009.02025.x/abstract.

Yin, W. (2009, August 20). Retrieved from http://onlinelibrary.wiley.com/doi/10.1111/j.1540-6210.2009.02025.x/abstract.

MIX
Papier aus verantwortungsvollen Quellen
Paper from responsible sources
FSC® C105338

If you have any concerns about our products,
you can contact us on
ProductSafety@springernature.com

In case Publisher is established outside the EU,
the EU authorized representative is:
Springer Nature Customer Service Center GmbH
Europaplatz 3, 69115 Heidelberg, Germany

Printed by Libri Plureos GmbH
in Hamburg, Germany